AMERICAN

SERENGETI

American Serengeti

THE LAST BIG ANIMALS OF

THE GREAT PLAINS Dan Flores

 UNIVERSITY PRESS OF KANSAS

Published by the

University Press of Kansas

(Lawrence, Kansas

66045), which was

organized by the Kansas

Board of Regents and is

operated and funded by

Emporia State University,

Fort Hays State University,

Kansas State University,

Pittsburg State University,

the University of Kansas,

and Wichita State

University

Portions of some of the chapters in *American Serengeti* have appeared in print in earlier and usually briefer versions. A version of chapter 1 appeared in *The Magazine of History* in 2013, a much-abbreviated take on chapter 2 in *Wild West* in 2015, and a treatment of chapter 3 in *Wild West* in 2013. An initial version of chapter 4 was in *Montana: The Magazine of Western History* in 2008. Significantly different and early grappling with the topics of chapters 5 and 7 here were in Dan Flores, *The Natural West* (2002) and *Horizontal Yellow* (1999), which provide some of the passages in these chapters. The same is true of chapter 8, which in places resembles an essay that was in Sherry Smith, ed., *The Future of the Southern Plains* (2003).

Library of Congress Cataloging-in-Publication Data

Names: Flores, Dan L. (Dan Louie), 1948–
Title: American Serengeti : the last big animals of the Great Plains / Dan Flores.
Description: Lawrence, Kansas : University Press of Kansas, 2016. | Includes bibliographical references and index.
Identifiers: LCCN 2015049990
ISBN 9780700622276 (hardback : alkaline paper)
ISBN 9780700622283 (ebook)
Subjects: LCSH: Animals—Great Plains—History. | Herbivores—Great Plains—History. | Predatory animals—Great Plains—History. | Natural history—Great Plains. | Human-animal relationships—Great Plains—History. | Nature—Effect of human beings on—Great Plains—History. | Environmental degradation—Great Plains—History. | Wildlife conservation—Great Plains—History. | Great Plains—History. | Great Plains—Environmental conditions. | BISAC: NATURE / Endangered Species. | NATURE / Animals / Wolves. | NATURE / Animals / Bears.
Classification: LCC QL155 .F55 2016 | DDC 591.50978—dc23
LC record available at http://lccn.loc.gov/2015049990.

British Library Cataloguing-in-Publication Data is available.

Printed in the United States of America

10 9 8 7 6 5 4 3 2

The paper used in this publication is recycled and contains 30 percent postconsumer waste. It is acid free and meets the minimum requirements of the American National Standard for Permanence of Paper for Printed Library Materials Z39.48-1992.

For Sara

CONTENTS

AMERICAN

SERENGETI

In the summer of 1843, four years after dazzling the world by completing a gigantic book that presented 435 American birds gloriously painted life size, the now world-famous artist John James Audubon was traveling up the Missouri River for an ambitious new project. An American raconteur, Audubon had just done a book tour of Europe dressed in buckskins, his hair cascading about his shoulders. Now he and his sons, Victor and John Woodhouse, had resolved to portray the continent's mammals in the same manner that Audubon had done with its birds. Because the genius behind *The Birds of America* was intimate, first-hand observation of his subjects in their natural state, Audubon knew he could not produce a grand book on mammals with paintings done from specimens. So it was authenticity that brought one of world's premier nature artists to the American Great Plains aboard the steam vessel *Omega*.

Here was a man who had spent almost his entire life in the wilds of America, closely observing nature, contemplating its moods, beauty, and meaning. He had read the great books on the West, including Lewis and Clark's account from three decades before, and fellow artist George Catlin's much more recent book, which irked Audubon and aroused his jealousy. Yet he was in no way prepared for what unfolded in front of them as the *Omega* made its way past the ruins of the Mandan and Arikara villages, destroyed by smallpox six years earlier, and chugged up the narrowing river, bound for Fort Union at the confluence of the Yellowstone and the Missouri, in the heart of the wild American Great Plains.

It was the animals that stunned him. Audubon had spent his life surrounded by wild creatures, but this was something different. Watching the country unwind in front of them from the prow of their vessel, the plains almost appeared to vibrate with life, so many animals of so many different kinds that the renowned bird painter simply could not believe what his eyes were seeing. In one stretch, two weeks downstream from Fort Union near the eastern border of today's Montana, this condensation from the journal he was keeping—I've excised some of his other commentary—lets us into his mind to experience what he felt about this American Eden:

> We passed some beautiful scenery and almost opposite had the pleasure of seeing five Mountain Rams, or Bighorns, on the summit of a hill. We saw what we supposed to be three Grizzly Bears, but could not be sure. We saw a Wolf attempting to climb a very steep bank of clay. On the opposite shore another Wolf was lying down on a sand-bar, like a dog. I forgot to say that last evening we saw a large herd of Buffaloes, with many calves among them; they were grazing quietly on a fine bit of prairie. They stared, and then started at a handsome canter producing a beautiful picturesque view. We have seen many Elks swimming the river. These animals are abundant beyond belief hereabouts. If ever there was a country where Wolves are surpassingly abundant, it is the one we now are in.

"In fact," Audubon wrote, "it is *impossible to describe or even conceive* the vast multitudes of these animals that exist even now, and feed on these ocean-like prairies." He closed a letter to his wife that summer with this sentence: "My head is actually swimming with excitement, and I cannot write any more."

In the phrase of the nineteenth century, Audubon had gone west and seen the elephant. What one of the country's premier artists was privileged to witness, and in truth what had him in such a state of euphoria, was no less than the American version of the wildlife-rich Serengeti Plain of East Africa. Not even two centuries back in the continent's past, it was one of the natural spectacles of the world, equaled only by places like the Serengeti, the Masai Mara, or the veld of South Africa. These landscapes were all similar, immense open grasslands extending to the curve of the earth, which was part of the appeal. But it was not just the settings, not only the vast opalescent distances, the blue pyramidal forms of mountains on distant horizons, the intersecting planes of horizontal, yellowed grasslands. It was presence of so much sheer life, the marvelous aggregations of big grazers and their predators, all of which you could clearly see interacting in the clean light and vast spaces of all these landscapes, including the interior grasslands of North America.

For millions of years before Audubon stood gobsmacked on the deck of the *Omega*, the American Great Plains had been the setting of giants. In 1855 Ferdinand Hayden discovered the first dinosaur bones from an American site very near Fort Benton, upstream of where Audubon had been in a swoon about nineteenth-century plains wildlife the decade before. The next year, Joseph Leidy named five new dinosaurs from the confluence of the Missouri and Judith's River, only 150 miles up the Missouri from Audubon's epiphanies. Edwin Cope, one of Leidy's students, came to Judith's Landing in 1876, followed by the celebrated Yale paleontologist Othniel Marsh in 1880. Barnum Brown of the American Museum of Natural History found the first T-Rex unearthed from the plains in the early twentieth century. The Great Plains, especially its exposed badlands, became crucial locales for the fossil discoveries that took evolution from theory to fact, and have remained the primary target of the modern dinosaur hunt, at least in the United States and Canada, today.

But of course it wasn't just dinosaurs they were finding. Up and down the plains, from West Texas to the Canadian border and beyond, the paleontologists excavated boxcars of fossil materials pointing to other giants that had lived much more recently than 65-plus million years ago. As nineteenth- and twentieth-century scientists began to re-create the world of the Late Pleistocene, they invented a term—"charismatic megafauna"—to characterize a suite of African-like animals whose bones they were unearthing. It turned out that the American Serengeti had possessed lions (*Panthera*, the giant steppe lion), elephants in the form of mammoths, cheetah-like cats related to modern cougars, along with saber-toothed and scimitar cats that preyed on mammoth calves, giant ground sloths, and probably huge, long-horned bison. Skeletal material showed what was a remarkably gracile short-faced bear that ambushed almost every prey species. The American Serengeti had hyenas, a fast, hunting version, and giant wolves called dire wolves, which pulled down distinctively American-evolved prey from bands of camels and the incredibly plentiful herds of wild horses. That American bestiary was the closest analogue of the creatures of the African plains and veld anywhere in the world. Teddy Roosevelt is supposed to have said of his train ride out of Nairobi in 1910 that it was a "railroad through the Pleistocene."

Because while the African grasslands had retained most of their charismatic megafauna, North America did not, or at least not all. The most high-

Mammoth and Pleistocene megafauna, Museum of Paleontology and Comparative Anatomy, Paris, France. Dan Flores photo.

drama extinction scenario in North American history since we humans have been here happened not during the lifetime of the United States, but instead between 8,000 and 14,000 years ago, when more than thirty genera of American Pleistocene animals completely vanished. There were survivors, to be sure, and across the next few thousand years evolution replaced that earlier version of the American Serengeti with a new one, the historic version that Lewis and Clark, Audubon, and many others left descriptions of from the 1530s on. Until we destroyed it, there was this other, historic version of the Serengeti on the plains, the poetry and spectacle of thronging bison playing the role of thronging wildebeests, pronghorns assuming the role of antelopes and gazelles, stallion bands of wild horses functioning ecologically much like wild bands of zebras, gray and red wolves filling the niche of wild dogs, and coyotes doing an almost exact impression of jackals. Africa might have retained its lions and elephants, hyenas and cheetahs, but the post-Pleistocene version of the American Serengeti had another king of beasts, the grizzly, which played a god-like, lion-like role on the prairies.

No wonder when certain Europeans read about the Great Plains of America in the early 1800s they thought: *safari!* Grand hunting adventures in the world's final primeval grasslands began in America at precisely the same moment they did in Africa, when British traveler Sir William Drummond Stewart commenced a luxurious, guided, high-end hunting trek into the West in the very years (it was the mid-1830s) when William Cornwallis Harris was doing the same in South Africa. Although "safari" (a Swahili word) didn't enter English until the 1850s as a result of Sir Richard Burton's books, all the elements of the luxurious, catered wilderness adventure were there from the beginning when elites like Stewart, the Irish nobleman Sir George Gore, and Russia's Grand Duke Alexis went on extended, celebrated safaris on the Great Plains from the 1830s through the 1870s.

Those elements are memorable to anyone who has seen the film *Out of Africa* or read Hemingway's *The Snows of Kilimanjaro*. Indigenous guides and "white hunters" were a core part of the experience. Stewart, who as Bernard DeVoto says "appears to have been the first wealthy British sportsman who found the West a splendid playground," originally used trader/trappers William Sublette and Joseph Reddeford Walker as his guides. Gore hired Henry Chatillon and Jim Bridger, two other famous mountain men, as his white hunters. For Grand Duke Alexis, son of the Czar of all the Russias, Lakota war leader Spotted Tail was on hand, and his white hunters were equally impressive: Bill Cody, Philip Sheridan, and George Armstrong Custer.

As Robert Redford's Denys Finch-Hatton instructed us in *Out of Africa*, the experience needed to be high-end. Stewart was a former military officer who had fought at Waterloo, but his foppish, laundered attire, tending to white frocks and hats, shocked the mountain men. On his first trip in 1833 he brought wagons of rare liquors, fine cigars, and a companion, a handsome "young English blood." DeVoto characterized Stewart's few surviving letters as brimming with "mysterious longings and melancholies, romantic passions, unhappiness and frustration" and (again this is DeVoto's razor-sharp reading) "an urgent but never quite focused unrest." Writing in the 1940s, he passed off Stewart's oddities to upbringing and a longing for military action. Apparently some of Stewart's companions on safari were not so sure those were the reasons.

On his own second safari to the West, in 1854–1855, Sir George Gore wanted to focus on a specific region of the plains, the Powder River drainage of the Yellowstone in today's Wyoming. His entourage included a staff of fifty—"secretaries, stewards, cooks, flymakers, dog tenders, hunters, servants"—along with imported foods and wines and an extensive library. En route to the Powder, the caravan of six wagons, twenty-one carts, a dozen yokes of oxen, fourteen dogs, and more than a hundred fine hunting horses would string out for more than a mile across the plains. Gore's Indian and white guides liked the man but found themselves sitting around camp until nearly noon while he slept in every day, then had to listen to him read from the classics by firelight at night. Even that degree of opulence got obliterated by Grand Duke Alexis's safari on the Nebraska and Colorado plains in 1871–1872, a party that included all manner of Indian and military dignitaries, more than 500 people, even a regimental band for hunting camp entertainment.

What made a safari, either on the African Serengeti or the American version, was not just servants, haute cuisine on fine china, or cultured companions whose taste ran to (or at least could tolerate) literature and music. Safaris were blood sports, and success was measured by body counts. To his credit, when Stewart was pursuing grizzlies or pronghorns that "could outrun a streak of lightning," he tended not to be obsessive about counting up his kills. On the Powder River in 1855, though, Gore stacked up animals like cordwood— 2,500 buffalo and 40 grizzlies alone. At least he didn't bother to keep tallies on all the pronghorns, elk, mule deer, and wolves he shot, but he shot so many the Crows and Lakotas in the region grew resentful, which ended the hunt. Short, corpulent Duke Alexis, hunting along the Republican and North Platte rivers at a time when the impact of the market hunt was well evident, was dissatisfied enough with the party's kill of only 56 bison that he made their train from Denver to Topeka stop on the Colorado-Kansas border for a second try. This time, in a single day, they murdered another 50 buffalo, along with 150 assorted pronghorns, elk, mule deer, wolves, and coyotes—in short, any living creature that appeared within range. That, not natural history or nights under the stars immersed in a 10,000-year-old ecology, made the duke's safari a success.

The nineteenth-century Great Plains was a slaughterhouse. In the years from the 1820s to the 1920s, this single American region experienced the largest wholesale destruction of animal life discoverable in modern history. The largest biomass of animal life on the plains took the form of bison, which in times of good climate reached 25–30 million and could fill the prairies to the horizons for days on end. By 1886 a few more than 1,000 remained. But the outright eradication wasn't confined to bison, usually the only plains animal you hear about in casual conversation. Pronghorn antelope numbers came close to rivaling those of bison and in 1800 were probably 15 million strong.

Crossing the best pronghorn country in the West, the Llano Estacado plateau, Bureau of Biological Survey biologist Vernon Bailey counted thirty-two in 1899. Grizzlies, which had once ranged across the plains from Texas and Kansas to the Dakotas and had a continental population of 100,000, reached the twentieth century with a few hundred scattered bears left, all those having fled to the mountains. At the time of the Civil War somewhere between a quarter-million and a half-million wolves filled the ecological niche of dominant predator on the Great Plains. Paid federal hunters trapped and poisoned the final few scattered plains lobos in the 1920s, the same decade the last wild horses on the plains ended up bound for dog food plants in the Midwest.

Only coyotes, survivors of the Pleistocene extinctions—and now the slaughterhouse—presented America a baffling predator no amount of persecution could defeat.

We had our reasons, of course, along with our excuses and our bravado about how we were doing it for civilization. But only a handful of charismatic big species ended up left on the plains, primarily the seven whose stories I tell here (I include us in that count), plus deer and cougars. Elk, which had once ranged across the plains through half of Oklahoma, most of Kansas, even into Iowa and Minnesota, survived only in the Mountain West. We hunted bighorns to local extirpation in the Northern Plains badlands by 1906. Both species survived, and we have reintroduced them back onto the plains when and where we could, at least, a mea culpa and penance, although we know their patchy presence is but a shadow of what once was.

I have always loved that Walter Prescott Webb's wonderful book from nearly a century ago now, *The Great Plains*, has a section about the animals of the plains, which to me meant he took them seriously rather than as some kind of lumpen fodder for the meat-grinder of history. But the march of civilization *has* been a meat-grinder. Much like evolution, it has been one of those processes that goes on around you whether you acknowledge it or not, or even believe in it. Commenting on the herds of bison he could see from the parapets of Fort Union in 1843, Audubon described an obvious depravity of human nature towards them, namely the sport of firing cannon shot into the distant herds when times around the fort were boring. Audubon was disgusted: "even now there is a perceptible difference in the size of the herds, and before many years the Buffalo, like the Great Auk, will have disappeared." He continued, "Surely, this should not be permitted."

But, to let Audubon's passive construction stand, it *was* permitted. We

The "American Serengeti"—the Great Plains, eastern New Mexico, in our own time an empty stage compared to the riot of wildlife that thronged here for millions of years before us. Dan Flores photo.

permitted it. We stood by and allowed what happened to the Great Plains a century ago, the destruction of one of the ecological wonders of the world. In modern America we need to see this with clear eyes, and soberly, so that we understand well that the flyover country of our own time derives much of its forgetability from being a slate wiped almost clean of its original figures.

What we did to the Great Plains was not some admirable conquest. It was a myopic, chaotic, unthinking destruction, and, I think, immoral. I mean this less in reference to what we consider modern moral dicta than with respect to the origins of morality, that evolution of a sense of fair play among members of a social species, which eventually led to our religious and social codes. The evolution of fairness early on came to include a human recognition that other creatures enjoy being alive, and that depriving them of life is a very serious matter. Some philosophers have called this Biophilia, a love of organic, biological life. In terms of the origins of morality, our slaughterhouse on the Great Plains was profoundly immoral.

This is another of those moments in history when we have a chance to make things right, though. We have mostly stumbled 'til now, but in the present century we have the best chance so far to re-wild and re-create an American Serengeti of the size, and in the template, of the world's first grand nature preserve, Yellowstone National Park. Doing so will take monumental will and statecraft. But the bison, pronghorns, and grizzlies are still here, horses of the original Spanish type that exploded across the plains still foal in the Pryor Mountains Wild Horse Range in Montana, wolves are on their way back—as of 2015, at least to parts of the Southern Plains—and coyotes haven't gone anywhere except into the streets of every big city in America.

Henry David Thoreau made an entry in his journal in 1857 that is appropriate for putting all of this into perspective. It's a sentiment I've come back to many times in thinking about the plains. Thoreau had been reading some of the accounts of the first settlers in New England, from two centuries earlier. Writing a journal entry one morning, he put his feelings this way: "I take infinite pains to know all the phenomena of the spring, for instance, thinking that I have here the entire poem, and then, to my chagrin, I hear that it is but an imperfect copy that I possess and have read, that my ancestors have torn out many of the first leaves and grandest passages, and mutilated it in many places."

Then he continued, in a way that anyone who drives across the plains today, but also knows something of its history, will well understand.

"I should not like to think some demigod had come before me and picked out some of the best of the stars. I wish to know an entire heaven and an entire earth."

I

In the 1980s and 1990s I lived on the Great Plains. I have never gotten over it. I grew up in southern forests and bayous, spent twenty years of my life in the Rocky Mountains of Montana, and presently live off the end of the Southern Rockies in New Mexico because I am passionately in love with deserts. And I travel to oceans, since like most of us I find something hypnotic and satisfying to my genetic memory in an ocean beach. But here's the thing: the sea, the woods, the mountains, all suffer in comparison with the prairie. What Romantic Age celebration of landscape aesthetics used to call "the sublime"—an awe capable of stilling the dialogue in the mind—is reachable more easily in vast, horizontal plains than in any other kind of landscape. That sublimity arises from the plains' unfathomable boundaries, a self-confident grandness of scale layered atop a kind of still, calm, monotony of sensory effect, and from the country's entire lack of echo and strange ability to deceive. In the years I lived there, I found that, deliberately taken in with all the senses, the Great Plains endlessly stunned me. The place is a sensuous feast of the minimal.

But I do understand that there is something bigger going on here. For the last 40,000 years, since we humans left Africa and began to explore the larger world, encountering and taking the measure of one landscape after another, we have been engaged in a search. Maybe it was the same search, as some believe, that compels us in this century to Mars and beyond. But the impulse may have been simpler, for once we began to write, in the literature of exploration the places that aroused our strongest passions were places that most resembled our original African home: yellow savannahs speckled to the limits of our sight with herds and packs of wild animals. Think of the Masai Mara and the Serengeti as our templates, and the diverse bestiary of Chauvet Cave, the site of some of our earliest artistic expressions, as a subsequent remembering of whence we'd come.

The American Great Plains may be one more reminder that we can find home again. Excepting East Africa itself, 200 years ago no part of the globe quite thrilled us in the same primeval way. Today the plains out east of the mountain divide is a drought- and dust-plagued habitat of big farm machinery, ignored and ridiculed, flyover country. But before it was de-buffaloed, de-wolved, and de-grassed, the nineteenth-century Great Plains was one of the marvels of the world. With its staggering ecology of charismatic animals, the plains enabled Americans and Europeans of all backgrounds to experience home base one last time.

It was here, on these sublime horizontal yellow sweeps, which extended eastward for 500 miles beneath the rain shadow of the Rockies, that we also have the strongest argument for the oldest continuous (or almost so) story of human life in North America. This debate actually revolves around several candidate places, in locations as diverse as Alaska, Pennsylvania, Virginia, and Texas, and it is a debate that may not be resolved in our lifetimes. But one overcast March day in 2005, an old friend from Montana, writer Steven Rinella, and I spent an afternoon tramping across one spot that, without any question, stands in the direct line of the founding of human history in America. The bleak, surprising setting of our immersion in Big History in America entirely lacked any of the schoolbook associations of a Jamestown or a Plymouth or a Santa Fe. But in the founding of America, it did have one great advantage not enjoyed by those more famous sites. Its story pushes definite human inhabitation of our continent back more than 13,200 years (Jamestown, 1607, and Santa Fe, 1610, seem yesterday by comparison). Thirteen-thousand years is also how long, for a certainty, we humans—the most charismatic Great Plains megafauna of all—have intertwined our lives and fortunes with the animal life of the North American plains. Once more, across a span of time that didn't finally end until a century ago, we lived off animals.

There are arguments, to be sure, for a continental culture even older than Clovis. Centered on a small scattering of sites elsewhere in America, one of them, the Friedkin Site in the Texas Hill Country on the southeastern edge of the Great Plains, may date to 15,500 years ago. But so far no older cul-ture we've found seems to have draped itself over the continent with the geo-graphic sweep of the Clovis Paleolithic hunters, whose excavated campsites range from Montana to West Texas and the Southwest. We barely know them as a people. One recent theory is that they were a "Northern Hemisphere wild-type." Think Siberian Vikings, a settler society of hyper-aggressive colonists whose descendants, once the giant bestiary of the Pleistocene collapsed, lost many of those traits. Analysis in 2014 of the DNA of a Clovis child from a Montana site indicated that the Clovis people were not only originally Siberi-ans, they are the direct ancestors of 80 percent of the native population of the Americas.

In search of Clovis America, Steven and I were out in my old home country, the Southern High Plains, although who knows what the ancient inhabitants might have called these flat prairies, seemingly endless as the ocean seas. In 1932, when archaeologists first discovered this ancient setting, near spring-fed wetlands in a shallow Pleistocene stream channel coursing these plains, the place was about to be mined for gravel to build roads through the nearby town of Clovis, New Mexico. Early settlers had named the winding, grassy channel Blackwater Draw. But as archaeologist E. B. Howard made discov-eries here that rocked the world, the scientists decided to name the people whose lives they were resurrecting the "Clovis People," after the nearby town. Eventually science would discover a "Clovisia the Beautiful" that had lasted some 400 years, almost twice as long as the modern United States has so far, and conclude that its residents had fanned out across most of America. But Blackwater Draw was where Clovis people reemerged out of the mists of the continent's forgotten past. This marshy little valley out in the middle of plains extending thirty miles to the horizons is where one of the templates for how to live in a grand grasslands took shape.

As Steven and I followed our self-guided tour around this famous site, it became clear that the Clovis people had arrived in America at a propitious time. Large cosmic forces have shaped Earth's Big History. There have been extra-terrestrial impacts that have reset the evolutionary clock more than once, wobbles in the Earth's spin around its axis that have effected clocklike climate shifts cycling between Ice Ages and the Pluvials between them, plate tectonics and continental drift to raise mountain ranges and spark volcanic fireworks. And of course amidst it all has been biological evolution, refitting life for all the endless changes. But the Clovis people were lucky enough to be

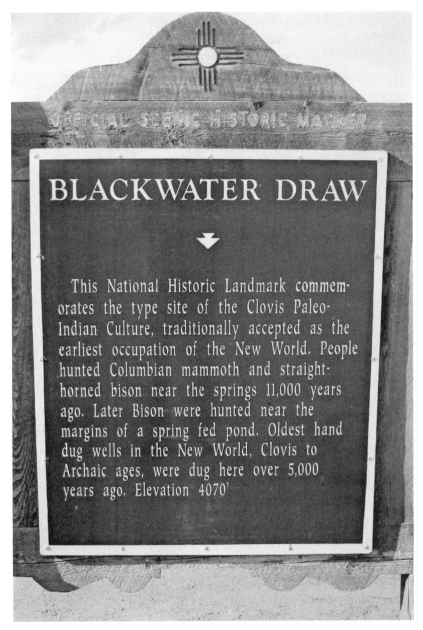

Blackwater Draw, eastern New Mexico, site of the original discovery of the Clovis big game hunting culture of North America. Dan Flores photo.

here when giants still roamed the continent. Indeed, it was the never-hunted Pleistocene megafauna of the Americas that had drawn the Clovis people out of Siberia in the first place.

Between 14,000 and 8,000 years ago, though, as the Wisconsin Ice Age began to wane and North America began to warm, many of the large, Africa-analogue creatures that inhabited the Americas were going extinct. But 13,000 years ago in what would one day be New Mexico, it was still possible for the Clovis people to specialize in elephants. It was the discovery of their large spear points embedded in the remains of mammoths, giant ground sloths, camels, and horses that had rocked the world in the 1930s. It confirmed something no one had believed previously, that ancient Americans had hunted giant creatures no longer found on Earth.

Walking along Blackwater Draw and gazing across these vast plains that March afternoon, the obvious observation to make was that the elephant hunt did not last. Indeed, in the early 1970s archaeologists uncovered more than 8,000 artifacts here from another culture, known as Folsom (also named after a New Mexico plains town, farther north), which succeeded the Clovis people in time. As indicated by the Folsom site, and many others like it across the West, the extinction of the elephants led the next inhabitants of this region to specialize in another of the great Pleistocene species, a massive, early bison known as *Bison antiquus*. But like the mammoths, in time *Bison antiquus* were also fated to become extinct across the Great Plains. While Folsom culture and its spinoffs perfected bison drives, corrals, and atlatl technology to enable them to survive some 2,000 years, around roughly 11,000 years ago this lifeway, too, was collapsing.

Looking around us at these immense, windy, usually brightly lit savannahs, now bereft of both elephants and giant bison (and on this particular day, even sunshine), it did not require much intellectual effort for Steven and me to discern some patterns in the deep time history of this place. Track any part of the world across the large expanses of time since humans arrived and a story begins to unfold that demonstrates a set of principles about history. First, because the grand forces mean that the Earth is an evolving and endlessly changing world, no place remains the same across Big History. The science of ecology once waxed eloquent about "climax," the biophysical reality of environments if left undisturbed. But every environment is endlessly undergoing disturbance, or recovery from it, so that what appear to be climaxes are merely snapshots in time.

Second, human beings—like every other living species—change the places where we live. The famous geographer Yi-Fu Tuan once composed a simple and elegant aphorism: space plus culture equals place. In truth, though, only the first human inhabitants to occupy a piece of ground on Earth ever got to interact with "space." Since we succeed one another in place after place, we end up interacting not with raw nature but with settings that have already been altered by the preceding inhabitants. Just as the Folsom people did in the wake of 400 years of Clovis life on the Great Plains, all of us who come later are engaging with someone else's previously-created "place." The Folsom people inherited a Great Plains without elephants, then bequeathed a plains country lacking giant bison.

A story that spans time-frames like these is the province of Big History—what French scholars have for many decades called la longue durée. In a part of the world now divided up into cities and towns and their spheres, by county and state lines—so that we tend to think of ourselves as being in "West Texas" or "the Oklahoma Panhandle" or "the Dakotas"—the plains has actually long functioned, and still does, as a distinctive ecological region that has produced a particular kind of history different from elsewhere, different because of the landscape itself. And its possibilities.

There is in fact a theory about human settlement that goes directly to the issue of possibilities for settler societies. Possibilism, as it's known, posits that regional environments like the Southern High Plains or the Dakota or Montana Badlands do not completely determine how people will live in them. Rather they offer a range of possibilities from which we choose based on the kind of culture we bring with us. Human cultural preparation can be so different that what one group sees as a valuable potential resource, another group may entirely ignore as worthless. A region like the Southern High Plains, say, does not offer unlimited possibilities. Whaling or an economy based on processing timber would not fall within the range of lifeways any human culture might follow here. Yet out on the expansive, sunlit grasslands of the Great Plains, whose offerings might strike many from forested, wetter regions as quite limited, 13,000 years of Big History shows a fair range of possible ways of living. Always, though, following a particular dictum of nature: like the Earth itself, life on the plains revolves around the sun.

The geology, topography, climate, and biology of the Great Plains have been fundamental keys to life of all sorts in a grassland setting. What appears an unrelenting, unremarkable flatness to the topography of the plains comes from its surface geology, which is sedimentary outwash from the Rocky Mountains. Over millions of years that outwash buried ancient, carboniferous life forms from the Permian, Triassic, and in a few spots the Jurassic periods, when the country that would become the Great Plains was then ruled by dinosaurs. The overlying erosional wash from the mountains also buried very old mountain stream runoff in the form of a gigantic fossil lake we now call the Ogallala Aquifer, which lies beneath the surface from Texas to Nebraska.

Because its surface has been washed down from high mountains to the west, plains topography gradually loses elevation from west to east. Despite appearances from a car window on interstate highways, though, the Great Plains is far from tennis court–flat. Rivers out of the Rockies—the Missouri, Yellowstone, Platte, Arkansas, Cimarron, Canadian, Pecos, and hundreds of their tributaries—had carved arroyo channels, canyons, and left vast stretches of eroded badlands on the plains eons before the Clovis people ever arrived. The Red River, Brazos, and Colorado of Texas, draining off an isolated plateau called the Llano Estacado on the Southern Plains—laid down another set of long, shallow channels before sluicing away a wild, tangled, vertical landscape on the plateau's eastern escarpment. For the last million years these smaller plateau rivers have spilled off that escarpment through deep, brightly colored canyons that expose the underlying Permian and Triassic rocks. The original Clovis site in New Mexico that Steven and I walked in 2005 is in one of the headwater channels of this system.

Geology and topography have remained fairly constant since humans got to the plains, but climate and biology have changed enormously, and often. Because the Great Plains is far inland from oceans, and the Rocky Mountains intercept much of the moisture flowing across the West from the Pacific, since humans have been here the plains has had a semi-arid climate. For the past 13,000 years it has been drier than the country on either side of it, typically bathed in 320 annual days of sunshine, and because of its slight topography and solar heating, usually very windswept. But like everywhere else on Earth, it has had a climate dramatically variable through time. The Wisconsin Glacial period produced much cooler, more lush conditions, with much more extensive tree growth across the plains then. One of the reasons we know this is because of relict populations of trees now associated with the mountains, like Rocky Mountain junipers, that still grow in wet, north-facing locations hundreds of miles out on the prairies. But there have also been hot, dry ep-

In a landscape that powers human societies with sunlight converted by grassland photosynthesis into energy, the most direct strategy for exploiting that energy is through hunting grazing animals. Dan Flores photo.

isodes that sometimes lasted not just decades but hundreds of years, and in the case of a drought called the Altithermal, for thousands.

Conditions like these have meant that the plains has been dominated by grasses, which by their nature require less water than woody vegetation. The closer to the mountains, where the rainshadow effect is pronounced, the shorter the grasses, which gradually increase to mid-height and then tall grasses on the eastern edge of the plains. A world dominated by grass and sky has meant everything in plains history. The equation is a very simple one. Biological life is dependent on energy, and since the energy that drives most terrestrial systems comes directly from the sun, grasslands in open terrain under cloudless skies tend to produce a very direct conversion of solar energy. In one simple step of photosynthesis, thermodynamic energy streaming from the sun is directly available to animals that eat grass. Hence when humans, omnivores rather than herbivores, looked to the resource possibilities on the Southern High Plains, what they readily saw were lifeways centered around converting the massive solar energy charge of the region into forms humans could use.

One final element influenced the world of possibilities on the plains: geographical context. Humans are not just social among our own groups, we seek out contacts with other human groups. And if those groups reside in environments different from ours, we trade what we produce and value for things we lack but value. Today our global market economy is the result. So it is not surprising that at signal moments in the human history of the Great Plains, its residents reached out to peoples who were following very different lifeways in very different biological regions to the west and east. The peoples of the plains, in other words, joined in regional economic systems that tied them by trade to peoples living elsewhere.

This is the framework for human history on the Great Plains from the time of the Paleolithic big game hunt, from the age of Clovis elephant hunters and Folsom bison hunters. The Folsom hunters inherited a *Clovis* place—"Clovisia the Beautiful"—that no longer offered the possibility of elephant hunting. In the time they dominated the plains, Folsom hunters and their several offshoots concentrated their economies on the remnant herds of Pleistocene bison, increasingly on a late subspecies, *Bison antiquus occidentalis*. But by 11,000 years ago the huge Pleistocene bison were gone.

Then over the next 3,000 years, one species of charismatic Pleistocene megafauna after another went extinct. Winking out in isolated little groups, the camels followed the bison, as did the giant ground sloths. Camelops, the last plains camel, sprang from a family of animals that, like horses and pronghorns, had evolved in the American West. Now this American native was extinct. Hanging on the longest, but whose disappearance is the most bizarre of all, horses were another American native that had absolutely dominated the Pleistocene grasslands. There are recently discovered horse kill sites in the West, but nothing on the scale of the Solutrean horse hunters of Europe, who left kill sites of 20,000 animals. Nonetheless, by 8,000 years ago horses became the last of the big animals to go. The predators that had pursued all these grazers and browsers—the steppe lions and dire wolves and long-toothed cats, the long-legged hyenas and "false" cheetahs—followed the ungulates to their graves. Viewed in fast-forward from space the extinctions would have appeared like wind-scattered embers dying out in a slow rain. And in the end, nothing.

The Pleistocene extinctions are obviously a big story. Isolated from the rest of the world since the breakup of the ancient supercontinent of Laurasia, the Americas had long lacked one significant charismatic megafauna that Africa had, and that Europe and Asia in time acquired: humans. North American wild creatures had evolved many wonderful special adaptations, like the long, curved fangs of the saber-toothed and scimitar cats, perfectly adapted for stabbing young elephants. Several prey species had evolved tactics against predators that hunted in packs, but none had evolved any adaptation at all to a pack hunter who used dogs and fire and topography and highly refined and deadly flint tools. Herds of animals that had never seen or smelled a human no doubt was the magnet that drew hunters from Siberia to search out pathways into America.

American Pleistocene animals seem to have been in no way prepared for that arrival. Sad outcomes from First Contact between sophisticated human hunters and unschooled animals have been a worldwide phenomenon in Big History, but of course on the Great Plains between 8,000 and 13,000 years ago, there was another elephant in the room. The Ice Age was ending. Climates were changing drastically, and some species clearly could not keep up. All we know is that across that 5,000-year-long span, thirty-two genera and at least fifty species of American animals vanished forever. A Great Plains that looked very much like Africa, was if anything maybe even more impressive than Africa, dwindled away to a few remnant species, which then went on to create their own grassland ecological marvel over the ensuing centuries and millennia. But it was a fairly faint reflection of what had been.

And to be honest, that is close to where our knowledge ends. Just why almost three-quarters of all the species of our large mammals and birds went extinct is still a mystery. There are theories, naturally, the most engaging of which is paleobiologist Paul Martin's "Blitzkrieg Overkill" model, positing that a fairly small population of hunters spread rapidly across the Americas, increased in population from the opportunities of this great frontier, and in a few hundred years wiped out millions of big animals. The warming, drying climate theory has a hard time matching that for drama. But the truth is, we just don't know. Martin's overkill hypothesis is on its firmest ground with mammoths. Elephant populations may not have been large, and a great many mammoth sites show evidence of human points and butchering tools. For most other species things are far less clear. An emerging line of thinking is that both hunting and climate were involved, climate because it generated patchy habitat that then isolated animal populations, which human hunters may have finished off— not in a few hundred years but across perhaps 5,000. Or, as paleomammalogist Ross McFee has more recently suggested, perhaps human migrations with domesticated dogs brought new diseases that produced epizootics among the native fauna.

It is the grand mystery of early America.

The most important part of this story for us is not so much what killed all these marvelous creatures, or that the Great Plains thereafter would never again quite duplicate the Serengeti, although both those ideas are fully capable of co-opting the mind. Down the timeline we inherited, the most important thing is that the Great Extinctions set in motion ecological ripples through space and time. Nature's response to the warming climate and the continued stress of hunting societies from the successors of the Folsom (some of them are the Plainview, Plano, and Cody cultures) and so many now-vacant ecological niches was to push the surviving animals to take advantage of the new circumstances. By about 5,000 years ago, with so many grazers now gone, a dwarfed species of bison (our modern animal) that possessed a faster reproductive turnover time and other traits better adapted to the new conditions evolved as a new, fully formed plains species. In the absence of serious competition the population of Bison bison grew exponentially, filled at least some of the vacuum left by the great extinctions, and multiplied into the enormous herds that so boggled the imaginations of all those who would later witness them. In an evolutionary sense, the historic bison was something of a "weed species," released by a major ecological disturbance. Later bison hunters were reaping the good life from a fairly unusual situation in world history, as it turns out. And as long as there were millions of them covering the river valleys and uplands of the plains beyond the eye's reach, a thousand generations of human beings really considered no other possibility.

This rise and fall of cultures on the Great Plains is a Big History fixture. Hence the pattern: each set of new inhabitants would inherit a place modified and changed by prior and accumulating human history, in effect a humanized landscape. After the Pleistocene had run its course, new peoples, a collection of slightly different regional cultural groups who are collectively known as the Archaics, would live, love, die, and transform the region by firing the grasslands and hunting the animals for almost 10,000 years, almost forty times longer than our own society, centered on what we call the United States, has existed.

At this point I want to focus the unfolding story more closely, specifically now on the Southern Plains, the part of the Great Plains south of the Arkansas River, in today's Kansas, Colorado, New Mexico, Oklahoma, and Texas. The Big History patterns here are the clearest of any plains subregion. Archaic peoples are generally known as gatherer/hunters who devoted more attention to plant gathering than had their ancestors, but on the sunny grasslands of the Southern High Plains it was still a grazing animal that converted sunlight most efficiently into energy. The cycles of wet and dry enormously affected the caloric energy in the grasslands. Sometimes the plains produced an enormous biomass of bison that spilled eastward and westward hundreds of miles. At other times bison entirely abandoned parts of the plains. But during times of good climates more than 8 million of them would convert sunlight into energy on the Southern High Plains. Across the past 5,000 years the bison's adaptation to the shortgrass and mid-height grasslands was such a perfect fit that the animals were able to survive every wild swing of the Grand Forces. No wobble in the Earth's spin took them out. No asteroid froze them in post-impact winters. In fact *Bison bison* was better adapted to the grasslands than were the Archaics who hunted them. Until a little more than a hundred years ago they would survive fifty centuries of climate swings and hunting and re-main the dominant, iconic, Great Plains megafauna of the new era.

The Archaics perfected a long-term, sustainable lifeway on the plains, one of the longest-running ways of extracting a living from nature that humans have ever practiced in America. But they did experience a changing world that at times led them to draconian decisions. Closely attuned to the feedback they read from nature, aware that times were not always good, they seem deliber-ately to have managed their populations, and the most common way they did so was through infanticide, a psychological burden they would seek to avoid when and if they could.

They also confronted a major climate emergency that demanded an ex-treme response. Beginning about 8,500 years ago, climate in the American West cycled into an extremely warm, dry phase that stuck in this climate cycle for a mind-blowing 3,700 years. This was the depths of the Inter-Glacial, a long slide down from the frozen wastelands of the Wisconsin Ice Age. But the Earth's rotational wobble now had the northern hemisphere slightly closer to the sun, so for almost forty centuries the plains cooked. The Altithermal, as it is called, came close to turning the entire plains into a true desert, and a vacant one. Not only did bison leave the region for wetter conditions to the east and north, evidence is strong that most of the Archaic peoples did the same. While a few villages of Archaics held on in Southern Plains wetlands like Blackwater Draw and Lubbock Lake, outmigration in fact became the preferred adaptation for both people and animals during this longest, hottest summer in Great Plains history. Pretty much everybody and everything left.

As the effects of the Altithermal began to wane and bison and Archaic peoples filtered back onto the Southern Plains, beginning about 2,000 years ago, significant changes occurring on both sides of the region set in motion new possibilities. About 4,000 years ago Mesoamerican cultures separately invented agriculture, a breakthrough step—probably forced by mounting human populations that pushed hunting to its limits—that had revolutionized human life in the Old World a few thousand years earlier. Crop growing as a new lifeway traveled northward with Mexican traders to the Mogollon and Anasazi peoples of the Desert Southwest and to the mound-building Mississippian peoples of the Mississippi Valley. With developing farming societies on either side of the Southern Plains, a new world of possibilities opened up.

In the 1,500 years following AD year 1, in present New Mexico just west of the open plains, corn-growing, pottery-making, pueblo-building societies of great sophistication and far-reaching trade networks grew up whose power began to influence the plains. At about the same time, agricultural, village-dwelling peoples in the South, Caddoan speakers in what is now East Texas, Arkansas, and Louisiana, likewise established vibrant societies that began to probe up the rivers towards the plains, looking for trading partners and new possibilities. The result of this stimulation for plains hunters was a suite of new ideas—new ways to think about resources, trade, even the kind of houses you lived in. There were dazzling new technologies, the most revolutionary one the bow and arrow, passed from group to group from the Far North. Plains Archaic people probably first saw bows in the hands of the Anasazi/Pueblo farmers in New Mexico.

The trade possibility was an obvious one for people living in different ways and in very different landscapes. The plains peoples had in profusion the products of the bison hunt. They had flints striped in maroon and blue from a famous quarry we would later name Alibates, also beautifully tanned robes, and especially dried protein in abundance. What plains hunters had always lacked to make them fully healthy were vegetables—carbohydrates. Now, with

The emergence of farming communities, like the one at Taos Pueblo, on both sides of the plains created new trading possibilities for Great Plains people a thousand years ago. Dan Flores photo.

agricultural societies on the scene, both hunters and farmers could overcome their dietary bottlenecks. Puebloan and Caddoan farmers longed for more protein in their diets. Plains hunters ate too much meat. Soon enough the meat-for-vegetables trade became mutually beneficial for everyone involved. Humans being human, luxury and status goods to help people differentiate themselves, like turquoise from the Pueblo mines, lubricated the exchange. The trade items would change over time but this immersion into far-flung regional trade networks was a whole new plains possibility. This Indian form of it would thrive almost a thousand years.

With a more imaginative take on the possible, plains people could now pursue lifeways of increasing complexity. One spur: from AD 1250 to 1525, as the climate drifted again towards droughts, bison once more migrated away from the Southern Plains to wetter locales to the east. The response of the plains hunters to this was fascinating, to say the least. Apparently the new lifestyles modeled by the farmers suddenly seemed attractive to folks living in the midst of the High Plains; maybe with buffalo gone some of the agriculturalists themselves decided to try to farm the prairie interior. But between 1200 and 1500 a famous experiment on the Southern Plains involved groups like the Antelope Creek people who set up farming towns out in the heart of the plains, along the Canadian River system near the Alibates quarries in the panhandle of present Texas and alongside the Republican River in today's Kansas. What makes these High Plains farmers a mystery is that their crops, points, pottery, and tools came from both the eastern *and* western farming traditions. Rather than the hide tipis of the hunters, they built rock-slab houses of multiple rooms, an architecture fairly evidently based on admiration of the Pueblo model from 300 miles farther west.

Crop growing was a strategy to extract solar energy as directly as possible. But growing crops requires consistent moisture, and whoever the Antelope Creek people were, they could not sustain farming in the deep heart of the plains. Drought, the cause that had undercut the great Chacoan Empire of the Pueblos farther west, eventually pressed the Antelope Creek people to abandon their experiment. Others, notably Caddoan speakers from their Mississippian homeland and Siouan speakers from the Great Lakes, would push farming villages up the rivers of the plains, too. But until the twentieth century, no one else would ever try to farm so far out on the High Plains in the midst of a hunting country of big animals.

After the 1500s, of course, radically new possibilities opened up on the Southern Plains and the Great Plains generally. When European Spaniards founded Santa Fe in 1610, and European Frenchmen commenced Natchitoches (1714) and New Orleans (1718) in Louisiana, the Big History story ratcheted into another phase. Two brand-new developments—domesticated animals brought from Europe, and the bottomless desires of a relentless international market economy—once again expanded the possibilities. One of the animals happened to be the old American native, the horse. Their evolution shaped by millions of years in North America, horses had survived in Asia and Europe, where the people who had once hunted them had finally domesticated them. Returned by the Spaniards to their original habitat, horses exploded across their old homeland, especially after the Pueblo Revolt of 1680 left Santa Fe's stock herds in Indian hands. It took fewer than twenty-five years after the Pueblo Revolt for the next dominant hunters of the Southern Plains, the Comanches, to arrive from the north in search of the country from whence an animal as magical and entirely perfect as the horse had sprung.

For peoples then living on (or drawn to) the Southern Plains, the horse was a revolution, and not just because it gave native peoples a more efficient beast of burden to replace the dog. The horse made possible a massive intensification in the human capture of solar energy streaming from the sun into the grasslands. It was a grazer itself, so transformed solar energy into power humans could harness. It competed with the food source animal, the bison, for grass and water, but it also became an efficiency multiplier for harvesting them. With the horse, plains humans had finally become as well-adapted to the grasslands as the bison themselves. Along with the pull of the market economy, the cycling climate of the plains, and growing human settlements encircling the plains that cut off the bison's migration refuges, the horse also was fated to cast a dark shadow over the bison herds. In the euphoria of the time, no Indian could see that shadow, but it was there.

For 150 years the new Comanche Empire of the Southern Plains availed itself of all the new possibilities. Occupying an ancient place and adding new elements, it built on old trade networks to exchange bison products both for crops and now for European industrial metal ware. Even the horses the Comanches rode, bred, and collected into herds of great personal wealth became a trade resource. Starting in the 1770s, the Comanche Empire traded tens of thousands of horses and mules annually to American traders from towns like New Orleans and St. Louis. The very success of the empire the Comanches built rested atop the most fundamental of Big History principles: with bison, and now an added grazer, the horse, theirs was an empire erected as directly as possible on most intense use of solar energy any humans had so far harnessed on the plains. The Comanches actually saw that connection and made the sun their primary object of religious veneration. Visitors to their villages said that in the morning Comanche men would hang their shields in full view of the sun. Through the day they would rotate them, like a field of painted leather sunflowers, to absorb streaming sun power—*puha*, or medicine.

For millennia the size of the bison population had been linked with climate, and except for a dry period in the late 1820s, the first four decades of the nineteenth century was a time of above-normal rainfall on the Plains. The carrying capacity for bison and horses was high. In retrospect, it was one last, brief, shining moment of 13,000-plus years of Indian life on the plains. Beginning in 1846, Southern Plains rainfall plunged as much as 30 percent below the median for nine years of the next decade, and did so for six of those years on the Central Plains. Drought on the Great Plains in the fifteen-year stretch

Nomadic villages of horse herders and bison/pronghorn hunters still characterized the Great Plains as late as the 1880s. Dan Flores photo of a Steven Spielberg movie set from *Into the West*.

before 1865 is one of the most severe "short" droughts on record. What was happening was that the Little Ice Age, which had cooled and moistened the plains for almost 300 years, was ending in a shockwave of dry and hot.

Beyond drought there was the global market's insatiable hunger for the animals of the plains, which it needed dead and at least modestly processed. The market hunt took out the bison first, then the elk and the sheep. Pronghorns were next. The remnant straggling grizzlies went quickly. Plains buffalo wolves took longer and significant effort, as did the rest of the wild horses. No amount of effort directed at them made any difference with coyotes, but their persecution hardly made them the lucky winners. All this plus the advance of the railroads, and American imperialist intentions towards the grasslands, made the endgame for the Comanches more complicated, if not less tragic, than was the case for Clovis or Antelope Creek people. As so many times before in plains Big History, when the end came it was sudden and shocking.

Big History patterns did not fade away just because Americans arrived to push aside the New Mexicans (who had quickly directed yet another grazer, enormous flocks of sheep, onto the grasslands). Out on now silent sweeps, like a stage abandoned by its players, Americans initially saw the grazing possibility and populated the region with cattle, trail drives, ranches. By the early

twentieth century on the Southern Plains, and the early twenty-first on the Northern, with deep-drilling (and ultimately fracking) technology available to them, American plains dwellers discovered the fossilized carbon wealth in the Permian and other formations buried underfoot. By the 1920s the realm of the elephant and bison had become a booming oil and natural gas bonanza that, burned for energy, began to contribute to a carbon buildup in the atmosphere that not only threatened Great Plains climate but that of the world. Along with de-buffaloing and de-wolfing the country, the new residents also came close to de-grassing it, turning much of the region into wheat and cotton grown by tapping the fossil lake beneath the surface. Did the new plains have anything of the romance and poetry of the earlier versions of the plains, with their grand herds and hunts and natural drama? Only if you're exceptionally unromantic and ahistorical.

It took 13,000 years but the one, singular charismatic megafauna that walked upright did finally succeed in vanquishing, indeed nearly obliterating, all the others and bending the plains to its will. An observation like that makes this sketch of *longue durée* human history seem more simplistic than it ever was, of course, but the thing about Big History is that inside its broad-stroke narrative, individual humans were still living out their lives, full of the pathos and drama inherent in the human condition. Events of such great importance to us that we mark the passage of centuries by them—the collapse of a civilization, the emergence of a religion, the invention of some technology that transforms how we live, the rise or fall of noteworthy figures, the demise of diagnostic regional animals—all these were playing out inside Big History. They were what we normally think of as "human history." Admittedly, thinking in these grand, sweeping terms does miss some of those more normal markers of the human trajectory, a kind of scent of flesh as we live it. What the story I've just told does do to compensate, though, is to give us a history of the human animal quite a bit more like the kinds of histories we ought to have about bison, wolves, horses—about species other than ourselves, in other words. Like us, each of the last big animals of the Great Plains has a biography, its own distinctive story. I am convinced their stories, too, are an essential part of North American history.

Standing out in the sunlit horizontal yellow sweeps today, far enough from roads that I can focus my mind on the matter, by an act of the imagination I can sometimes conjure up the historical imagery that played out here. Out in the physical space where all those dramas unfolded, the Big History of the Great Plains can make you feel as if you're standing at the end of an immense line of dominos, which wind and curl far beyond your sight, but you know stretch back to elephant hunters, to giant animals, to vast panoramas of grass and distance and unbelievable animals in unfathomable abundance, the whole tableau domed by an endless blue that everyone from Clovis times until now must have paused to marvel over.

These are spans of time vaster than most of us can imagine and ways of living we may struggle to recognize as part of our past. The eerie emptiness enveloping a place like Blackwater Draw does not lie, though. This is who we are, and across a stupendous setting where millions of charismatic creatures once made up one of the wonders of the planet, this is what we've done.

2

"From the accounts of all the Indians, I have seen, it is probable there may be a species of Antilope near the head waters of R. River." Those words, penned for the eye of President Thomas Jefferson, were written by Dr. Peter Custis, the official naturalist attached to Jefferson's "Grand Expedition," the president's follow-up to the Lewis and Clark exploring expedition into the Louisiana Purchase. When Custis conveyed to Jefferson accounts from the Indians and their guides about the mysteries that lay farther up the Red River of the Southwest, he was writing at one of the portentous moments in the early exploration of the West. His brief line, it turned out, also captured a critical point in time in the long history of one of the true marvels of the American Great Plains, the pronghorn antelope.

The year was 1806, and Custis was with a fifty-man party of scientists, soldiers, and guides that had just been turned back at the edge of the Great Plains by a Spanish army. In almost a final, dying gasp of its North American empire, Spain had risen to the occasion to keep expansionist-minded Americans out of the Southwest and away from Spanish treasures like Santa Fe and the California missions. Naturalist Custis was taking one last wistful look upriver before heading back to civilization. And one of the misses on his mind clearly was this rumored, African-like "Antilope" that roamed the horizontal yellow prairies just beyond his reach as an Enlightenment Age scientist.

When Americans finally made it to the Great Plains at the turn of the nineteenth century, we called these fabled animals

Pronghorns evolved on the Great Plains with 70 mph predators like American cheetahs. When their predators vanished in the Pleistocene extinctions, pronghorns continued into our own time with evolutionary adaptations modeled around a vanished world. Dan Flores photo.

antelope for good reason, since in size, form, and speed they resembled no other creatures quite so much as the antelopes and gazelles of Africa. But pronghorns turned out not to be true antelope. The Antilocapridae ("antelope-goats") emerged as a distinctly American family of animals roughly 25 million years ago, but paleontologists still do not agree on their earlier provenance. An older super-family, the Cervoidea, may have produced both the Antilocapridae and the Cervidae (the deer family), but there are some modern biologists who argue for an Asian bovine line of ancestry for pronghorns. Others think their closest living relatives are in the family Giraffidae—the giraffes, whose legs resemble pronghorn legs.

Whatever their origins in ancient America, modern pronghorns are a rarity in nature, a species that is today the sole remaining survivor of an entire family of animals. Fossil records in North America demonstrate that the Antilocapridae actually consisted of two major subfamilies. The earlier of these subfamilies, the Merycodontinae, or "pronglets," included several species of graceful, dainty ungulates with teeth that were very different from deer, but possessed of permanent, multi-branched, antler-like horns. The various species of the exotic little Merycodontinae were all extinct by the end of the Miocene, around 5.3 million years ago, but their line had given rise to the other subfamily, the Antilocaprinae, which soon replaced them on the great grasslands that were emerging in western America. The various species of Antilocaprinae were larger "antelope-goats," very definitely high-speed runners still, but with quite different horns made around a deciduous sheath. Some Antilocaprinae species sported four and sometimes six of these horns, whose sheaths (but not the cores) were shed annually. One dwarfed four-horned version, *Tetrameryx*, not much larger than a jackrabbit, still sprinted across the Great Plains as late as 10,000 years ago but vanished soon after. Very rarely four-horned animals are still born to modern pronghorns as genetic reminders of this varied deep past. But *Antilocapra americana*, our present-day pronghorn from an evolutionary family dating back 25 million years, is now the single living representative of the entire family—consisting of two subfamilies, at least fourteen genera, and many dozens of species—of the Antilocapridae.

In 1997 biologist John Byers, after years of studying pronghorn behavior and natural history on western Montana's National Bison Range, offered up a provocative argument that explained much about an animal that has long seemed somehow inexplicable, almost "alien," even to its admirers. Pronghorn watchers had long noted the animals' inability to jump fences and attributed it to pronghorn evolution. A grasslands creature shaped by the open country niche it occupied, pronghorns never experienced any selective pressures to be able to jump obstacles, which ultimately became a maladaptation to the modern world that played a central role in pronghorn history across the past 150 years. Byers found many other deep-time adaptations that help explain pronghorn oddities on the modern plains.

Pronghorns are one of only a handful of Great Plains species that managed to survive the truly epic extinction crash that ended the Pleistocene 10,000 years ago, a bestiary simplification that stands as the most profound ecological alteration in western North America since the extinction of the dinosaurs. In the biography of this species, however, the Pleistocene extinctions were only a few heartbeats in the past. So what if much about the behavior of modern pronghorns has little at all to do with the present circumstances of the plains? What if most of their physical characteristics and behavior are adaptations to a lost world that winked out around them 10,000 years ago, leaving pronghorns still living out their existence among us reacting to a world of ghosts?

The primary predators of pronghorns for the past 10 millennia have been wolves and coyotes, neither of which is capable, flat-out, of running more than 45 mph. Pronghorns, on the other hand, are the Ferraris of the natural world. Their delicate bones and frames and remarkably low body fat keep them light, while broad nostrils and a huge windpipe deliver turbocharged oxygen to their outsized lungs and heart. Pedal-to-the-metal they top 85 kilometers per hour, some 55 mph for the 120-pound males and possibly as high as 65–70 mph for slighter females, which is as fast as the cheetah. They can run at 90 percent of top end for more than two miles. Like horses, to detect predators at great distances they evolved gigantic eyes. But why so much protective excess?

Pronghorn behavior features other peculiarities. Like Thompson's gazelles and other African ungulates pursued by big cats, pronghorns have a powerful inclination towards a form of grouping known as the selfish herd, with much of their expression of dominance and rank focused on their physical position inside the groups. The lower-ranking, less dominant animals get pushed to the outer margins where, if pronghorns were on the African veld, the low-ranking group members would be in much greater danger from predatory attacks. But as adults, American pronghorns have no predators. Because of their impossible speed once they're grown, pronghorns are subject to predation only as fawns. If a pronghorn fawn survives to six or eight months of age it will join all other surviving fawns in living to the ripe old age of eleven or twelve years old. Yet pronghorns still group, and fight for position in the center of them, and persist in joining groups as if predation mattered when (except for fawns) it simply doesn't.

The fascinating question, then, is whether the whole suite of pronghorn behaviors, not just their lack of jumping ability, has something to do with the lost world of the Pleistocene Great Plains? Pronghorns emerged in their modern form at a time when the American Great Plains was the scene of one of the grandest assemblages of savanna-steppe creatures anywhere on earth, a more diverse collection of animals than are present in the African Serengeti or Masai Mara today. Along with the elephants and long-horned bison and the enormous herds of horses and zebras, along with bands of numerous types of camels and deer, and of course elk and pronghorns, the Pleistocene Great Plains of the past 2–4 million years featured an array of truly formidable predators that hunted and scavenged among the millions of ungulates. Pronghorns spent the better part of 4 million years perfecting their ability to survive where large and fast predators looked hungrily at them over bright teeth.

There were gracile, active, and aggressive short-faced bears (*Arctodus simus*), the *Smilodons* or saber-toothed cats that attacked mammoth calves, and a steadily changing lineup of wolf and coyote packs. Jaguars and cougars were present, along with the steppe lion (*Panthera leo atrox*), a far larger version of the African lion. Predators of the fastest grazers, the horses and pronghorns, included a slender-limbed, lion-sized running cat known as the scimitar cat (*Homotherium serum*), along with a particularly rapid and leggy American "hunting" hyena, *Chasmaporthetes ossifragus*. And there were two species of large American "false" cheetahs, *Miracinonyx trumani* and *M. inexpectatus*, cats from the same evolutionary line that produced cougars, but with elongated, curved spines, long legs, and wide nostrils for gulping air in open country pursuit or in rockslide ambushes.

These vanished creatures of the ancient plains—so biologists have begun to argue—however long ago they passed the veil of extinction, are the cause for why pronghorns seem so alien and unusual to us now, why they struck early observers like Lewis and Clark as possessing a speed that resembled more the flight of birds than anything else. Pronghorns are at once breathtakingly beautiful yet outrageously overbuilt relics that have outlasted the conditions that created them. They offer almost our only remaining glimpse of the American Pleistocene.

Like most wild ungulates then, or now, pronghorns follow a route that varies considerably by the seasons. At the conclusion of the September rut, the exhausted bucks, which would once have been prime targets for predators, disguise themselves by mimicking the females. They shed the outer husk of their horns and join the female herds. Since the Pleistocene, winter has been a time of migration for northern pronghorns. A few years ago, with a friend who lives in Jackson Hole, I photographed the famous Sublette pronghorn herd, which summers in Grand Teton National Park but still migrates almost

200 miles south, near Green River, Wyoming, in winter. This inclination to migrate before severe winter storms was adaptive in the wild, but coupled with their inability to jump obstacles ultimately would produce tragic die-offs in the late nineteenth century, when legendary winters in the 1880s sent pronghorns southward by the thousands into a new era of barbed-wire strung across the plains.

In the spring, from a year old until they are three, young pronghorn bucks segregate themselves into bachelor bands and spend most of their time in all-male groups. There they express group position dominance just as females do, but they also spar and practice moves they will later use in earnest. Around three years of age, pronghorn males become solitary for most of the spring and summer, during which time—at least in most pronghorn country—they set up territories of perhaps 150 acres whose perimeter they scent-mark and will use to cloister a harem of females to hide from other males during the rut. In other circumstances, male pronghorns protect harems of females but without defending a territory itself. Rather than a prime resource location, pronghorn territories seem to be merely tactical space for defending females. Pronghorn bucks fight over females, too, in violent, quick, and quite often mortal (as high as 15 percent of the encounters) fights. Reproduction success is the prime directive, and some pronghorn bucks win the lottery. Others spend their entire lives without ever siring any offspring at all.

Then there is female selection behavior. Female pronghorns, which reach sexual maturity at eighteen months of age and give birth every spring for the rest of their lives, find themselves in harems that male pronghorns judiciously protect during the brief September mating season. During the rut females repeatedly break away from their cloistered harems, however, joining the other harems of other males and inviting males to compete for them. What are they looking for? Apparently they are setting up contests of stamina, speed, and resolve between various males and observing the outcome before surrendering themselves up to be bred by "the winner"—the pronghorn male that demonstrates his genetic fitness by running faster and longer than his rivals. But if you are already almost 20 mph faster than your fastest predators, why would females set up games of natural selection and choose who will impregnate them based on fitness as demonstrated by speed?

Pronghorn females have evolved another strategy that is interesting with respect to what it says about both past and present. After a remarkably long gestation period of some 252 days, they give birth not to single offspring but

With no predators in adulthood but shrewd coyotes as predators of their fawns, pronghorn females commonly give birth to twin fawns as insurance. Dan Flores photo.

to "litters," specifically litters of two fawns every spring, and do this through-out their reproductive lives. Twinning as well as the weeks-long "hiding" of fawns, which lie motionless and silent for most of a day, are clearly responses to serious predation and they, too, probably emerged as adaptations to the distant past, when pronghorns lived in a world where they were prey for three or four different predators. Today it means that coyotes, the principal predators of pronghorn fawns for probably the last million years, are able to pull down as much as 50 percent of a pronghorn fawn crop, sometimes as much as 70–80 percent, without appreciably affecting pronghorn popu-lations. With "litters" and with their extremely high adult survivability rates, pronghorns were anciently prepared to survive the culling of even so efficient a predator of fawns as coyotes.

While a mother pronghorn will attack and fight a coyote to keep it from her fawns, pronghorn bucks do not defend fawns. Some biologists argue that this is another leftover behavior from the Pleistocene, when fast predators scattered groups of pronghorns across wide territories and a male pronghorn thus could not be sure that a fawn it defended was its own.

As cud-chewing ruminants capable of processing forbs and shrubs, pronghorns demonstrate yet another adaptation to the ancient savanna ecology of western America. For at least 800,000 years, since bison had followed the Bering land bridge from Asia into America, pronghorns had been evolving a mutualistic relationship with the bison herds. Bison, too—albeit a smaller, shorter-horned, "dwarf" species of them—had survived the Pleistocene extinctions and had increased dramatically in their wake, in numbers (depending on the climate cycles) that likely ranged somewhere between 20 and 30 million animals. Waves of bison and waves of pronghorns cropping the same country produced mutually beneficial results. Cropping the grasses and ignoring the often-poisonous species like locoweed, rabbitbrush, and sagebrush, bison grazing encouraged forbs and shrubs in their wake. Coming along after the bison herds and concentrating on the flowering plants and shrubs, pronghorn browsing shifted the advantage back to the grasses. Both preferred areas that were freshly burned, when pronghorns would avidly crop new grasses, too.

Thus deep-time history created an entirely unique situation for pronghorn antelope. Since pronghorns had out-survived almost all their predators, had ended up with few competitors for the often toxic shrubs and forbs they preferred, they spread everywhere there were vast, horizontal yellow plains, and they increased into the millions. Ernest Thompson Seton famously estimated that in 1800, the moment in time when pronghorns were on the verge of discovery by formal western science, there were 40 million of them in America. More recent estimates have advanced original figures of 15 to 35 million. But all these are wild guesses, as no one then or now can say with any certainty. What we probably can say is that on the Great Plains, where their ranges overlapped most precisely, pronghorn numbers very likely matched those of bison. We've long thought of the historic-era Great Plains as the Great Bison Belt. In truth it was just as much the Great Pronghorn Savanna.

Nineteenth-century exploration and travel literature speaks of bison and pronghorns so often as a matched set on the Great Plains that we've tended to imagine them as co-inhabitants of the West, but actually their ranges were not identical. Pronghorn bands and bison herds created their mutualistic foraging pattern on the Great Plains, but the two iconic prairie animals spilled in different cardinal directions on the continent. Bison were able to graze mid-height grasses like little bluestem and to a lesser extent the knee-high bunch-grasses west of the Rockies. When the climate was favorable and times flush on the plains, overflow bison populations could pool westward but primarily went eastward, to the Mississippi River and even beyond it.

Pronghorns, by contrast, are animals of the shortgrass plains and desert grasslands. They don't appear to have advanced eastward beyond about the 97th meridian in Texas and Mexico and the 93rd meridian (into Iowa and Minnesota) farther north, but ranged westward all the way to Baja California and eastern Oregon and Washington. Better adapted to tundra climates, bison survived winters much better on the Canadian plains than pronghorns. But southward on the continent, pronghorns were able to colonize the desert grasslands of Mexico all the way to the vicinity of Mexico City at 20 degrees latitude, considerably south of where bison ever ventured. Although pronghorns can derive adequate water from the plants they browse in optimal, wet conditions, contrary to rumors about them, they need to drink about 3½ quarts of water a day during hot weather, which limited their numbers in the Great Basin and the Mojave, Chihuahuan, and Sonoran deserts.

The truth is that, as with their evolutionary behavior, we have only recently come to understand something about the role pronghorns played in the Indian world in the West in the 10,000 years after the Pleistocene extinctions. Abundant and widespread, they attracted the attention of Indian hunters from the beginning. There are butchered pronghorn remains in some of the Clovis and Folsom archaeological sites, particularly those around lakes and marshes on the plains, so at least some Paleo-hunters did take the occasional pronghorn to vary a diet of mammoth cuts and steaks from giant bison. But it required fifteen to twenty pronghorns to equal the caloric possibilities of a single giant bison, and since pronghorn flesh was so very lean, pronghorns commonly ranked well down the list of commonly pursued prey. Among Southwestern peoples pronghorns ranked lower than rabbits, even though it took sixteen jackrabbits to match the edible flesh of a pronghorn.

Archaic hunter-gatherers and even historic-era Indian hunters, understanding from hundreds of generations of experience with pronghorns how to exploit their weaknesses, nonetheless killed them in large numbers and utilized pronghorn leather, horns, and hooves for a variety of purposes. One aspect of pronghorn evolution that made them vulnerable to Indian hunters was their inability to jump. Another was their disinclination to leave their home ranges. That deep cultural lore meant that even foot-bound Indians long ago figured out techniques for hunting pronghorns successfully. Parts of the West yet show fading evidence of ancient pronghorn corrals such as the Fort Bridger trap site in southwestern Wyoming, where local Indians enclosed pronghorn herds and pushed them to run in circles until they were exhausted and could be clubbed to death. Another technique involved a V-shaped pair of fence wings, often miles long, made from piled-up sagebrush that sent stampeded pronghorns into corrals or pits.

There are also references from a variety of sources of horse-mounted Plains Indians engaging in the kind of historic "surround" often used for bison to hunt pronghorns successfully, again with the goal of getting a pronghorn band to run in circles until the hunters could ride down the spent and stumbling animals with their horses. According to Richard Irving Dodge, when pronghorns collected into the thousands in wintertime, some tribes even used rifles in pronghorn hunts from horseback. Reacting as if pursued by predators, the "antelope crowd together in their fright," Dodge wrote, and hunters easily shot them down. Because local herds could end up completely extirpated by mass techniques like these, hunters among the Navajos often spared a couple of animals.

When bison were scarce, plains hunters preferred antelope to deer because you could take an entire herd of pronghorns at once, but a small hunting party might prefer to jog an individual pronghorn to exhaustion by relentlessly pursuing it on foot, or lure always-curious antelope within gunshot range by waving flags or performing odd gymnastics. Whatever the technique, the problem of lack of fat remained. Unlike bison or elk, pronghorns butchered out as all protein and very little precious fat. Their lean body mass may be the reason no tribe bothered to domesticate pronghorns, which are easier to tame than any African antelope.

Leather was certainly tanned from pronghorn skins, but both Indians and white market hunters thought antelope hides were inferior to those of bison or deer. Nonetheless, when Thomas Jefferson's Indian agent for the Orleans Territory, Dr. John Sibley, held a council for the Southern Plains tribes in Natchitoches in 1807, among the group that assembled was a soon-famous plains tribe, the Comanches, who had a division known as the Kwahadis or Antelopes. Sibley went on to write that "they dress the skins of the Antelope most beautifully and Colour them of every shade from light Pink to Black of which they make their own and Husbands Clothing, the edges Pinked and scalloped resembling lace. . . . you would take them for fine Black velvet."

The Indian peoples of the West had thus known pronghorns intimately for thousands of years. Among Europeans it was the numerous Spanish travelers on the Great Plains and in California who first encountered them and called them *berrendos*, while French travelers all across the Great Plains referred to them as *chevreuilles* or *cul blanc*. Francisco Hernandez's 1651 natural history of Mexico, which also provided the literate world its first description of the North American coyote, described and even provided an initial illustration of the western pronghorn. But as was the fate of so many natural history descriptions in the period before the eighteenth-century Swedish naturalist Carolus Linnaeus codified science with his binomial classification system, pronghorns—like the other charismatic animals from the American West—did not come to the official notice of the Enlightenment Age until the Lewis and Clark expedition. While President Jefferson's naturalist on the Red River, Dr. Custis, only heard reports of "a species of Antilope," fellow explorers Meriwether Lewis and William Clark had direct experiences with pronghorns and, critically, collected a type specimen that they shipped to the East in 1805.

About the time Custis was writing Jefferson to tell the president he had heard stories of "Antilope" in the West, in Philadelphia Charles Willson Peale was unpacking Lewis's specimen and preparing a mount for it. The Lewis and Clark party had seen their first pronghorns on September 5, 1804, not far from today's Niobrara, Nebraska, during the same two-week stretch when they crossed that magical boundary from woodlands to prairies and first encountered (and began collecting) a whole suite of Great Plains animals: bison, prairie dogs, coyotes, mule deer, and magpies among them. A pronghorn buck's turn came on September 14 when William Clark, fruitlessly searching for a volcano that was supposed to be in the vicinity, shot what he called "a (Buck) Goat which is peculiar to this Countrey. . . . verry actively made . . . his Norstral large, his eyes like a Sheep—he is more like the Antilope or Gazella of Africa than any other Species of Goat."

Finding "Antilopes . . . feeding in every direction as far as the eye of the observer can reach" but discovering them to be "extreemly shye and watchfull," Meriwether Lewis a few days later would pen a classic line about pronghorns. Hoping to collect a female for science, Lewis had the buck harem of seven he was stalking whirl away and disappear. Within minutes he spotted them more than three miles distant. "I had this day an opportunity of witnessing the agility and superior fleetness of this animal which was to me really astonishing," he wrote in his journal. "When I beheld the rapidity of their flight along the ridge before me it appeared reather the rappid flight of birds than the motion of quadrupeds."

Lewis and Clark would go on to make more than 200 pronghorn entries in their journals of their exploration, although they found them—like elk and deer—far less numerous west of the Continental Divide than on the Great Plains east of the Rockies. This was a phenomenon that appears to have had something to do with the relatively large population of Indians west of the mountains, and the fact that much of the Northern Plains from the Mandan villages westward was in the early nineteenth century a zone of warring tribes, which kept extensive hunting rare and allowed an unusual buildup of wildlife.

It was not so much "discovery" of the pronghorn by Lewis and Clark as their collection of a specimen they sent to eastern scientists that finally brought this several-million-year-old animal to the attention of modern scientific classification. It fell to George Ord, a Philadelphia naturalist and ornithologist who at the time was vice president of the Philadelphia Academy of Sciences and was working up many of the Lewis and Clark specimens from the West (among them the prairie dog and the grizzly) to publish a scientific description and propose a Linnaean name for the pronghorn in 1818. To his credit, Ord recognized that despite their similarities to African antelopes and gazelles, pronghorns were unrelated to any existing family of animals then known. Antilocapridae, the family name he devised, and *Antilocapra*, the genus Ord fashioned for a creature that seemed to combine the traits of both antelopes and goats, have stood ever since.

Surprisingly enough, although pronghorns came in for various mentions and notices, many western travelers in the nineteenth century had little additional information to add about pronghorns. That was a consequence in part of the pronghorn's wildness and speed, which made it a difficult animal for many travelers to lay hands on, and also because—compared to more familiar animals like elk or deer—pronghorns were so unusual they were almost alien in the minds of many travelers. But there were some interesting takes.

When the failure of Jefferson's Red River expedition brought Jeffersonian exploration to a close in 1806, Americans were almost fifteen years getting another scientific expedition into the West. But in 1819–1820 a party led by Stephen Long, which included naturalists Thomas Say and Edwin James and painter-illustrators Samuel Seymour and Titian Ramsay Peale, explored across the Central Plains from Iowa to the Front Range of the Rockies in present Colorado and New Mexico before returning eastward across the Southern Plains.

Long's party encountered pronghorns regularly and noted of them that "The antelope possesses an unconquerable inquisitiveness, of which the hunters often take advantage to compass the destruction of the animal." Significantly, from his own animal drawings and a landscape sketch by Seymour, Peale completed a painting that became the American public's first exposure to what pronghorns actually looked like in the wild. Peale's painting was also one of the country's first visuals of what an exotic place the American West could be.

The naturalists John Kirk Townsend and Thomas Nuttall, journeying across the plains with inventor/fur trader Nathaniel Wyeth's party, on the Platte River on May 15, 1834, saw pronghorns for the first time and also gave the world an impression. Townsend wrote that the pronghorn "is one of the most beautiful animals I ever saw. . . . The legs are remarkably light and beautifully formed, and as it bounds over the plain, it seems scarcely to touch the ground, so exceedingly light and agile are its motions. This animal . . . inhabits the western prairies of North America exclusively."

John James Audubon, with The Birds of America under his belt to rave reviews both in America and Europe, was on the Missouri River in 1843 attempting to add western animals to the book he was then working up on the mammals of North America. Audubon's initial encounter to secure a pronghorn specimen to paint didn't quite work out. He lured "a superb male" pronghorn from 300 yards out to less than 60 yards by taking advantage of its curiosity: "I lay on my back and threw my legs up, kicking first one and then the other foot, and sure enough the Antelope walked towards us." His shot missed, however. Before finally completing another of the early visual representations of the pronghorn, Audubon noted that they "often die from the severity of the winter weather" and were "caught in pens in the manner of Buffaloes, and are dispatched with clubs" by Indian women.

One of the best-selling books of the West in the nineteenth century was the trader/naturalist Josiah Gregg's Commerce of the Prairies, first published in 1846. It included sections on the wildlife of the Great Plains that often served up critical information on them. This is what Greg had to say about the pronghorn: "That species of gazelle known as the antelope is very numerous upon the high plains. This beautiful animal . . . is most remarkable for its fleetness: not bounding like the deer, but skimming over the ground as though upon skates. . . . The flesh of the antelope is . . . but little esteemed: consequently, no great efforts are made to take them. Being as wild as fleet, the hunting of them is very difficult."

The commercial market hunt of wildlife in the West, initiated by the fur and robe trade, got under way on the Great Plains in earnest in the 1820s, but for almost three-quarters of a century—as long as beaver lasted, bison roamed in numbers enough to produce robes, hides, and tongues, and wolves and coyotes still were targets of traps and poison bait—it left pronghorns largely alone. Unlucky ones of course got shot by emigrants on the western trails, or were gunned down by foreign hunters on safari in the American Serengeti, or killed to provide food for railroad workers. By the 1850s and 1860s pronghorns were reaping the whirlwind in mining areas like California, where market hunters corralled and killed them to feed miners. But it was not until bison numbers began to drop, first on the Central and Southern Plains in the 1870s, then on the Northern Plains in the 1880s, that pronghorns finally began to attract attention in the slaughter of Great Plains animals for profit.

With more than 5,000 professional hunters in the West in the 1870s and 1880s, and Indians all across the plains not only invested in the market hunt but attempting just to stay alive on their new reservations, when every last buffalo had been pursued to ground, hunters looked to see what they might turn their guns on for a final killing spree. Without the bison herds as prey, wolves were going fast. Bighorn sheep in the Badlands lasted only a handful of years. Elk and even deer had mostly fled the plains to the safety of the mountains. In the 1880s only two primary charismatic animals remained on the Great Plains: wild horses and pronghorns. The horses would end up caught by mustangers and sold to overseas buyers whenever Europeans were involved in wars, or by the 1920s get rounded up as a source of dog food in the American pet industry. Or they were simply shot down by cowboys as nuisances. But pronghorns? They had evolved on the Great Plains, survived fearsome predators, lived through the Pleistocene extinctions. Erasing them from America was going to require some effort.

Naturally we were up to the task. As with the extinctions and close calls for so many birds and animals during this free-wheeling period of American history, there were multiple causes for what began to happen to pronghorns. Homesteading in places like western Kansas and Nebraska steadily tore up the prairie, and with it pronghorn habitat. Ranchers overstocked the plains with cattle and sheep that undermined vegetation pronghorns depended on. Those causes weakened pronghorns, but there were others that killed them directly, and in vast numbers. The new barbed-wire fences demarcating a West that was fast becoming private property went straight to the pronghorns' evolutionary weakness. Fences that were loose or partly down they could wriggle through, but tight fences captured them, preventing the herds from migrating and from escaping winter blizzards. Without bison to tromp down the snow, in winter pronghorns couldn't get at the plants they ate. Add fences to block their migrations and the horrific western winters of the 1880s devastated them. In an event that had become all too common, homesteaders in the Texas Panhandle discovered and killed 1,500 pronghorns trapped against a fence in the winter of 1882.

Then there was the market hunt. The generally poor opinion of pronghorn leather and their slight amount of meat had long kept pronghorns out of the rifle sights of men who killed animals for money. But with everything else gone and a deathly silence beginning to fall across the Great Plains, market hunters finally turned their rifles on pronghorns. The story is too familiar: sporadic but relentless and remorseless rifle fire echoed across a western landscape gradually emptying of animal life from the 1870s into the 1890s, and what had once been millions of wild creatures fell for a pittance in returns.

With bison dwindling and hunters looking for targets, winter concentrations of pronghorns around places like the Black Hills got wiped out in two or three seasons. A single hunter in California killed 5,000 for their hides when a drought drove pronghorns there to a few remaining waterholes. Hunters desperate to keep their lifestyle going sold pronghorn meat to butchers in Kansas for 2–3 cents a pound. In 1873 an Iowa firm shipped some 32,000 pronghorn and deer skins via railroad from the plains, barely selling them for more than $1 apiece for all that effort of hunting, skinning, and shipping. As always, the arrival of railroads to ship animal products coincided with a rising crescendo of gunfire, which happened when the Union Pacific reached Wyoming, the Santa Fe line reached New Mexico, and the Texas and Pacific became a market source that funneled pronghorn meat and hides from the Llano Estacado and all of West Texas.

When George Bird Grinnell alerted conservationist and future president Teddy Roosevelt to the impact of market hunting, a step that would eventually lead to the formation of the Boone & Crockett Club to protect American game animals, one of the victims he mentioned was the pronghorn. That had put pronghorns before an influential group, but by the time Roosevelt had become president, pronghorn numbers had dropped frighteningly low, to an estimated 13,000 remaining animals out of what had once been at least 15 million across the entire West. Rescuing them from almost certain extinc-

Pronghorns on the High Plains of New Mexico in 2015. Fifteen million pronghorns had plummeted to barely thirteen thousand a century ago. Dan Flores photo.

tion required, initially, cooperation between the states in the West, which Roosevelt facilitated, along with pronghorn stocking in Yellowstone, on the national wildlife refuges that TR created, and eventually on the scattering of national and state parks on the Great Plains. Real efforts occurred primarily between 1925 and 1945 and were commonly small-scale and regional, often spearheaded by state or provincial game departments, to use existing pronghorns to recover the animals in places where they had disappeared.

Every western state has a version of this story, but one example is Texas, which for millions of years absolutely swarmed with pronghorns. Biologist Vernon Bailey, representing the Bureau of Biological Survey in the Southwest in the years before it evolved largely into an anti-predator agency, crossed the Texas Panhandle by train in 1899. In the 100 miles between Canyon, Texas, and Portales, New Mexico, traversing premier antelope country across the Llano Estacado, Bailey counted only 32 pronghorns. Ten years before they had been fairly common in Trans-Pecos Texas; by 1899 they were all but gone there. It took a 1903 law against shooting them and expensive efforts to save pronghorns in Texas. By 1924 a census found only 2,407 in a state that had formerly held 20 percent of the continent's pronghorn population. State efforts to restock them using a funnel net capture technique invented by the nearby New Mexico game and fish commission began in 1939. By 1944 there were 9,000 pronghorns in Texas, and by 1960 12,000. By the year 2000 the figure was 13,000, mostly in the Trans-Pecos and the Panhandle, better than none, certainly, but a faint echo of the millions that once were found in the region. Other states, particularly Wyoming and Montana, have fared better, and the US and Canadian population of pronghorns today hovers around 700,000 animals, half of them in Wyoming, with another 1,200 in Mexico. A series of highway overpasses now allows some of them to continue their winter migrations.

But I am still transfixed by a moment, for a few years in the 1880s and 1890s, when the two ancient Americans, pronghorns and mustangs, had still held out, finding themselves—along with coyotes—almost alone on the vastness of the American prairies. In April 1884 a cowboy named George Wolfforth, rounding up strays for the Kidwell Ranch in West Texas's Yellow House Canyon, rode his horse up over the rim of the canyon about where Lubbock now stands. The scene he saw seared itself into his memory. "As far as we could see," he wrote, "there were antelope and mustangs grazing in the waving sea of grass," the whole tableau "rendered misty and unreal by the mirage that hovered over the plains."

They were almost the sole survivors of the Pleistocene megafauna of the Great Plains. Many of their compatriots had died out in that mystifying extinction crash 10,000 years before, and almost all the rest had suffered extinction or extirpation across the previous 30 years. Here the two survivors still were in 1884. But even that moment was brief, soon enough was nothing but a romantic vision set down in a memoir. Those last herds extending as far as the eye could see proved as fleeting as Wolfforth's mirage.

3

August and September of 1804 loom large in the natural history of the American West, and indeed in the history of western science. In the short stretch of three weeks, ascending the Missouri River in what is now Nebraska and South Dakota, the American explorers Meriwether Lewis and William Clark described for Enlightenment science many of the diagnostic wildlife species that made the Great Plains so unique in North America. On August 23, encouraged by President Jefferson to seek out and collect plants and animals not found in the Atlantic states, the party had downed the first bison most of them had ever seen. By September 7 they'd encountered their first prairie dogs, or "burrowing rats," in Clark's rather less-flattering description. A week later it was a "Buck Goat of this countrey . . . more like the Antilope or Gazella of Africa than any other Species of Goat." That was of course the pronghorn. It was followed three days later by "a curious kind of Deer of a Dark Gray Colr . . . the ears large & long." Thus did the mule deer come to the notice of science.

The day following, somewhere in the vicinity of present Chamberlain, South Dakota, one more American Original emerged from the wilds of the Great Plains to arrest the attention of scientists in Philadelphia, Paris, London, and Stockholm. For most of that month the party had reported seeing what they had assumed to be a kind of fox. The more they observed these sleek, beautiful canines, however, the less fox-like they seemed. So on the morning of September 18, Clark finally decided to collect one. With the animal in the grass before him, the explorer was mystified by its ambiguity. Although in size about like "a gray fox," it looked more like a small wolf than any fox. Yet just as obviously, it was not the large wolf these Euroamericans knew both from Europe and the East. Clark finally decided to call the creature a "prairie wolff." And he then went on to correct his journal: "What has been taken heretofore for the Fox was those wolves, and no Foxes has been seen."

This account of the discovery of the American coyote is well known in biological and ecological literature, but it cannot carry the burden of standing as Book of Genesis for what has become, two centuries later, America's most widely observed wild predator. Like the other animals Lewis and Clark "discovered," coyotes had hardly been invisible to the native peoples in the West across the previous 15,000 years. Nor, like pronghorns, had they escaped the notice of previous French traders, traversing the plains since the early 1700s, or the Spanish colonists in New Mexico and California, who had borrowed the Nahuatl (Uto-Aztecan) name—coyotl—for the animal.

The literary accounts Jefferson's explorers penned—Meriwether Lewis would go on to write a lengthy coyote description a few months later—and the expedition's fame help explain why the coyote's history so often begins in 1804. But because neither Lewis nor Clark wrote up a scientific description or proffered a Latin binomial for their 1804 coyote, they did not become its official discoverers even in western science. That honor fell to Thomas Say, naturalist on the later Stephen Long expedition to the Rockies, who in 1823 officially described the type specimen of Clark's "prairie wolf" from a Nebraska coyote he trapped using a bobcat as bait. Despite competition from other naturalists of the era, who believed the coyote might actually be a North American jackal—and even an African biologist today who, upon seeing a coyote in Yellowstone, said flatly, "that's a jackal"—Say's binomial, Canis latrans, has been the accepted scientific name for the coyote ever since. Science should get its due, certainly, but a 200-year-old name simply can't do justice to an ancient American Original like the coyote, whose evolutionary roots lie 5 million years deep in America, and whose furtive profile western Indians had known as a commonplace for perhaps 15,000 years.

William Clark's 1804 description of his "prairie wolff" does, however, tantalize us with three elements of the coyote's remarkable story that are still with us. The first is that this was an animal, unlike the wolves, unknown to Euroamericans. No European brought centuries' worth of preloaded myths and stories about coyotes to North America. Second, Clark and his compatriots found the coyote confusing, ambiguous. Was it a fox? A wolf? A jackal? Something else? That ambiguity has played a marked role in almost every facet of the coyote's biography ever since. Finally, nineteenth-century Euroamericans had to get halfway across the continent, to the Great Plains, before they ever saw a coyote. That becomes most interesting given the arc of the coyote's modern story.

In the beginning the coyote was as western as sagebrush or deserts, and that it played such a significant—and ancient—role in the indigenous religions of North America is a testament to how powerfully this small, crafty wolf captured the human imagination. Virtually everywhere in North America Indian peoples had lived side-by-side with coyotes, over time the animal assumed the guise of a mythic human avatar being. In the form of Coyote (or Old Man Coyote), it became a crucial character in native cosmology. The Trickster figure is a very old human religious deity, so old it was in place long before the invention of agriculture. In fact it dates to the Paleolithic, in America the time of the elephant and giant bison hunters. Anthropologists have found Tricksters in pantheistic religions around the world, where they usually take the form of animals—hares, spiders, bluejays, ravens—although in Old Norse traditions the Trickster is a human-like god called Loki. But in America, at least from Oregon and the Columbia Plateau southward through California, the Great Basin, the Great Plains, the Southwest, and far into Mexico—in short, everywhere coyotes ranged—it was the western song dog that ancient native peoples chose for their Trickster deity. Across 10,000 years of stories that constitute the oldest literary canon in American history, Coyote emerged as a distinctive continental figure, crucial to the Indian grasp of human nature and the animal within.

In hundreds of mythic native stories, Coyote almost never was the Ultimate Cause god. More often, in traditions like those of the Salish and Nez Perce, he was the immortal, earthly helper to a more abstract divine being, and he inhabited the world before humankind. In these stories Coyote created the very terrain of the American West, causing rivers like the Missouri to flow one direction, but not both. In a famous Nez Perce story Coyote defeated monsters whose body parts he forged into various tribal groups. For some people, like the Karuks, he invented fire; he taught others how to hunt bison. And in stories from the Yanas, Navajos, and others, Coyote famously introduced death in the world to preserve Earth from human over-population.

As one of America's most ancient deities, and an avatar for humans, coyotes like the one portrayed in this Pueblo Indian petroglyph starred in the oldest literary canon in American history. Dan Flores photo.

It is obvious who Coyote really was, but in the event you were a bit dense, his description left no doubt. Coyote stood upright on two legs, had arms and hands, and although he brandished a tail and a wolfish head, he spoke every human language known. His mythical function in the beginning of time was creation. Coyote took the basic structure of the world as set in motion by the Creator, then "improved" on it and gave it the natural laws that make it work. That done, his larger purpose in the many oral stories about him was to reveal all the complexities of human nature. Rather than a perfect deity, set up as role model for humans, Coyote was the personification of the full suite of humanity's traits, good and bad. He was admirable, inspirational, imaginative, energetic, a whirlwind biophysical force with a large capacity for taking sensuous pleasure in life. But he was also selfish, vain, cunning, deceitful. And quite often envious, lustful, ridiculous, and possessed of an overconfidence that got him into endless fixes. Old Man Coyote's major flaw as a god, indeed, resulted from a combination of both his positive and negative traits. He found cause, sometimes admirable, sometimes laughable, never to be quite satisfied with the way things were. But he was also fallible. Because he was invariably unable to predict outcomes with any degree of accuracy, his tinkering with nature often produced disaster. Especially for him.

The truth is that Coyote is very probably North America's oldest extant deity, who bequeathed us down the timeline a continental world of imagination, creation, artistry. Unfortunately, because of Coyote's hubris and selfishness, his best-laid plans for improving the world endlessly produced consequences he never intended. In other words, in Coyote ancient Americans possessed an unusually instructive deity. It was easy for native peoples to see the Coyote impulse writ large in human nature. In every way, Coyote functioned as our stand-in figure in the world, and he has done so almost since human time began here.

To history and religion we can also add the sciences as critical to understanding why we can't turn our eyes away from the coyote. Consider coyote evolution. This is an animal whose co-evolution with North America is as deeply embedded as ours is with Africa, indeed more deeply, since unlike us the coyote has never left the continent that gave it birth. The Canidae family that produced wolves, jackals, and coyotes is a 5-million-year-old family of American proto-wolves. By a million years ago various groups of this family did migrate, following land bridges across the Bering Strait into the Old World and becoming golden jackals and Asian and European gray wolves there. The ancestors of the gray wolf (*Canis lupus*), particularly, became cosmopolitan and eventually colonized almost the entirety of the planet. But there was a line of canids that never left America, and by 800,000 to a million years ago they began to diverge into larger forms. There were true American wolves like the eastern wolf (*Canis lycaon*) and the red wolf (*Canis rufus*), which became hunters of most of America east of the Great Plains. And there was the smaller American wolf—the coyote—that came to occupy the same niche in western America that jackals did in the Old World. In evolution a million years between siblings is not a very long separation, and that would produce consequences in the coyote/wolf story, too.

The coyote's closest relation, which explains many things about the coyote's history and present, is undoubtedly the red wolf, whose original range stretched from the edges of the Southern Plains across the South to Florida, and up the Atlantic shore all the way to eastern Canada. As famous Kansas naturalist E. Raymond Hall wrote of the American red wolf, it differs from the world traveler gray wolf in featuring a "smaller size and more slender build." Its nose is sharper and longer than the gray wolf's, its foot pads are smaller, and its "general coloration [is] more tawny." While the red wolf became a long-legged hunter of deer in the forests and swamps of the South and East, its evolutionary sibling, the coyote, became the jackal of the American plains and deserts.

The advantages of life on the Great Plains may have been the same for both coyotes and humans. During the Pleistocene, the great savannas were where the action was. In America, elephants, giant bison, herds of wild horses, and a diverse bestiary of smaller animals flocked to the plains. Perhaps by spawning the small, quick coyote, evolution allowed North American canines to compete in a situation with a great many predatory opportunities. And, eventually, to function alongside larger gray wolves, which 20,000 years ago began to return to their evolutionary homeland.

The paleontological record indicates that Pleistocene coyotes had to be especially creative adapters, and that, too, has had consequences. About the same time that extreme climate stresses (caused by volcanic eruptions on the island of Sumatra 71,000 years ago) led our ancestors to transform their cultural lives, in what Jared Diamond has popularized as our "Great Leap Forward," coyotes were acquiring some of the traits that made them so unique, resilient, and successful in North America.

Like humans, who are intensely social but whom anthropologists describe as having developed a unique kind of social life—"fission-fusion societies"— coyotes became the very rare predator to do the same. Fission-fusion capability allows for unusual flexibility to individuals, who can be either gregarious or solitary, depending on what circumstances call for. In such societies, individuals cooperate to take on large endeavors, but flexibility allows for more individualized effort in different situations. The gray wolf, which evolved and became specialized as a pack animal to pursue large prey, is not a fission-fusion carnivore. Indeed, that would become a near-fatal flaw in wolves in the modern age, as their pack instincts made them vulnerable. Most other predators are either solitary or social, not both.

We humans, and coyotes, are exceptions. Our successes come from our plasticity. Coyotes could be solitary hunters, focusing on the kind of small prey an individual animal could capture. Given different opportunities, coyotes could also become pack animals when prey like deer called for cooperation. It is the adaptation that made them, like us, opportunists that could encounter wholly new situations and thrive. It is one of the adaptations that allowed them to survive twentieth-century America's war on predators when wolves could not.

And it seems to have been in place way back in the Pleistocene. Coyotes then were distinct from the animal Lewis and Clark would see in 1804. Their skulls and jaws were thicker, their teeth wider, most likely because their initial response to life on the plains was to pursue larger prey, in packs. This was, unfortunately, a niche that newly returning gray wolves also filled. So in the wake of the Pleistocene Extinctions of 10,000 years ago, when scores of animal species on the American Plains disappeared, competition between gray wolves and coyotes intensified. The genius of the coyote was to back away and seek out the new strategy of individual effort. Wolves remained big, 5- to 6-foot-long pack hunters weighing 80 to 120 pounds. Coyotes became 3- to 4-foot-long, 30- to 40-pound solitary foragers for small game, even omnivores. Fission-fusion—and sheer, crafty intelligence—turned out to be especially effective in turning coyotes into canids that could survive a wolf-dominated world, and eventually a human-dominated one.

Coyotes would go on to evolve an array of other traits we would take special notice of, certainly because of their similarities to the traits of wolves, which were after all our first animal domesticate. Like our dogs, as well as ourselves, coyote young require lengthy childhoods—neotony is the biological term—to learn culture and critical information about the world from their parents. The social life of canids is so similar to ours that we understand it on many levels, even when it features a kind of census-taking. Coyotes become mated pairs, but they do something else quite remarkable. Average coyote litter size is 5.7 pups, but coyotes seem to have an autogenic mechanism that allows them to assess the ecological possibilities around them. If they sense fewer coyotes relative to resources, they give birth to larger litters. Their classic yodeling howl, which has so long stood as the iconic night sound of the starry-skied West, has many functions, but one is assessing the size of the surrounding coyote population. Coyotes also evolved an ability, under intense pressure to survive, to go into a "colonization" mode featuring not just large litters but migration into new settings. It would take halfway through the twentieth century but biologists would eventually conclude that as a result of these adaptations, eradicating coyotes is virtually impossible. To wipe out a regional coyote population, 75 percent of all coyotes have to be removed—not once but every single year for fifty straight years—to produce even a momentary impact.

Their ready identification with the social lives and survivability of wild coyotes is the reason for the Old Man Coyote traditions of Indian peoples in North America. Ten thousand years ago, native cultures would have had many scores of animal candidates for their deity figures. But for Indian peoples in the American West, something about coyote survivability in a general Pleistocene collapse obviously captured their imaginations. Once they moved into coyote country, American explorers, settlers, government officials, and literary figures also found coyotes worthy of fascinated attention, but usually with very different ends in mind.

With our evolutionary background as hunters, we may be fascinated by predators, but we long ago recognized them as danger, and as competition. Given our Old World experiences with wolves, we were suspicious of coyotes from the first. But while the coyote seemed too small to arouse our fears, it was without doubt a competitor, especially so when our domestic livestock were involved. In churches and bars and over polite conversation, as well as in the ranch houses of the West of a hundred years ago, no North American predators escaped a general excoriation. But for intriguing reasons, coyotes struck everyone as particularly vile. With no imported mythology and scant knowledge of Indian ideas of a Coyote deity, Americans in the West found coyotes ripe for original interpretation. And for half a century after 1872, a very unflattering one emerged.

It was Mark Twain's description in his 1872 book *Roughing It* that seemed to provide the foundation for an American coyote assessment that only grew worse as time went on. In Twain's view, the coyote's choice of homes defined him, for he lived "chiefly in the most desolate and forbidding deserts." He went on: "The coyote is a long, slim, sick and sorry looking skeleton, with a gray wolf-skin stretched over it, a tolerable bushy tail that forever sags down with a despairing expression of forsakenness and misery, a furtive and evil eye, and a long, sharp face, with slightly lifted lip and exposed teeth. He has a general slinking expression all over. The coyote is a living, breathing allegory of Want."

Wanting meant becoming a target. Strychnine, first available in the 1830s, by the 1850s had become a regular commodity at western trading posts. As a result, predator pelts began to join the international fur trade in that decade. The commercial buffalo harvest of the 1860s–1880s created boom-time conditions for Great Plains canines, but also inaugurated the initial campaign of extermination against them. The real target was wolves, but strychnine did not discriminate: a poisoned bison carcass in Kansas yielded thirteen wolves, but also fifteen coyotes and forty skunks. They weren't always collateral damage. Coyote pelts functioned as a medium of exchange on the Great Plains after the Civil War, their value set at $1 in the fur trade; tens of thousands of plains coyotes met that fate. But many more were killed by wolfers as by-products of the trade in wolf pelts. No one knows for sure, but western writer George Bird Grinnell estimated that wolfers killed hundreds of thousands of coyotes on the Great Plains during these years.

Meanwhile both cattlemen and sheepmen were taking their herds and flocks into the West. Cattle ranchers never got too heated up about coyotes so long as wolves remained, but sheepmen—who regarded coyotes as a "parasite on civilization"—early on pushed for bounties. Most western states enacted bounties on both wolves and coyotes in the late nineteenth century. Montana for its part went even farther, trying deliberate introductions of sarcoptic mange, an early form of biological warfare.

According to the *Salt Lake Weekly Tribune* in 1887, the ranchman's view was not universal in the West. Near Fillmore, Utah Territory, farmers had poisoned coyotes to scarcity, only to find their croplands invaded by rabbits "which have multiplied into swarms, so that the farmers pray for coyotes now." But stockmen prayed (and did more) to effect the opposite outcome. It was only their fury towards wolves that delayed the coyote's turn until the twentieth century.

Gone now was the Indian deity who created the world. Observing the same animal, what Americans saw was a sick, despairing, forsaken, miserable creature, an animal (as we warmed to the task) that took on traits of both cunning and cruelty. Articles by popular writers like Ernest Ingersoll and Edwin Sabin described coyotes as "contemptible" and "especially perverse." Their howls were "eerie" and "blood-stilling," even defiant. Coyotes supposedly lacked "higher morals," and were "cowardly to the last degree." Exploring ideas for commercial gain from coyotes, a 1920 article in *Scientific American* asserted that coyotes were not worth the price of the ammunition to shoot them, then went on to add the ultimate insult for the age (and a patriotic reason for shooting them anyway): the coyote, the writer avowed, was the "ORIGINAL BOLSHEVIK."

Eradication of such an unsavory animal seemed the logical next step, and a century ago everyone was on the bandwagon. Nature writer John Burroughs argued that predators "certainly needed killing." William T. Hornaday, a conservation hero who saved the last bison and led the charge to replace market hunting with sport hunting, thought that for coyotes, "firearms, dogs, traps, and strychnine [are] thoroughly legitimate weapons of destruction. For such animals, no half-way measures suffice." Not even John Muir, who found coyotes "beautiful" and "graceful," came to the defense of predators. With packets of strychnine available in every hardware store in America, it had become almost a patriotic duty to scatter a few to beat back the continent's wild predator horde.

By the twentieth century, however, there were many Americans who believed that exterminating animals like coyotes was too big for individual effort. It seemed too big for livestock associations or state bounty programs, too. Coyotes, in particular, seemed somehow impossible even to thin out. In Ernest Thompson Seton's allegorical story in an issue of *Century* magazine in 1900, a coyote "Moses" who had learned all of civilization's designs against the "coyote kind" was the explanation for the coyotes' seeming invincibility. Getting rid of predators appeared to call for experts in mass techniques.

If ever there was a poster child for the stereotypical government agency that hangs on even when the tides of both science and public opinion threaten to drown it, it was the Bureau of Biological Survey. The bureau's quite benign roots lay in the 1880s, and until 1905 its mission was to conduct a nationwide survey of the flora and fauna of America. But doing pure science threatened it with extinction every time appropriations votes came up. Stockmen in the West particularly blamed the federal government's new public lands system—national forests and national parks—for creating a system of mountain refuges for wolves and coyotes fleeing persecution on the Great Plains. In a search for an economic mission, the bureau's Vernon Bailey began to position it as an agency of national wildlife experts with solutions to the "problem of predators." The first large congressional appropriations went to the bureau in 1914, to be used "on the National Forests and the public domain in destroying wolves, coyotes, and other animals injurious to agriculture and animal husbandry." The next year it hired 300 hunters across the West to engage in this new federally mandated war against the wild, then asked Congress to allow it to accept additional funding from stockmen's associations and state legislatures. And the bureau's PR campaign spread the idea to hunters that its project of destroying predators would produce bumper populations of game animals for sport hunters, bringing new allies to the cause.

Since the quickest way to mass-kill wolves and coyotes was not shooting but poison, the bureau built a plant in Albuquerque to produce strychnine tablets in volume. In 1921 it relocated its so-called Eradication Methods Laboratory to Denver, where it would perfect an amazing witch's brew of ever more efficient and deadly poisons. Hunters first engaged in "pre-baiting," or strewing cubes of fat and meat across the countryside to get coyotes habituated to them. The poison bait stations went in next. Stanley Young, a field hunter who became a coyote specialist and public relations figure for the bureau, found that using strychnine it was possible to kill 350 coyotes in ten days. Approaching his bait stations, he found every dead coyote frozen in a signature strychnine convulsion, their tails sticking straight out as if they'd been electrocuted.

That scene, the visual imagery of a coyote extermination campaign, was about to be writ large across the West. As wolves melted away before the onslaught, Señor Coyote's turn had now come. Although federal hunters had initially concentrated on the wolves that stock associations particularly wanted wiped out, by 1923 wolves were so scarce on both the plains and in the mountains that thereafter the hunters never killed more than a single wolf a year. Nonetheless, in Colorado alone the bureau set out 31,255 poison baits in 1923.

The truth was, bureau arguments for making coyotes public enemy #1 may not have been mere propaganda. With the keystone predator, the gray wolf, now gone or nearly so, an ecological revolution was under way across America. With their competitors eradicated by the bureau, coyotes now exercised their ancient "fission-fusion" capabilities. At least some coyotes began to form packs and hunt larger prey—including sheep and, on very rare occasions, newborn calves. And with wolves gone, not only did the coyote population bloom in the West, in the decade of the 1920s coyotes began an unprecedented and historic expansion of their range—eastward across the Mississippi River, where they would gradually begin to fill the wolf's vacant niche in the East and South.

With wolves eradicated and the Denver plant cranking out the strychnine, the bureau's Predatory and Rodent Control hunters by 1924 had set out 3,567,000 poison baits across the West—figuratively a scorched-earth policy against coyotes. In that decade the bureau was averaging 35,000 poisoned coy-

Almost without interruption since 1915, a federal agency today called Wildlife
Services has waged an unceasing war on coyotes using guns, traps, poisons,
and airplanes. Since the 1850s Americans have killed untold millions of coyotes,
prompting them to spread across the entire country. Dan Flores photo.

otes a year. But even with such a campaign, coyotes were not so easily erased as wolves, whose strong, pack-based social ties had doomed them. Like Old Man Coyote in the native traditions, the real coyote somehow seemed immortal. Newspapers like the *Rocky Mountain News* in Denver would run stories with titles like "U.S. Agents Stalk 'Desperadoes' of Animal World thru Deserts and over Mountain Ranges of West," but somehow, against the lowly, slinking, immoral coyote, the bureau could not win the war of civilization.

And unexpectedly, coyotes began to acquire champions. At their annual meeting in 1924, the American Society of Mammalogists debated whether predators served essential functions in nature, and whether American policy was tragically wrong in pressing for their eradication. Scientific luminaries such as Joseph Grinnell, E. Raymond Hall, Olaus Murie, and Aldo Leopold began to demonstrate with their field studies that, lacking predators, the natural world often swung precipitously to new and often very fragile paradigms.

The reaction of the bureau to this threat from the scientific community was to double-down on denials of a role for predators and propose a shocking final solution. "Large predatory mammals, destructive to livestock and to game, no longer have a place in our advancing civilization," the bureau's E. A. Goldman thundered. Ignoring the accumulating science, in 1928 the bureau offered up its faunal end-game. If Congress would fund the bureau at $10 million for a decade, it would wipe out coyotes—"the archpredator of our time" Goldman called them—once and for all.

The proposed 10-Year Plan for coyote eradication was the final straw for the scientists and ecologists. One of them, Olaus Murie, working as a bureau biologist since 1927, was known for his conviction that scientists must above all be ethical. Now Goldman wanted him to study coyotes, hoping to buttress the bureau's position. In his report Murie evaluated "the factions interested in [the] coyote question" and concluded that there was an emerging group he called "The Nature Lovers." Murie argued that these people might actually represent a state of human evolutionary enlightenment. As he put it, "I firmly believe that it is working against the best interests of humanity to . . . ridicule those who see beauty in a coyote's howl."

In 1931, however, Congress passed the famous Animal Damage Control Act, appropriating $1 million a year for ten years for the bureau to pursue "the eradication" of coyotes, the "Gangsters of the Animal Kingdom" in the media's phrase. As it turned out, the bureau pursued its coyote mission relentlessly well beyond a single decade. World War II produced an explosion of knowledge about chemicals, and in 1946 it offered up thallium sulfate as an improved predacide. Its advantage was that dying coyotes did not alarm other coyotes, as with strychnine. Instead, the new poison killed them slowly, often causing their hair to fall out first. (Hairless coyotes, dying of thallium sulfate poisoning, were sometimes found huddled, freezing, in outbuildings of ranches.) A second new poison, sodium fluoroacetate, was called Compound 1080 because it had taken the lab 1,080 tries to create it. With Compound 1080 the bureau got closer, sometimes approaching local coyote extirpation. A third technique, the "humane coyote getter," was designed to close the deal. It featured an upright tube capped by scented cloth that coyotes found difficult to resist, and fired a mist of sodium cyanide directly into a coyote's face.

But wasn't overconfidence too often the downfall of Old Man Coyote's plans to change the world? The new poisons killed vast, unknown numbers of coyotes, but coyotes not only weren't exterminated by the 10-Year Program, they actually continued to expand their range. Unlike wolves, coyotes are fertile by a year old. Poisoned to scarcity, they simply had larger litters. With fission-fusion adaptability, they could turn to a large array of prey, particularly the massive rodent population. They readily hunted as loners or pairs, making them harder to wipe out. And without question they had the huge American public lands, where thanks to the scientists national parks, at least, had been off-limits to bureau hunters since 1936, as refuges for rebuilding their populations.

So coyotes held on, and meanwhile the cultural pendulum began to swing. Rachel Carson's legendary 1962 book, Silent Spring, dramatically changed the way many Americans felt about poisons. By then scientists had published sufficient work about the role of predators to begin to change how people felt about them, too. And in the 1960s and 1970s the science of ecology and the environmental movement created a whole new appreciation for a species' innate right to exist. Surfing this wave, President Richard Nixon not only banned the use of poisons in federal predator control on public lands in 1972, he supported the Endangered Species Act in 1973, one of the most important and controversial environmental laws in US history.

A superficial view of the decades since might lead one to say that little has changed for coyotes in America. That would be a mistake. Like so many policies, coyote control has become a marker of politics and the culture wars. Nixon's poison ban did not survive the Reagan years, although many restrictions remain and a continuing ban on blanket poisoning has made shooting coyotes from airplanes and helicopters the strategy of choice since the 1970s. The Endangered Species Act and changing public attitudes now protect coyotes from the invention of some new form of extermination. But the coyote war is far from over. Congress during Reagan's terms separated Animal Damage Control from the Fish and Wildlife Service, relocating it in the Department of Agriculture where in the 1990s the USDA renamed it "Wildlife Services." So on behalf of agriculture, particularly on behalf of a shrinking but still powerful sheep-raising lobby, federal coyote control continues. Between 2006 and 2011, Wildlife Services' hunters "controlled to death" 512,710 coyotes in the United States. From all causes (including increasingly popular "coyote hunting contests") we still kill about one-half million coyotes a year, every year, in the United States.

The response of the coyote to all this has been downright remarkable. Starting in the 1920s, coyotes began mysteriously showing up in places where the animals had never been known before. In 1949 a Wisconsin biologist collected a coyote on the Apostle Islands. Within another two years marginal records of coyotes had cropped up in Indiana, Illinois, and 200 miles east of the Great Lakes, in eastern Ontario. With some confusion, a 1955 work on mammal distributions noted coyote appearances in Virginia, West Virginia, Tennessee, the Carolinas, and Georgia, Alabama, and Mississippi. As a kid growing up in Louisiana, I first saw coyotes there in the early 1960s. Now they are in every province in Canada, and by 2011 they colonized their last continental state, Delaware, which became the forty-ninth US state to list coyotes as part of their twenty-first-century fauna. Coyotes now blanket North America from Alaska to Panama, a distance of 7,500 miles. In the United States they now drink from Pacific, Atlantic, Arctic, and Gulf waters. In response to 150 years of persecution, more coyotes now exist than at any time in history.

For those used to thinking of coyotes in Mark Twain terms, this former resident of the "most desolate and forbidding" plains and desert wildernesses has done something else equally astonishing. Confronted with a continent transformed by humans, coyotes adopted mankind as a lifestyle and moved in amongst us. Since 1940 virtually every city and town in America, starting with Los Angeles and now even including New York City, has acquired a resident coyote population. Studying this urban coyote phenomenon, Ohio State biologist Stanley Gehrt realized a few years into his work that it wasn't a few dozen coyotes he was studying in Chicago, but that "hundreds, even thousands" of coyotes were roaming the streets and alleys of the Windy City. By

Unlike every other charismatic Great Plains species, the small North American wolves we call coyotes not only survived the nineteenth- and twentieth-century war against them but also have spread across the continent and into major cities from coast to coast. Dan Flores photo.

the early twenty-first century, the most common large wild animal most urban Americans had ever encountered was a coyote, and as often as not it was in their backyards.

The coyote's final demonstration of its smarts and adaptability is the best evidence yet that the American Original truly is a continental totem animal—not just for the ancient West, but in our time for the whole country. In a striking nod to Lewis and Clark's puzzlement in 1804 about just what kind of animal coyotes were, coyotes are now mirroring our own multicultural patterns in modern America. Just as the United States is rapidly becoming a nation of blended ethnicities, coyotes have become the active agents in a blended wild canid population in America. What scientists call a "canis soup" is their version of our "melting pot." Careful genetic work among eastern coyotes indicates that by interbreeding with dogs and with their remnant, close relative wolf cousins (like the red wolf), the last 75 to 140 generations of coyotes have thoroughly mixed wild canids in the East and South. Remnant eastern species of wolves are now 40 to 75 percent coyote—in truth, "coywolves." Recovery efforts for the endangered red wolf, which coyotes appear to have hybridized with both anciently and during their migrations eastward in the mid-twentieth century, have had to feature such massive interventions to keep coyotes and red wolves apart that in a modern America now saturated with coyotes, pure red wolves will likely never be recovered across any significant part of their former range. And that's mostly a result of the coyote's remarkable success story.

Among the charismatic Great Plains animals, the coyote's story stands alone—not just separate, but in shocking contrast to the situations of bison, pronghorn antelope, grizzlies, wild horses, even wolves. Human thoughtlessness, or economically driven impulses, saw us stoically push the other last surviving charismatic plains megafauna to the edge of extinction. But the same level of exploitation and focused persecution that drove wolves, grizzlies, and wild horses off the Great Plains produced another response altogether from coyotes. Like native pronghorns and bison, coyotes are still on the Great Plains. But now they're also everywhere else.

Coyotes are still wild and numerous and playing their ancient role on the plains, but in the world we humans transformed, they are also practicing their new urban lifeway here, as well. In the Queen City of the American Great Plains, Denver, coyotes started to become an urban presence in the 1980s. As of 2015, the estimate—which urban biologists think probably too conservative by maybe 20 percent—is that there are 112 coyote packs with established ranges in the Denver Metro Area. Those 112 coyote packs have a summer population of more than 1,000 coyotes living, hunting, and thriving in the plains' biggest city.

That's a stunning tribute to "the prairie wolf." But then, almost everything about coyotes is a stretch for superlatives.

4

In the summer of 1834, just two years after his now-famous adventure visiting and painting the tribes of the Missouri River and Northern Plains country, the prototype western artist George Catlin got his first opportunity to observe and paint that counterpoint world, hundreds of miles to the south, on the Southern Plains of what is now western Oklahoma. Accompanying an American military expedition hoping to treat with peoples like the Comanches and Kiowas, fate and luck offered Catlin a singular chance to see first-hand the similarities and differences between these two regions of the early nineteenth-century American West.

On the Missouri, Catlin had traveled and lived with fur traders from the big companies that were engaged in a competition for wealth stripped from the backs of beavers, river otters, muskrats, and bison. And the artist had duly painted (and mourned) the great destruction then under way there. In the different ecology of the Southern Plains in 1834, however, Catlin saw only a small-scale facsimile of the great economic engines that were stripping the northern landscapes clean of valuable furbearers. Instead, on these southern prairies an altogether different animal caught his attention. Traveling in the vicinity of the Wichita Mountains that summer of 1834, this was how he described his impression of the difference between the Missouri drainage and the Red River country of the southern prairies: "The tract of country over which we passed, between the False Washita and this place, is stocked, not only with buffaloes, but with numerous bands of wild horses, many of which we saw every day." He went on with obvious admiration: "The wild horse of these regions is a small, but very powerful animal; with an exceedingly prominent eye, sharp nose, high nostril, small feet and delicate leg; and undoubtedly, have sprung from a stock introduced by the Spaniards."

No other denizen of the plains was "so wild and so sagacious as the horse," Catlin wrote. "So remarkably keen is their eye, that they will generally run 'at the sight,' when they are a mile distant . . . and when in motion, will seldom stop short of three or four miles." Like many wild horse observers, the artist was struck with the sheer beauty of the horse in its wild state, which somehow seemed amplified by the difficulty of possessing them: "Some were milk white, some jet black—others were sorrel, and bay, and cream colour—many were an iron grey; and others were pied, containing a variety of colours on the same animal. Their manes were very profuse, and hanging in the wildest confusion over their necks and faces—and their long tails swept the ground."

At roughly the same point in time that Catlin expressed admiration over the wild horses of the Southern Plains, back in the horse country of Kentucky, John James Audubon, Catlin's fellow painter (and, in private, thorn in Catlin's side), wrote that he'd become acquainted with a man who had just returned from "the country in the neighbourhood of the head waters of the Arkansas River" where he'd obtained from the Osages a recently captured, four-year-old wild horse named "Barro." While the little horse was "by no means handsome" and had cost only $35 in trade goods, Audubon was intrigued enough to try him out. He proved a delight. He had a sweet gait that covered forty miles a day. He leapt over woodland logs "as lightly as an elk," was duly cautious yet a quick study in new situations, and strong and fearless when coaxed to swim the Ohio River. He was steady when birds flushed and Audubon shot them from the saddle. And he left "a superb" $300 horse in the dust. Audubon quickly bought Barro for $50 silver, and gloating over his discovery, concluded that "the importation of horses of this kind from the Western Prairies might improve our breeds generally."

With an audition like Barro's, one is tempted to say, no kidding. But historically, what is most intriguing about Catlin's and Audubon's wild horse epiphanies is that they came so late. In fact, nearly simultaneous with the evolution of the fur trade on the Northern Plains, the remarkable wild horse herds of the Great Plains had generated an economy of capture and trade (and often, theft) that from the 1780s to the 1840s fairly dominated the region. Wild horses from herds like those Catlin saw in Oklahoma had been driven up the

Returned to the American West by Spanish settlers, horses quickly went wild and rejoined the ecology of the Great Plains where they had evolved. Artist George Catlin painted these wild herds in present southwestern Oklahoma in 1834. Courtesy Smithsonian Institution.

Natchez Trace to the horse markets in Kentucky at least as early as the 1790s, half a century before Audubon's test-ride on Barro. That neither man seemed aware of this in the 1830s is fairly strong evidence for the long-standing underground character of the early horse trade in the West. Which is why historians have missed it, as well.

Yet on the sweeping plains both south and north of the Arkansas River, during the period when Americans were becoming such a presence in the West, this was the fur trade's equivalent, schooling many diverse Indian peoples in the nuances of the market economy, providing Spanish Texas a revenue base, intriguing a famous American president, and drawing itinerant American mustangers—who quite literally carried the flag with them—into vast, horizontal yellow landscapes whose ownership seemed up for grabs.

The Great Plains' wild horse trade had first come to the official attention of the United States in the period, and in the same flurry of motion, that would eventually add the Louisiana Purchase to the early republic. Since at the turn of the nineteenth century bands of western wild horses were still confined to the California valleys, the deserts of the Southwest, and the prairies of the Southern and Central Plains, identifying them as a feature of the natural history and economy of the West emerged during the years when Thomas Jefferson, as vice president in the John Adams administration, was contemplating various schemes for understanding and eventually exploring the West, both north and south.

In conversations about the West with informants like General James Wilkinson, as early as 1798 Jefferson had begun to hear stories about an intriguing individual known as "the Mexican Traveller." His real name was Philip Nolan, and he was an Irish-American adventurer who, Jefferson discovered, had made a series of journeys far into the unknown Southwest, returning time and again driving herds of captured wild horses into Louisiana and then up the Natchez Trace to the horse markets of Kentucky. Wilkinson had raised Nolan in his own household, where he had no doubt absorbed dinner talk of revolution and westward expansion. That may have given Jefferson pause. He asked for other opinions about Nolan.

The image that emerges of this shadowy and rather legendary figure is of a literate, athletic, and adventurous young man who was confident enough in his wide-ranging abilities to attempt things other men only speculated about. William Dunbar, the Mississippi scientist who became Jefferson's primary associate in assembling information on the southwestern reaches of the Louisiana Purchase, knew Nolan and told Jefferson he thought the man lacked sufficient education and that he was flawed by eccentricities "many and great." Nevertheless, Dunbar wrote, Nolan "was not destitute of romantic principles of honor united to the highest personal courage." Another Jeffersonian who knew Nolan, Daniel Clark, Jr., of New Orleans, told Jefferson he thought Nolan "an extraordinary Character," one "whom Nature seems to have formed for Enterprises of which the rest of Mankind are incapable."

What Jefferson learned from these informants was that as early as 1790, when he was barely twenty years old, with a passport in hand from Esteban Miró, the Spanish governor of Louisiana, Nolan had embarked on a two-year journey into the Southern Plains, ultimately meeting and traveling with Wichita and Comanche Indians and providing them with an initial, apparently very favorable, impression of Anglo-Americans. Judging from what seem today very precise descriptions of a part of the continent then almost unknown to anyone except tribal people, Nolan got all the way to New Mexico, along the way learning that the numerous Southern Plains Indians were dissatisfied with Spanish trade and very desirous of replacing their former trading partners, the French, with a new source of guns and European goods. The Osages, enemies of many of the groups farther west, were well-armed themselves and making every effort to block traders from St. Louis from establishing trade relations with the tribes of the deep plains. Apparently Nolan had in mind addressing that opening from a different direction.

But—and this was what had caught Jefferson's attention—the vice-president learned that Nolan had not returned from the Southern Plains with the usual Northern Plains trader's packs of Indian-processed furs. Instead it was horses he'd brought back from these forays, some of them wild ones that he and his associates had captured, others traded from the Indians.

Although he'd found "the savage life . . . less pleasing in practice than speculation" (he could not "Indianfy my heart" as he put it), Nolan had gone on a second expedition into the deep plains in 1794, and a third one in 1796. He'd brought back only 50 horses in 1794, but the number had jumped to 250 in 1796, several of which he'd decided to take to Frankfurt, Kentucky, to sell, which had brought him and his horses to the attention of important people who clamored for more of his product. So in 1797, packing $7,000 worth of trade goods, "twelve good rifles, and . . . but one coward," and a sextant and a timepiece, "instruments to enable me to make a more correct map" (which caught the attention of suspicious Spanish officials), Nolan launched a fourth expedition. This time, when he returned in 1798, he was driving a herd variously estimated at between 1,000 and 2,500 western horses, which in the Kentucky horse markets reportedly brought between $50 (for ordinary animals) and $150 for truly outstanding horseflesh.

When Philip Nolan returned from his fourth mustanging expedition, a letter awaited him, requesting—in a fine, clear, and famous hand—natural history information on the wild horses of the West at "the only moment in the age of the world" when the horse might "be studied in its wild state." What Jefferson really wanted was a visit with Nolan, and he eventually hatched a plan to effect one, writing Nolan in a follow-up letter that he was most desirous of purchasing one of Nolan's animals "which I am told are so remarkable for the singularity & beauty of their colours and forms."

The small handful of western historians who've been aware of Philip Nolan have long assumed that Jefferson's letter produced the expected response.
According to both Wilkinson and Daniel Clark, Nolan and an "Inhabitant of
the western Country" who was a master of the fascinating language of Indian
hand signs (he was probably Joseph Talapoon, a Louisiana mixed-blood), departed for Virginia in May 1800 with a fine paint stallion for Jefferson. However, neither Nolan nor the paint horse ever got to Monticello. For a reason
that is not clear—one is tempted to speculate that Nolan may have lost Jefferson's stallion in a game of chance—he got no farther than Kentucky, then
turned back. The West's "Mexican Traveller," in other words, stood up the
Virginian about to be elected the country's third president.

By October 1800 Nolan was in final preparations for a fifth, and as it would
emerge, final, expedition to the western plains. He told a confidante before
he left Natchez that he had two dozen good men, armed to the teeth, and was
taking a large quantity of trade goods. This time he did not have a passport
from Spanish officials, who had grown increasingly alarmed at Nolan's contacts among the expansionist Americans. Since the 1780s Spain had sought
to control and regulate the western horse trade for her own purposes, so the
lack of a passport meant that any horses Nolan captured would be illegal contraband. To his contact Nolan enigmatically added: "Everyone thinks that I go
to catch wild horses, but you know that I have long been tired of wild horses."

By December the party was far out onto the Southern Plains beyond the
Trinity River. Following a visit to a Comanche village on one of the branches
of the Red River, they returned to what seems Nolan's favorite mustanging
country in the Grand Prairie south of present-day Fort Worth, where they built
corrals and began running horses. In March 1801, Indian scouts operating for
a Spanish force sent out to arrest Nolan located the Americans' camp. When
Nolan refused to surrender the Spaniards attacked, killing Nolan and capturing more than a dozen of his men, although seven of them—including a pair
of American mustangers named Robert Ashley and John House—escaped
into the vastness of the plains. Philip Nolan's intriguing adventures were over.

For Thomas Jefferson, who assumed the presidency at almost the same
moment that Nolan was dying amongst his wild horse corrals, the intriguing
knowledge that horses had gone wild in the West sifted about in that blow-
torch mind for years to come. Following Nolan's death, Jefferson's hopes for
understanding wild horse natural history, and his growing sense that in the

southern West the horse trade might play an economic, diplomatic, and geo-political role similar to the one the fur trade did in the northern West, were embedded in his plans to send a Lewis and Clark–type exploring expedition into the Southwest. With Peter Custis, the young University of Pennsylvania naturalist he attached to his 1806 "Grand Expedition" into the Southwest, Jefferson no doubt thought to put a scientific observer amongst those herds. But of course as we know now, during the same summer that Lewis and Clark's party was returning from the Pacific, Jefferson's second major expedition into the West encountered an immovable obstacle on the Red River in the form of a Spanish army four times its size. Regrettably, Peter Custis would never get to be Thomas Jefferson's eyes amongst the teeming wild horse herds towards the Rockies. Nonetheless, as with the fur trade, wild horses and Jefferson's dreams for the West would remain linked for years to come.

Jefferson never got to know what history now can reconstruct, however im-perfectly, about the nineteenth-century West's wild horses. Deep-time horse history commences with an irony. Euroamericans like Jefferson understood that their ancestors had brought the horse to the Americas, and that after initial fear of it, many indigenous peoples in both North and South Amer-ica had adopted the animal into their lives, where it had revolutionized their cultures. And yet, back into depths of time that Jeffersonians never suspected lay a surprising story. Unlike so many of the post-Pleistocene animals of the Great Plains, including even the bison, which had come to the Americas from an evolutionary start in Asia, horses joined pronghorns and coyotes as true natives of North America. The ancestors of the horses Philip Nolan sold in Kentucky had begun their evolution into the modern horse 57 million years earlier as distinctively American animals. If anything the irony was even more profound than that. After millions of years of North American horse evolu-tion, indeed by 10,000 years ago into animals so similar to modern horses that paleontologists have difficulty telling them apart, horses unaccountably went extinct throughout the Americas. Equally perplexing, the American horses that had migrated into Asia, Europe, and Africa survived that same extinction episode. So the Barb horses that danced and nickered beneath the Spaniards in their first entradas in the West, although not precisely the same animals that had become extinct here ten millennia earlier, were still ancient America's cabelline horses, returning to their evolutionary homeland. Except that when they galloped onto the seventeenth-century Great Plains, while the prairie ecology still included wolves and cougars and grizzlies, many of the horses' Pleistocene predators were now gone.

That Big History is why horses were so phenomenally successful in going wild in the American West. From their primary seventeenth- and eighteenth-century distribution centers in the Spanish settlements of northern New Mexico, Texas, and California, escaped horses had run away into the very landscapes that had shaped their ancestors' hooves, teeth, and behavioral patterns millennia earlier. When the Pueblo Revolt of 1680 drove the Spaniards out of New Mexico for more than a decade, liberated livestock and horse culture famously got traded to tribes northward up the Rockies, passing from Pueblos to Utes, and from Utes to Shoshones and Salish and Nez Perce, and within a half-century to Blackfeet, Crows, and Crees. But in the chaos of the revolt, many animals also ran loose into the High Plains. Similarly, when Spain abandoned its initial, 1690s attempts at missions in Texas, the fathers simply turned mission livestock out in the wild. Spaniards commonly did not geld stallions, and when they returned to Texas in 1715 they found the stock they'd left had increased to thousands, in places blanketing the whole countryside with animals. Three-quarters of a century later, a similar phenomenon was well under way in California.

By Jefferson's day, across the southern latitudes of the West, wild horse herds had become enormous. In Texas, Spanish bishop Marin de Porras wrote in 1805 that everywhere he traveled there were "great herds of horses and mares found close to the roads in herds of four to six thousand head." By 1794, the California missions and presidios—having commenced with virtually no horses in the 1770s—found themselves surrounded by such growing bands of feral animals that beginning in 1806 in San Jose, then in Santa Barbara in 1808 and 1814, in Monterrey in 1812 and 1820, and generally throughout the California settlements by 1827, ranchers and colonists annually slaughtered large numbers of horses in the surrounding countryside as nuisances and threats to grass and water for domestic stock. On the Southern Plains, with a century's natural increase, wild horses had become a memorable sensory phenomenon, one observer noting that "the prairie near the horizon seemed to be moving, with long undulations, like the waves of an ocean. . . . [T]he whole prairie towards the horizon was alive with mustangs." And another: "As far as the eye could extend, nothing over the dead level prairie was visible except a dense mass of horses, and the trampling of their hooves sounded like the roar of the surf on a rocky coast." And a third: "Wandering herds of wild horses are so numerous that the land is covered with paths, making it appear the most populated place in the world."

It is fascinating to imagine a Great Plains ecology that once again replicated the Pleistocene (or Africa with its wildebeests and zebras) by integrating bands of wild horses in amongst the bison, herds of pronghorns and deer and elk, wolves and cougars and coyotes and grizzlies. How large a component of that ecology they became in the eighteenth and nineteenth centuries is difficult to judge because we have little other than anecdotal descriptions to go on. In the Pleistocene horses had sometimes comprised as much as 25 percent of the biomass of grazing animals, and they may have been on their way to approximating that. No one has been able to suggest historic-era horse numbers in the same way we have worked out bison estimates. The writer J. Frank Dobie speculated that by 1800, some 120 years after the Pueblo Revolt, there were at least 2 million wild horses in the West, and that a million of them were on the prairies south of the Arkansas River, although he made no effort to track wild horse expansion over time or the effects of changing climate on their numbers. A million wild horses on the Southern Plains would have been about 12 percent of bison numbers there in those years. As with other ungulates, wet weather and droughts no doubt affected them, and from seed herds—not just on the Southern Plains but in California, the Columbia Plateau, and Wyoming's Red Desert—wild herds were spreading out across the West.

In the early years of the horse trade, before 1825, however, the best mustanging grounds were still on the Southern Plains and in the "Mustang Prairie" of South Texas, especially the former because it possessed both wild horses and herds of bison. Like favorite bison ranges, huge herds of horses concentrated in particular ecoregion settings produced profound cultural and ecological effects. The Southern Plains herds drew Indian peoples from all over the West, bringing Utes, Shoshones, Crows, Arapahos, Cheyennes, Lakotas, even Blackfeet to the country below the Arkansas River. Ecologically, as wild and Indian horse herds increased over the decades, their numbers cut into the carrying capacity of the plains for bison and other grazers.

As with bison and beavers and other furbearers farther north, useful animals in such enormous numbers as were found with wild horses filled the human mind with thoughts of acquisition, wealth, and power. In other words, with thoughts of a potential economy.

The "Great Horse Funnel" of this early western economy took in tens of thousands of horses from its flared end on the Southern and Central Plains and then funneled them to trade marts like St. Louis, Natchitoches, Natchez, and New Orleans. Its historical origins are found in a simple equation. There was the supply, the horses, an example of American limitlessness, feral horses begetting horses across all the immense, horizontal yellow plains of the West. And there was the demand, in the form of human desire—the desire for wealth and status on the parts of newly emergent plains people like the Comanches, the desire for a source of revenue on the part of Euroamerican colonial officials, the desire for profits on the part of ambitious American traders, and the demand for the product (in this case animal-powered energy) by Americans on the homesteader frontier pushing westward between the Appalachians and the Mississippi. The trick, eventually, would be to get the horses from the high plains of the West to the farms of the woodlands of the American frontier. With one exception, the details of how it would all work are entirely familiar because it was so similar to the functioning of the fur trade. The exception, which is the reason we have never heard much in western history about this particular economy, is the presence of corporate involvement in the fur trade, and its absence in the horse trade.

A fundamental characteristic of the American fur trade regardless of geography was the role Indian people played as procurers of the resource. With the creation of trapping brigades by the Hudson's Bay Company, and the American Rocky Mountain Fur Company's reliance on free trappers and the rendezvous system, eventually the fur trade produced a group of non-native, company employees who acted as procurers of furs. But Indians began as and remained major players in the nineteenth-century fur trade system. In good part that was because the Euroamerican stage of the fur trade was based on a preexisting native economy involving inter-tribal exchange of animal pelts and related trade items.

Precisely the same pattern evolved in the western horse trade. Virtually from the start, horses became such revolutionary cultural agents, and so valuable to tribal ethnogenesis in the European age, that barter exchanges of the animals became a central feature of western Indian life. Annual trade fairs in places like the Black Hills, and at fixed villages like those of the Mandan-Hidatsas on the Missouri, funneled horses in huge numbers from the Southwest to the Northern Plains. Even middleman groups emerged. The horse

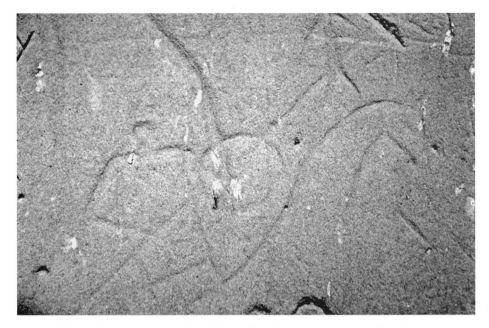

Captured, domesticated, and trained by plains Indians, horses entirely transformed human lifestyles on the Great Plains. They also became the principal subjects of Indian art, as in this petroglyph from Texas. Dan Flores photo.

trade, for example, contributed to the segmentation of the previously agricultural Cheyennes into two geographic divisions, a northern and southern one, because the southern bands became central players in distributing horses northward up the plains.

The various bands of the Comanches, another people newly drawn to the eighteenth-century plains because of horses, quite literally reconceived themselves in the context of horses and trade. They raided other tribes and Spanish colonists both for horses and captive children, training the latter as herders in an economy that became more pastoral by the decade. The Cheyennes and Comanches not only became famous catchers of wild horses, like the Nez Perce they became horse breeders, selecting animals for conformation, speed, and markings. From the heart of the Southern Plains they marketed their animals northward to horse-poor Northern Plains tribes, westward to the New Mexicans via trade fairs in places like Pecos, Picuris, and Taos. And eventually eastward to the Americans.

No one duped these native peoples into the market economy. Indeed, to a significant degree, they *created* the western horse trade, built their own internal status systems around it, and for a century used it to manipulate the geopolitical designs of competing Euroamericans anxious for profits and alliances with them. Of course, for native people, the nineteenth-century western market economy came with many decided downsides. As with the fur trade, access to ever-more animal resources meant that the horse trade ultimately would produce inter-tribal raids, wars, and territorial expansion. Eventually the Southern Plains tribes would raid hundreds of miles southward, liberating new supplies of horses from Mexican ranches. And because winters on the Northern Plains could be so hard on horses, raids for replenishment of tribal stock rippled from north to south every spring. As was always the case, when American traders entered these kinds of situations, things could be dicey.

One result was that soon after prototype American horse traders like Philip Nolan joined the economy, initially procuring their horses from the native people via a process carefully regulated and managed by Indian band headmen, a point came when the Americans attempted the same step the fur men did: with millions of wild horses running free on the plains, they would try to procure the resource themselves. Just who originated the technique for catching wild horses in trade-sufficient numbers is difficult to ascertain; it may have begun as a North African or Iberian equine art. By the time Americans entered the horse economy, many different peoples seem to have mastered it. The Wichita Indians taught trader Anthony Glass how to build pens and run wild horses; Nolan and others appear to have learned the art from the French and Spanish settlers of Louisiana towns like Bayou Pierre and Natchitoches. Indeed, while the artist George Catlin and others provide us with accounts and paintings of single horse capture by Southern Plains Indians, the best descriptions we have of early trade-volume mustanging strategies come from a third group involved in the horse trade: the Hispanic residents of Texas.

As the wild horse herds of the plains had grown into the hundreds of thousands across the seventeenth and eighteenth centuries—and private horse hunters began to capture and drive more and more of them to Louisiana and Missouri to supply the emerging American frontier market—Spain acted to declare the animals *mesteños*, or the king's property. In a move that neither the United States nor Canada ever effected with bison, Spain proclaimed the vast wild herds of horses to be national property (*Real Camara y Fisco de su Magesta*), subject to government regulation. This interesting development was part of the famous Bourbon Reforms to strengthen the economies of Spain's colonies. The edict of 1778 required Spanish officials of the northern provinces (*Provincias Internas*) of New Spain to place a tax of six reales on every wild horse captured from Spanish domains, thus creating the famous "Mustang Fund." Since captured wild horses were worth only three reales at the time, the initial tax was something of miscalculation. So to grow the economy, in 1779 officials reduced the tax to two reales, a mere 67 percent rate! Spain required a license for citizens, plus a passport for noncitizens who sought to catch or trade for its horses. Without the license or the passport, the trade was illegal and contraband.

Enforcing this law proved impossible for a small Spanish population in an enormous setting. Yet, given how lucrative the mustang trade was, Spain needed to be able to enforce it. Nonetheless, it worked after a fashion. In the first six years of the tax, by January 1787, mustangers had paid taxes to Spain on 17,000 captured wild horses, some of which became colonial remounts, but most of which appear to have ended up east of the Mississippi River, carrying American farmers and merchants and supplying mounts for southeastern Indians like the Chickasaws and Seminoles (in fact, the "Chickasaw horse," a foundational type that led to the quarter-horse, sprang directly from this trade). As one San Antonio official put the matter in 1785, "The number of mustangs in all these environs is so countless that if anyone were capable of taming them and caring for them, he could acquire a supply sufficient to furnish an army. But this multitude is causing us such grave damage that it is often necessary to shoot them."

Catching wild horses in this kind of volume required the same sort of natural history understanding of the animals that trapping did. It also obviously required organization and carefully honed skills. Like trapping, in effect it became a kind of wilderness art form, with its own material culture, its own internal terminology, but one that differed from trapping by aiming at live animal capture. We know all of this in some detail because of a French scientist named Jean-Louis Berlandier, who saw and described the process of volume wild horse capture in the 1820s. What Berlandier recounts is so like Indian techniques for impounding bison and pronghorns that the source of the technique seems obvious. But wild horse capture had clearly developed some nuances all its own.

Once mustangers were on the plains, amongst the herds and stallion bands, the first step was understanding the landscape sufficiently to know how to site what Berlandier called the *corrale*. "These are immense enclosures situated close to some pond," he wrote. Commonly they were built of mesquite posts lashed together with rawhide, and were large enough that once inside, a herd could be swept into a circling, milling confusion in its center. "The entrance," Berlandier tells us, "is placed in such a way that it forms a long corridor, and at the end there is a kind of exit." That corridor often consisted of brush wings that fanned out a half-mile or more from the capture pen itself, usually oriented towards the south so that prevailing southwesterly winds would envelop an approaching herd in its own dust cloud, blinding it.

To start the action, Berlandier relates, mustangers divided themselves into three groups, each with different roles to play. After reconnoitering a likely herd, one group of well-mounted riders, the *adventadores*, had the task of startling the herd into flight and pushing it towards the brush funnel leading to the pen. Once the action was in motion and a direction established, the herd would find itself squeezed into a flight path by a second group of mustangers, the *puestos*, who were the most skilled riders and whose "role consists of conducting that dreadful mass of living beings by riding full gallop along the flanks and gathering there, in the midst of suffocating dust, the partial herds which sometimes unite at the sound of the terror of a large herd." Finally, at the moment of truth, as the white-eyed, terrified horses were sweeping at breakneck speed into the trap, a third group of mustangers, the *encerradores*, were charged with closing the gate, sometimes dashing in to open it for an instant to allow stallions and older horses to escape.

What followed were scenes of such emotional impact that mustangers had a specialized vocabulary to describe them. Captured wild horses "squeal terribly and rage like lions." They also died. Hispanic horse-catching jargon was rife with the language of death—horses that died from *sentimiento* (broken-heartedness over capture) or from *despecho* (nervous rage over capture). Then there was the term *hediondo* (stinking), whose meaning Indians who impounded bison would have well understood. It designated a corral ruined for use from the aftereffects of having been too often jammed with panicked and dying animals.

Berlandier's description continues: "When these animals find themselves enclosed, the first to enter fruitlessly search for exits and those in the rear . . . trample over the first. It is rare that in one of these chases a large part of the horses thus trapped do not kill one another in their efforts to escape. . . . It has happened that the *mesteñeros* have trapped at one swoop more than one thousand horses, of which not a fifth remained."

Exhausted by their efforts to escape, surviving horses were then roped one by one. "After some hours of ill treatment," Berlandier concludes, "these *mesteñeros* have the ability to render them half-tame a short while after depriving them of their liberty."

The rhythmic creaking of saddle leather, the rustling and tinkling of swaying packs of trade goods, and the snick of hooves on the cobbled prairie surface must have paused for a few moments on the Southern Plains in early August 1808. After a five-week outward journey, Anthony Glass and his party of ten traders, driving sixteen pack horses carrying more than $2,000 in goods and a riding remuda of thirty-two animals, had finally come in sight of the thatched-roof village complex on the Red River, inhabited by peoples the American horse traders and their government knew as the "Panis." In the horse trade this complex was the equivalent of the Mandan/Hidatsa towns on the Missouri, a trio of villages occupied by people who called themselves *Taovayas* and *Iscanis* (as prairie Caddoans they were related to the Pawnees farther north). Today we refer to them, collectively, as the Wichitas, and know them as the plains people Coronado found in his sixteenth-century search for Quivira. To make them more accessible for Euroamericans embarking westward from Natchez and Natchitoches, a half-century earlier French traders had persuaded them to move from the Arkansas to this location on the Red. In 1808 their acknowledged headman was Awahakei, or Great Bear. And he had been expecting these Americans.

Whether they built corrals and ran wild horses, or traded for them from the Southern Plains tribes, American horse traders like Philip Nolan had preceded the Louisiana Purchase in getting Americans into the horse-trade economy. But in the 1806 aftermath of Jefferson's failed "Grand Expedition," horse traders like Anthony Glass—who would ride down into the Wichita villages this August morning wearing the uniform of a US military captain, his party of a dozen men traveling under an American flag—became private but overt agents of Jeffersonian geopolitical designs on the West. In the Northern Rockies, of course, the trading posts and trapping parties of the American, Missouri, and Rocky Mountain fur companies consciously advanced US claims for territory and tribal alliances in a sharp competition with the posts and brigades of the Northwest and Hudson's Bay companies, agents of the British empire. On the Southern Plains, however, it was itinerant horse traders like Glass to whom the task of advancing America's empire fell. Indeed,

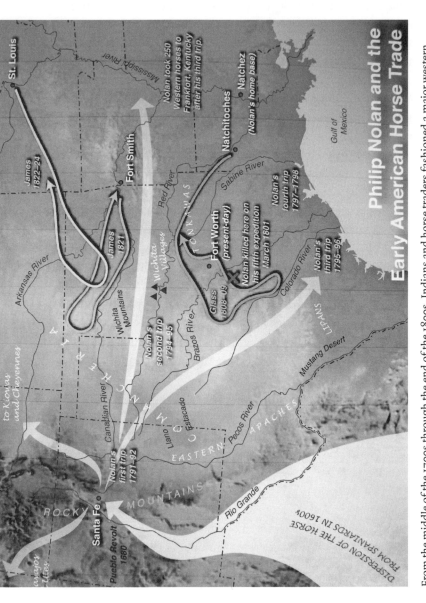

Philip Nolan and the Early American Horse Trade

St. Louis

Mississippi River

Fort Smith

Nolan took 250
western horses to
Frankfort, Kentucky
after his third trip.

Natchitoches
(Nolan's home base)

Natchez

Gulf of
Mexico

James 1822–24

James 1821

Arkansas River

Red River

Sabine River

Wichita
Villages

Wichita
Mountains

Nolan's
second trip
1794–95

Fort Worth
(present-day)

Nolan killed here on
his fifth expedition
March 1801

Nolan's
fourth trip
1797–1798

Glass
1808–09

T O N K A W A S

Canadian River

Brazos River

Colorado River

Nolan's
third trip
1795–96

C O M A N C H E S

Llano Estacado

Pecos River

Mustang Desert

LIPANS

E A S T E R N   A P A C H E S

to Kiowas
and Cheyennes

Nolan's
first trip
1791–92

Santa Fe

Pueblo Revolt
1680

Navajos
Utes

R O C K Y   M O U N T A I N S

Rio Grande

DISPERSION OF THE HORSE
FROM SPANIARDS IN 1600s

From the middle of the 1700s through the end of the 1800s, Indians and horse traders fashioned a major western economy around the wild horse herds of the plains, with traders like Philip Nolan, Anthony Glass, and Thomas James initiating the trade. Map courtesy Montana: The Magazine of Western History.

in the decades following the Jefferson administration's clash with Spain over territory and boundaries, a whole series of almost unremembered American horse-trading expeditions worked as a kind of economic/diplomatic wedge to assert the interests of the new American republic against a Spanish empire distracted and overwhelmed by colonial revolutions across the Americas.

How successful the strategy was of allowing private economic interests to advance state geopolitical design is open to question (although one could argue it has remained a fundamental of American foreign policy for two centuries now). On the Southern Plains between 1806 and 1821 it seems to have worked pretty well. In the aftermath of the events of that summer of 1806, with a Spanish army halting and turning back an official American exploring expedition, and the ensuing escalation that in the fall would put an American force of 1,000 troops eyeball-to-eyeball with a Spanish army of 1,400, Spain seemed to blink. In 1807 it instructed frontier officials in its northern provinces to avoid any more "noisy disturbances" involving the Americans, and to direct their ire and retribution over the contraband horse trade towards participating tribes rather than American traders. Hence when Jefferson's Indian agent, Dr. John Sibley of Natchitoches, authorized and helped plan the Glass expedition, the captain's coat and American flag (which Glass was to present to Awahakei to fly over their villages) reflected a Jeffersonian's musings about how to turn the horse trade to state advantage. As Sibley would go on to remark, sagely: "whoever furnishes Indians the Best & Most Satisfactory Trade can always Control their Politicks."

Of course it was profit rather than statecraft that motivated American horse traders, and that required no official sanction. In addition to Nolan, Glass had been preceded in the West by several other American horse-trading parties. We know little about them now, but in 1794–1795, for instance, a twenty-seven-year-old Philadelphia gunsmith named John Calvert had spent fourteen months pursuing horses with the Wichitas and Comanches before a Spanish patrol snagged him. As far as the documents inform us, Calvert's example was followed in 1804–1805 by a very active plains trader named John Davis and a Corsican carpenter, Alexandro Dauni, who seem to have also prospected for minerals in the Wichita Mountains. They were followed by one of Philip Nolan's mustangers, John House, who successfully drove a herd back from the plains in 1805 at the age of twenty-five. Then there were trading parties led by Francisco Roquier in 1805 and John Cashily in 1806, who ingeniously planned to tell Spanish officials that the horses they were driving eastward were intended to help them bring their families west as new Spanish emigrants.

Almost in the middle of the uproar over Jefferson's attempts to explore the Red River, Dr. Sibley licensed yet another horse-trading party, led by John Lewis and William Alexander and guided by Nolan's sign-language expert, Lucas Talapoon. Lewis and Alexander seem to have been the Jefferson administration's first experiment with traders as official government emissaries: they also took US flags to the western Indians, and in Sibley's name they invited the tribes of the Southern Plains to a grand council in Natchitoches in 1807. In June 1807, three of this party (the rest were still on the plains, running horses) arrived in Louisiana driving a herd of mustangs. Did they pay the Spanish tax on their horses? Of course they did not. As Sibley noted, a few years earlier Spanish records had shown 1,187 horses officially *leaving* for Louisiana, but somehow more than 7,300 horses had managed to *arrive* there! Helpless to stem the tide, one Spanish official estimated the number of the king's horses herded into the United States in the first decades of the nineteenth century at a thousand a month, which gives some idea of the size of this economy.

The paucity of surviving information on so many of the horse traders both before and after Glass does mean we ought to linger on Glass a bit. In apparent contrast to many of his contemporaries in the economy, Glass was literate. Remarkably, Sibley had persuaded him to keep a journal, which he did—sporadically—during his ten months on the plains. This document not only gives us a sense of the early horse trade, but leaves an impression of Glass himself as a sort of John Colter figure of the Southern Plains.

Glass was more solidly middle-class than most American horse traders. He and a brother were hardware store owners and merchants in the river town of Natchez, the terminus of the famous wilderness trail of the same name that funneled western horses into Kentucky and Tennessee. In 1808 he was about thirty-five and a recent widower. Either legitimately, or perhaps as an explanatory ruse in case Spanish officials captured him, the year before he had inquired about emigrating to New Spain. How much experience he had with horses, Indians, or the West is difficult to determine, but there is little doubt he viewed his 1808–1809 trading expedition as high adventure.

If Glass's experiences were typical, the horse trade of the early West *was* at least as much adventure as entrepreneurial enterprise. Judging from the address he describes making before the assembled peoples of the Wichita villages in August 1808, despite the conflicting territorial claims with Spain over the southern boundary of the Louisiana Purchase, the United States was convinced these western tribes were already *economic* allies of the Americans. Jefferson was their "Great Father," Glass told them, and as for him: "I have come a long Journey to see you & have brought with me some goods to exchange with you and your brothers—the Hietans [Comanches], for Horses if you will trade with us on fair and Equal terms."

Establishing those terms took some effort and caused some arguments, but within a few days Glass was assembling his herd—twenty horses one day, thirteen the next, eleven a few days later, and apparently at that rate for week after week. There were also losses. Osage raiders, whom the Wichitas reported had driven off 500 of their horses shortly before Glass arrived, took 29 of his best horses late that August. A month later, during a second Osage raid on the Wichita horse herds, Glass was chagrined to find that "one of them was riding a remarkable Paint Horse that used to be my own riding Horse, which was stolen with those on the 22d of August."

After two months of daily trade negotiations with the Wichitas, Glass's party—accompanied by a large Indian contingent—headed deeper into the plains in search of Comanche bands to trade with. While horses were his main goal, Glass clearly had another objective, too. The Wichitas had told him about a remarkable object far out on the plains, a large metallic mass they and the Comanches regarded as a powerful mystery, and after much verbal persuasion Glass had prevailed on them to take him to it. As he describes the scene, "Our whole party now became very numerous containing of men women and children near one thousand souls and three times that number of Horses & Mules," so many of the latter it became impossible to remain in a camp because the herds so quickly ate down the grass. Diverted from horses for the moment, Glass cajoled the Indians to lead him on, and "observing considerable ceremony" they finally took the Americans to the place where the metal was. Glass was as mystified as anyone else, but what he was seeing in fact was a 1,600-pound iron-nickel meteorite, a major healing shrine for Southern Plains Indians. Fancying it a giant nugget of platinum, some of the members of Glass's party would return two years later and contrive to haul and float it back to civilization.

Discontented with their inability to trade for horses from the Comanche bands they were encountering, in mid-October Glass's party divided their goods, several of the experienced horse traders among them heading off in search of particular Comanche trading partners from previous trips. Glass continued on southward, camping with increasingly larger numbers of Comanche bands from the north and west, although he reported with disappointment, "trade dull[,] the Indians are unwilling to part with their best Horses." They were, however, willing to part him from his, stealing twenty-three one night in late December, and smaller numbers later on, although the chiefs did manage to return some to Glass's possession.

During the dead of winter, 1809, with snow six inches deep on the plains, Glass finally attempted the mustanger's ultimate art—catching wild horses himself. Wild ones by this point "were seen by the thousands," and Glass, two remaining companions, and the Indians traveling with them built a strong pen and spent many days attempting to corral the wild herds around them. But "the Buffalo were so plenty and so in the way we succeeded badly in several attempts."

Unfortunately—one suspects quite by design—Glass remained vague on the number of horses he ultimately drove back from the plains in May 1809, but the sense is of a herd of many hundreds of animals, including several of those best-quality $100–$150 ones. It is difficult to say just how typical his horse-trade experience was. But in an economy for which so few other day-by-day accounts exist, Anthony Glass's journal provides a quite remarkable look at an early nineteenth-century western experience. He allows us to imagine a history where one had barely been imaginable before.

It would be a full decade later, when Spain and the United States finally agreed on the Red and Arkansas rivers as the official boundary between them (in the Adams-Onís Treaty of 1819), before another American horse trader would leave us an account rivaling Glass's. In the interim, scores—very likely hundreds—of unknown and undocumented American mustangers traversed the plains, running wild horses, trading for horses from the Indians, and encouraging such a general theft of horses across the West that one source estimates 10,000 were stolen from Spanish ranches in a single year. Murky references exist for a few of these traders. Ezra McCall and George Schamp (who had been with Glass) were back on the plains in 1810. The Osages plundered Alexander MacFarland and John Lemons's mustanging party in 1812. Auguste Pierre Chouteau, Jules DeMun, and Joseph Filibert opened up a significant horse trade with the Comanches and Arapahos between 1815 and 1817. Caiaphas Ham and David Burnet became modestly famous horse traders in the same years, and so did Jacob Fowler (who left us a journal written in phonics) and Hugh Glenn. When Mexico finally achieved its independence from Spain and moved to open up its markets to the United States, the man who opened the Santa Fe Trail— William Becknell— could do so because he, too, was an old plains horse trader.

What made these Southern Plains horse trade expeditions shadowy and Northern Plains fur trade activities well known was actually a simple difference. Since the horse trade featured live, not dead, animals, horses became their own transportation to markets. There was no need, as in the fur trade, for corporate investment in freight wagons, steamboats, or shipping. That difference not only created a documentary disparity for later historical writers, it affected the comparative fiduciary risk involved at the time.

Consider, for instance, one more example from the early western horse trade, that of Thomas James of St. Louis, who gives us another fine-grained look at the mustanger's Great Plains before Mexico's revolution changed the ground. James, intriguingly, was both a mountain man and a mustanger. He'd first gone west by ascending the Missouri to the Three-Forks in 1809–1810, and didn't make his first trip onto the Southern Plains until 1821, riding out from Fort Smith to the Salt Plains of present Oklahoma before he was confronted by Comanches under Spanish orders not to allow Americans to approach Santa Fe. Eyeing those splendid Comanche horse herds appreciatively, Thomas James got a sense of the possibilities.

Invited to return the next summer to trade for horses, James did, and the result was a three-year expedition (1822–1824) financed with $5,500 in goods. Ascending the various forks of the Canadian River, James's party of twenty-three finally met the Wichitas under their headman, Alsarea, and the trading commenced. Four yards of British strouding and two yards of calico, along with a knife, a mirror, flint, and tobacco, was the going rate for a well-broken horse, and James quickly bought seventeen that he knew would fetch $100 apiece back in the settlements. Eventually the Wichitas introduced James to the Comanches, a Yamparika band under Big Star, and James got his first taste of a little twist the Comanches put on horse trading: they were perfectly willing to trade their best horses since they had every intention of stealing them back! At one point he watched the Comanches drive 100 wild mustangs into a ravine corral, at the end of the day riding them about the prairie. According to James, despite the frustrations, the life of a nineteenth-century horse trader on the Southern Plains held a real allure. He was smitten: "I began to be reconciled to a savage life and enamored with the simplicity of nature. Here were no debts, no Sheriffs, no Marshals; no hypocrisy or false friendships."

Once he had assembled a drove of 323 high-quality animals, James departed for the settlements, but not before Alsarea made a present of his own fine war horse, "Checoba," and urged James to return the next year to the headwaters of the Red, where the Wichitas grazed 16,000 fine ponies. That would have been the horse trader's Promise of the Golden Fleece. But James never returned. Pushing his herd eastward he lost all but seventy-one to stampedes and what must have been a Biblical attack of horseflies. More attrition followed as he penetrated the woodlands. If James can be believed, when he finally reached St. Louis, for his troubles he had just five horses left. That happened to be precisely the number he'd started with.

James's account, published under the title *Three Years among the Indians and Mexicans*, may explain the lack of corporate interest in the horse trade. At least until the Mexican Revolution ended Spain's hold on the plains in 1821, the volume trading of horses on the Spanish border was probably too risky a business to attract corporate interest. Although Philip Nolan and his backers possibly made as much as $40,000 to $60,000 (figuring 1,000 horses at a minimal $40 each) from a $7,000 trade goods investment in 1797–1798, the cost-effectiveness figures for other early traders look a lot less impressive. And Nolan's speculated profits do not take into account the work, fatigue, and personal risk factors in a dangerous wildlands vocation like the wild horse trade.

The reason literary men like Catlin and Audubon had missed the full dimensions of the early horse trade of the Great Plains was that it was an example of what we might call a "concealed economy," in this case one that emerged where different empires—a fading Spanish one and a vibrant, emerging American one—overlapped. In this kind of situation, shadowy freelances, Indian traders, and even American presidents all ended up dealing with one another, at least indirectly. But there is a coda to this story. The wild horse trade on the Great Plains and in the West did not evaporate after 1821. If anything, as wild horses spread farther north and west, the horse trade expanded geographically and even in volume. The markets evolved, too, as overland emigrants plying the trails across the plains needed a constant supply of fresh horses, and the US Army of the West searched for remounts for its cavalry during the Mexican War.

So from 1822 to 1850 the plains horse trade began to shift to the Arkansas

River and northward. The trading firm of Bent, St. Vrain & Co. got its license in 1834, the same year that the Trade and Intercourse Act for the Indian Country made horses a legal trade item. They built Bent's Fort on the north side of the Arkansas River in 1835 and especially after the Cheyenne peace with the Comanches and Kiowas in 1840 facilitated Indian trade at the fort, the horse and mule trade became key to their success.

The Central Plains traders benefitted from wild-caught and Indian horses from off the surrounding prairies, but they also reaped profits from the large numbers of horses that adventuring mustangers were rounding up and driving eastward from California. The mountain man Old Bill Williams told artist Richard Kern years later that his "greatest coup" was stealing 4,000 horses from California ranches and driving them to Bent's Fort. Eventually both Bent's Fort and the town of Pueblo became horse trading destinations for army quartermasters. The adopted Crow, Jim Beckwourth, arrived at Pueblo in May 1846, with 1,000 horses from California, and traded almost all of them to Colonel Steven Kearny's Army of the West. So did mountain men Solomon Sublette and Joseph Walker, who arrived at Central Plains trading locations with ten drovers and 400–500 California horses about the same time. Meanwhile, local horse traders like William Tharp worked the Cheyenne villages at the Big Timber on the Arkansas for horses and mules to trade to the army at Bent's.

Over time the Great Plains horse trade shifted even farther northward. In the mid-1830s the artist Alfred Jacob Miller, accompanying British adventurer William Drummond Stewart to the Green River rendezvous, found wild horses numerous among the bison and pronghorns of the Wyoming plains, marveled at "the beauty and symmetry of their forms," and rendered several lovely, ghostly paintings of them. By the early 1850s the epicenter of the trade was in Wyoming, as far north as Fort Laramie, where the former Southern Plains traders and Arkansas River drovers began journeying to trade animals to the emigrants on the overland trails. By then, and in the decades after the Civil War, wild horses were undergoing the same kind of population explosion on the Northern Plains they had a century earlier farther south, and the Red Desert of Wyoming and the badlands of Montana and the Dakotas filled with wild stallion bands.

Like the other charismatic megafauna of the nineteenth-century Great Plains, the mustang herds did not survive very long into the twentieth century. In the 1880s, in the Southern Plains country where Nolan, Glass, and others had founded the horse trade economy, there were still an estimated 50,000 wild horses running free in the breaks along the Llano Estacado escarpment in West Texas. But wild horses had gone from being a resource to being pests, and what happened to those 50,000 horses is a predictable finale: ranchers paid their cowboys to shoot them on sight and to bait the carcasses with poison to kill wolves and coyotes. It was cold-eyed murder, pure and simple, but it was doubly efficient if you dreamed of a world without wild horses or wolves in it.

In some parts of the Great Plains the wild horse herds—and an economy of capturing them—lasted longer. During World War I, Miles City, Montana, on the edge of the Northern Plains badlands, furnished Allied buyers some 32,000 wild horses that sold, green broke, at between $145 and $185. American horses helped the British and the French hold the Germans off till the Yanks arrived. After the Ken-L-Ration company began to build pet food plants in the Midwest in the 1920s, most of the remaining wild horse capture and trade in the West fell to mustangers who at first seemed unaware of the fate of their captured stock. (That led to the sad, bizarre story of Montana/Wyoming mustanger Frank Litts, who—on realizing the wild horses he was bringing to Miles City were ending up slaughtered for pet food—actually caught a train to Illinois with 150 sticks of dynamite to blow up a dog food plant there.) Pet food was a billion-dollar-a-year industry in the 1930s, and since any horse at all brought $50–$60, mustangs once again became the target of an economy, only this time the mesteñeros herded them to capture with pickups and planes, with slaughterhouses and tin cans as their final destinations.

Thanks to a Californian named Velma Johnston ("Wild Horse Annie"), and an expose in the form of the Marilyn Monroe/Clark Gable movie The Misfits, the Wild Horse and Burro Conservation Act of 1959 finally brought an end to the practice of airplane mustanging. Richard Nixon took the next step, signing the Wild Free-Roaming Horse and Burro Protection Act of 1971, which recognized wild horses as "living symbols of the historical and pioneer spirit of the West [and] . . . as an integral part of the natural system of the public lands."

Wild horses now had a tenuous place in the West based on their history, along with a series of new federal wild horse refuges, including the Pryor Mountains Wild Horse Range, with its herd of zebra-striped dun mustangs from the earliest days of wild horses in the West, at the edge of the Northern Plains. But as has repeatedly been the case with the Great Plains, the scarcity of public lands on the grasslands east of the Rockies has relegated wild horses largely to other places than the setting where most of their history actually played out. Too, many biologists and land managers still ignore the horse's evolutionary history. Neither paleontology nor molecular genetics lends any support whatsoever to the idea that horses evolved into their modern form anywhere but in North America. Nonetheless, most state and federal land agencies continue to insist that horses, with 50 million years of evolutionary history here, are still "non-native." That's a shortsighted view, not a Big History one, but so far it still prevails.

The National Park Service, committed to the idea of preserving American nature in the presumably magical form in which Europeans first saw it, for decades religiously removed "feral" horses from every national park where they were found, including Theodore Roosevelt National Park in North Dakota, a plains badlands where Roosevelt himself had watched horses "as wild as pronghorns" in the 1880s. But since this particular park is a historic park, beginning in 1970 its managers recognized wild horses as part of the historical setting its namesake had witnessed in the area. Since then a mustang population that park management keeps between 70 and 110 animals preserves the ancient/historic relationship between wild equines and bison on at least this piece of the plains. A Great Plains national park with wild horses is a grand thing, but without their predators, park managers have had to control both horse and bison populations at the park artificially. Not so grand a thing.

And the Southern Plains, where so much wild horse history played out? The Wichita Mountains National Wildlife Refuge there, a 59,000-acre paradise of rolling plains and granite mountains in southwestern Oklahoma— exactly the country where George Catlin found himself so bedazzled by wild horses in the 1830s—is one of the oldest federal wildlife refuges in the country. In 2001, on a tour of the Special Use Area in its backcountry, I got to see many of this famous refuge's 500-plus bison, descendants of the very animals that preserved bison from extinction in America a century ago. We saw a beautiful royal bull elk herding his band of cows across a high, grassy ridge, animals reintroduced here from the Rockies and a stunning and historic sight on the Great Plains once again. And of all things, we even had longhorn cattle amble sullenly away from the trails we were hiking on in the backcountry, the refuge's nod to ranchers and cowboys and the role longhorns and nineteenth-century cattle drives played here.

But wild horses? Here in the precise Great Plains country where Catlin had exulted over wild horses and painted them with their manes in wild confusion over their faces and their tails sweeping the ground? Where Philip Nolan and Anthony Glass had traded for mustangs to drive all the way to Kentucky, and pursued them through clouds of dust into mustang corrals that had dotted this very landscape by the score? The very place where Thomas James heard tales of a wild horse Elysian Fields, and about which Thomas Jefferson had marveled, on top of his Virginia mountain, over this rare "moment in the age of the world" when the horse could "be studied in its wild state"?

Evidently not. Why, after all, would anyone expect wild horses roaming across a country like the Southern Plains?

THE MOST DANGEROUS BEAST

THE GRIZZLY, THE GREAT PLAINS, AND THE WEST

5

Wednesday 11 Sept. 1805. a beautiful pleasant morning. . . . passed a tree on which was a nomber of Shapes drawn on it with paint by the natives. a white bear Skin hung on the Same tree. we Supose this to be a place of worship among them.

—Joseph Whitehouse

In 1874, on a steamer heading up the Missouri River in Montana Territory, a western artist and illustrator named William de la Montagne Cary witnessed a scene one bright morning that he never forgot. From the boat deck, through good, sharp field glasses, Cary and his companions for several minutes watched a drama unfold that transfixed them with a chill Cary could not shake off: "about a mile off an immense grizzly bear [was] making for a cotton wood miles away and behind the bear came two men superbly mounted, armed to the teeth. . . . We could see distinctly the horses straining every muscle to overtake the bear who was equally anxious and making every effort to escape his pursuers."

On the American Serengeti of the last century, this was a sight of sights, and as an artist of the West, Cary well knew it. What he was seeing ranked with western spectacles like buffalo stampedes, prairie wildfires, or cavalry or Indian charges, and for the same reason: all implied furious activity with mortal outcomes at stake. But what required buffalo in mass numbers to effect, a grizzly bear—even one running for its very life— could evoke solitaire, and that was what transfixed Cary and his companions. The grizzly was then—and still is—the historic Great Plains counterpart to the lion or leopard of the Masai Mara or the striped tiger of the steamy jungles of the Bengal: the largest and most powerful creature of the landmass, fully capable of killing humans, fully capable under certain unusual conditions of consuming humans, too. In Cary's time on the plains most Americans were still hunters—George Armstrong Custer took time off from chasing Indians to shoot a grizzly in South Dakota that same summer— but in the nineteenth century we still understood that we had been prey almost as much as we'd been predators. Naturally we look especially closely and with a certain primal dread at any animal that might configure us as a meal. And especially so at an animal like a bear that is so much more human-like in its attack than big cats or sharks.

Even at a distance, William de la Montagne Cary felt the adrenaline of that kind of genetic memory, but he clearly also felt a sympathy for the bear as it crashed across the prairie fleeing its pursuers. The artist was one of a legion of nineteenth-century disciples of James Fenimore Cooper, and with two friends had first made a trip up the Missouri River in 1861. Returning home with sketches and some paintings, he'd gone on to become a magazine and newspaper illustrator in New York, working for publications like *Scribner's* and *Harper's Weekly*. These assignments had sent him into the Northern Plains again in 1874, this time to Fort Benton. The grizzly encounter was one of the high points of his trip, and—imagining the end result of the chase—he ended up executing a beautiful oil painting of what he believed the outcome might have been. Variously titled *Cattle Men Tracing Grizzly to Den* or *Mother Bear Guarding Cubs*, it became the prize piece of the artist's exhibit at the American Museum of Natural History in New York in 1917. No less than the famous writer/ conservationist George Bird Grinnell wrote the accompanying text for the exhibit. By 1917, Grinnell wrote, far from being the aggressive giant carnivores of the early wilderness West, grizzlies "have become the shyest of game and are well-nigh extinct." Somehow, in barely more than a century, the West's most imposing creature stood at the very brink of disappearing. On the Great Plains by 1917, the setting where the reading world had first imagined *Ursus arctos horribilis*, the giant bears were entirely extirpated.

How we react to animals is in part primate hard-wiring. The thump in the dark, the start to full waking, the pounding heart can transport us back to our African origins in a fraction of a second. But mostly what we think when "bear" comes to mind emerges from the tangled mess of software programs that is culture. What we've heard, what we've read, what we've inferred, what

The grizzly inherited the mantle of most fearsome animal of the American Serengeti from the short-faced bear, which became extinct during the late Pleistocene. Dan Flores photo.

others have implied, for some of us what we've experienced—all these and other ways of absorbing information—go into creating a construction in our minds like "bear." When an Idaho governor publicly opposed recovering grizzly bears in the Bitterroot Mountains at the turn of the twenty-first century because he said he didn't want "massive, flesh-eating carnivores" in Idaho, the bear he imagined was a very specific kind of historical memory. But many other kinds of bears look back at us, a maddening but fascinating aspect of the world.

Fascinating is the right word. It's hard to characterize the history of the grizzly bear in America in any other way, really. There is the grizzly bear out there in nature, the king of beasts in North America (at least once the truly fearsome short-faced bears and steppe lions went extinct), but a bear existing in a bear's world. And then there is the bear in the mirror, the bear that humans see when we look at grizzlies through the lenses of our minds and cultures.

The future predicts a vanishing act for the grizzly, now confined in the contiguous United States to just two small pockets in dense mountains near Glacier and Yellowstone parks in the Northern Rocky Mountains. A few years ago a friend and I crossed the Flathead River as early in the summer as it was possible to wade across it with backpacks (which was August) and then spent a week traversing Glacier Park from its western to its eastern boundary. We hiked up a stream called Nyack Creek to the Continental Divide, through country with one of the densest grizzly populations in America, the whole way ruminating about how much edginess, how much sheer adrenaline, this Glacier landscape would lose without big bears in it. That scenario is not difficult to imagine, because out east of Glacier, the Great Plains from Alberta to West Texas was once the domain of America's kingly bears and today harbors not a single grizzly. I have backpacked many times in the Great Plains. Those experiences weren't remotely like pushing through neck-high thimbleberry bushes up Nyack Creek, with piles of fresh grizzly scat still steaming in the trail.

How was it that the grizzly once thrived and was widespread across the Great Plains when in our own time only a few hundred bears exist only in national parks deep in the mountains? The answer is a variation on a too-common story here, with one very big difference. Pronghorns and coyotes are plains survivors in our time, and re-wilding the future Great Plains may be possible to some extent even with gray wolves and bison. But judging by the difficulty we've had getting new populations of grizzlies going even in other Rocky Mountain locations, restoring grizzlies to the Great Plains appears to be the longest of long shots. Almost all we can do in this instance is recall the bear's past, one not very distant in time but now growing ever fainter in the imagination, and reflect on how it all happened. At least we can do that much with grizzly bears, whereas with steppe lions, mammoths, camels, long-legged hunting hyenas, gazing across a rolling Great Plains landscape and trying to re-create in mind's eye what it must have been like, even dreams fail.

There must have been a powerful cultural psychology at work in nineteenth-century America, a Freudian feedback loop with respect to the continent. North America's wildness produced enough unease about the thinness of civilization's veneer that we reacted with a numb, almost instinctive orgy of destruction aimed at the animals that embodied the wild continent. "Nonhuman nature," writer D. H. Lawrence once wrote, "is the outward and visible expression of the mystery that confronts us when we look into the depths of our own being." For much of American history that exercise, when we've indulged it, has not pleased us, producing a self-hatred that we've deflected outward. As another writer who sought to understand our relationship with nature, Paul Shepard, put it in one of his last books, "By disdaining the beast in us, we grow away from the world instead of into it." That line stands as an evocative summary of much of the history of the American Great Plains.

A few representative human/grizzly stories from Great Plains history may help to reconstruct the way Americans reacted to the West's king of beasts. The bears of our evolving historical imagination have arguably been more important to what has happened to the grizzly—and what might happen to the grizzly in the future—than the flesh-and-blood bears in the real West. History doesn't allow for re-dos, but if it's true that the great bear was in some significant part a creation of our cultural imaginations, was there perhaps a way out, a path not taken? Perhaps a path we might still consider so that humans and the most formidable and awe-inspiring big animal on the continent can co-exist, even if uneasily, and even if elsewhere than on the plains?

Maybe. Grizzlies are obviously a special case. But fear, respect, even morbid fascination ought not be allowed to stand as reasons for outright eradication of an animal that defined a whole ecoregion. Perhaps we should start with American stories about grizzly bears, stories that explain why, from an estimated continental population of 100,000 grizzly bears five centuries ago, from Alaska southward into Mexico and across the entire Great Plains as far east as Kansas, today fewer than 1,000 grizzlies are left in the Lower Forty-Eight, none of them on the plains. In laying out these stories I have no intention of ignoring other ways, Indian ways, for example, of "seeing" bears. But I'd like to consider those other, older ways of understanding bears not so much as a starting point from which we've traveled, but instead as a potential destination.

Despite a scattering of encounters with grizzly bears as early as the seventeenth century, for two centuries after Europeans settled the continent, grizzly bears were little known to folk knowledge and only existed as rumors in the scientific grasp of North America. The first known description of grizzlies we have by a European was left by Spanish explorer Sebastian Viscaino in the year 1602. Sailing along California's Central Coast, in the bay where Monterrey and Carmel (and Pebble Beach) would one day stand, two centuries before the Lewis and Clark expedition would bring "white bears" to the attention of Enlightenment science, Viscaino watched grizzlies clamoring with astonishing nimbleness over the carcass of a whale washed up on a Monterrey Bay beach. Almost a century later, in 1690 and far, far inland, a Hudson's Bay Indian trader named Henry Kelsey was traveling overland on the grassy yellow plains of Saskatchewan when his party encountered a grizzly. This was not a view from the safety of a sailing vessel, but face-to-face on the ground, and Kelsey's first reaction was to shoot. He thus became the first European of record to kill a grizzly bear, an event pregnant with portents for the future of bears and of the Great Plains. Kelsey's act greatly alarmed his Indian companions, who warned him that he had struck down "a god."

Other unknown Russian, English, and American traders along the Pacific Coast no doubt encountered grizzlies by 1800, and the Spaniards in California and New Mexico and French traders penetrating the plains certainly had experiences with grizzlies by then. But at the beginning of the nineteenth century, journal-keeping Anglo-Americans began to push by boat and on foot into grizzly country. Archaeology and paleontology since have established firmly that the entire western half of North America, including the river corridors spilling from the Rockies out across the Great Plains, and even the island stepping-stone mountain ranges of the Southwest, was all grizzly country then. Except for Santa Fe and Taos and the Spanish missions along the Pacific Coast, no European settlements lay within this immense sweep of country. In 1800 it was inhabited by perhaps 2 million Indians, 25–30 million buffalo in times of good weather, and perhaps 50,000–60,000 grizzlies. So many grizzlies, indeed, that Ernest Thompson Seton says Spanish travelers along the rivers of Northern California could easily see 30–40 grizzlies in a single day.

Biologists believe grizzlies were far out on the Great Plains because there were bison to scavenge there, so as soon as Americans reached the buffalo country, they were in grizzly country, too. Although not the first Americans to encounter grizzly bears, Lewis and Clark occupy a prominent place in this story, in good part because they stand as such an obvious cultural template for this country's reaction to an animal so formidable.

American attitudes toward wildlife like bears by the Jeffersonian Age were complex and deeply internalized across thousands of years of human history. Genetic programming from as far back as the Paleolithic obviously preserves a human memory of giant bears. Mammals of the Northern Hemisphere, they would have been a new thing for modern humans migrating out of Africa and into Europe and Asia 45,000 years ago. Our Neanderthal ancestors would have long since been familiar with bears, but our own species likely first confronted them in southern Europe. Among the oldest painted art lo-

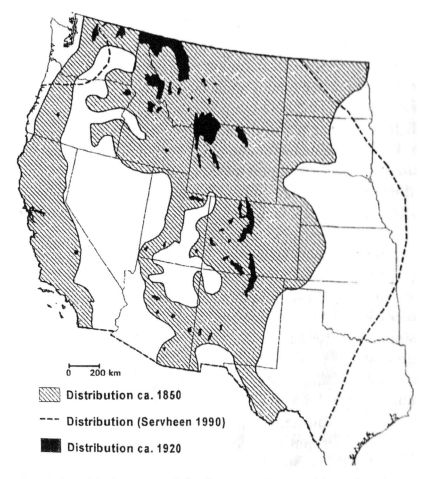

The grizzly's original range extended as far out onto the Great Plains as the Dakotas, Kansas, and Texas, where they scavenged bison carcasses up and down the American Serengeti. From *Conservation Biology*, August 2002.

cales anywhere in the world, the walls of Chauvet Cave in the Ardeche Valley of southern France preserve images that may be 37,000 years old. The large paintings here breathtakingly represent cave bears along with bison, horses, rhinos, lions, mammoths, and ibex. Indeed, Chauvet Cave was a cave bear den. When spelunkers discovered the site in 1994, the Chauvet floor preserved bear skeletons, bear footprints that looked days old, and a cave bear skull the ancient artists had placed atop a boulder as a kind of shrine. Cave bears were formidable beasts as large or larger than grizzlies.

As for North America's own Pleistocene bear, the gracile and active short-faced bear, the Canadian biologist Valerius Geist believes that until it went extinct 14,000 years ago, this super-aggressive bear may have single-handedly kept humans from migrating across the Bering land bridge in America.

Atop such a long-standing animus, whose outlines are sketchy but in pagan Europe indicate that bears once served as both totems and gods, later traditions like Judaism and Christianity, and eventually the scientific way of understanding the world, layered on a very complex cultural matrix about bears for Europeans. Almost all these strands are evident in the Lewis and Clark encounters, which were so widely read in early America that they became a kind of nineteenth-century guidebook to how to think about the West, its Indians, and its wildlife.

Jefferson's explorers had heard before they ever left the East Coast about the possible presence of a bear in the West that was different from the well-known black bear. Wintering at the Mandan villages in 1804–1805 they got exposed to more direct evidence by the Indians. Indeed, they had already seen the tracks of a "white bear" in eastern South Dakota, where some of the hunters claimed to have wounded one. But Lewis and Clark's firsthand experiences with grizzlies actually began in April 1805, in present Mountrail County, North Dakota, about halfway between Minot and Williston.

According to the University of Nebraska's new edition of the *Journals of the Lewis and Clark Expedition*, edited by Gary Moulton, this is how Americans and grizzly bears interacted for the first time on the Great Plains:

April 13, 1805: [Lewis]. *we found a number of carcases of the Buffaloe lying along shore, which had been drowned by falling through the ice in winter an lodged on shore by the high water. . . . we saw also many tracks of the white bear of enormous size, along the river shore and about the carcases of the Buffaloe, on which I presume they feed. we have not as yet seen one of these anamals, tho' their tracks are so abundant and recent. the men as well as ourselves are anxious to meet with some of these bear. the Indians give a very formidable account of the strength and ferocity of this anamal, which they never dare to attack but in parties of six eight or ten persons; and are even then frequently defeated with the loss of one or more of their party. the savages attack this anamal with their bows and arrows and the indifferent guns with which the traders furnish them, with these they shoot with such uncertainty and at so short a distance, unless shot thro' head or heart wound not mortal that they frequently mis their aim & fall sacrefice to the bear. two*

Minetaries were killed during the last winter in an attack on a white bear. this anamal is said more frequently to attack a man on meeting with him, than to flee from him. When the Indians are about to go in quest of the white bear, previous to their departure, they paint themselves and perform all those supersticious rights commonly observed when they are about to make war uppon a neighboring nation.

Over the next few days, as the party traced the Missouri across North Dakota towards the present Montana border, grizzlies continued to tease their imaginations. On April 14, Clark wrote in his journal that they had at last seen "two white bear running from the report of Capt. Lewis Shot, those animals assended those Steep hills with Supprising ease & verlocity." On the 17th Lewis was moved to write that although they "continue to see many tracks of the bear we have seen but very few of them, and those are at a great distance generally runing from us . . . the Indian account of them dose not corrispond with our experience so far."

The party's first real encounter came on the morning of April 29, 1805, in what is now either Roosevelt or Richland County, near the far eastern Montana town of Wolf Point. Lewis describes their mounting adventures this way:

I walked on shore with one man. about 8 A.M. we fell in with two brown or (yellow) bear; both of which we wounded; one of them made his escape, the other after my firing on him pursued me seventy or eight yards, but fortunately had been so badly wounded that he was unable to pursue so closely as to prevent my charging my gun; we again repeated our fir and killed him. it was a male not fully grown, we estimated his weight at 300 lbs. . . . The legs of this bear are somewhat longer than those of the black, as are it's tallons and tusks incomparably larger and longer. . . . it's colour is yellowish brown, the eyes small, black, and piercing . . . the fur is finer thicker and deeper than that of the black bear. these are all the particulars in which this anamal appeared to me to differ from the black bear; it is a much more furious and formidable anamal, and will frequently pursue the hunter when wounded. it is asstonishing to see the wounds they will bear before they can be put to death. the Indians may well fear this anamal equiped as they generally are with their bows and arrows or indifferent fuzees, but in the hands of skilled riflemen they are by no means as formidable or dangerous as they have been represented.

That optimistic arrogance, so classically American, coupled with a typical national faith in scientific technology's ability to prevail where the tools of lesser cultures left them vulnerable, weren't destined to last. On May 5, 1805, in present McCone County, Montana, the American explorers were given considerable pause when they had their first encounter with a full-grown grizzly bear. Again, let Meriwether Lewis tell the story:

Capt. Clark and Drewyer killed the largest brown bear this evening which we have yet seen. it was a most tremendious looking anamal, and extremely hard to kill notwith-standing he had five balls through his lungs and five others in various parts he swam more than half the distance acoss the river to a sandbar & it was at least twenty minutes before he died; he did not attempt to attact, but fled and made the most tremendous roar-ing from the moment he was shot. We had no means of weighing this monster; Capt. Clark thought he would weigh 500 lbs. . . . this bear differs from the common black bear in several respects . . . the heart particularly was as large as that of a large Ox. his maw was also ten times the size of the black bear, and was filled with flesh and fish.

In his own journal, Clark called this bear "a Brown or Grisley beare" and "the largest of the Carnivorous kind I ever Saw." Lewis noted that after campfire discus-sion that night:

I find that the curiossity of our party is pretty well satisfyed with rispect to this ana-mal, the formidable appearance of the male bear killed on the 5th added to the difficulty with which they die when even shot through the vital parts, has staggered the resolution several of them, others however seem keen for action with the bear; I expect these gentlemen will give us some amusement shortly as they soon begin now to coppolate.

Six days later, on May 11, having passed the mouth of the Milk River—which some biologists of pre-Columbian America believe was a kind of epi-center of grizzly bear range and numbers on the Great Plains, perhaps because it had long been in a buffer zone between warring groups like the Blackfeet, Shoshones, and Mandans where Indian hunting parties seldom ranged—the party had an experience that cemented the evolution in attitudes that was tak-ing place. Once again, let's let Lewis describe it:

About 5 P.M. my attention was struck by one of the Party runing at a distance to-wards us and making signs and hollowing as if in distress . . . he arrived so much out of breath that it was several minutes before he could tell what had happened; at length he informed me that in the woody bottom on the Lard side about 1 1/2 [miles] below us he had shot a brown bear which immediately turned on him and pursued him a considerable distance but he had wounded it so badly that it could not overtake him; I immediately turned out with seven of the party in quest of this monster, we at length found his trale and persued him about a mile by the blood through very thick brush of rosebushes and the large leafed willow; we finally found him concealed in some very thick brush and shot him through the skull with two balls . . . it was a monstrous beast . . . we now found that Bratton had shot him through the center of the lungs, notwithstanding which he had pursued him near half a mile and had returned more than double that distance and with his tallons had prepared himself a bed in the earth . . . and was perfectly alive when we found him which could not have been less than 2 hours after he received the wound; these *bear being so hard to die reather intimedates us all; I must confess that I do not like the gentlemen and had reather fight two Indians than one bear; there is no other chance to conquer them by a single shot but by shooting them through the brains.*

This initial American confrontation with the largest predator on the continent continued to worsen, primarily because the members of the party seem not to have learned the rather obvious lesson, and kept on shooting grizzlies. On the 14th six hunters spotted a grizzly on open ground and went after him, approaching to within forty yards. According to Lewis:

two of them reserved their fires as had been previously conscerted, the four others fired nearly at the same time and put each his bullet through him, two of the balls passed through the bulk of both lobes of his lungs, in an instant this monster ran at them with open mouth . . . the men unable to reload their guns took flight, the bear pursued and had very nearly overtaken them before they reached the river . . . [they] concealed themselves among the willows, reloaded their pieces, each discharged his piece at him as they had an opportunity they struck him several times again but the guns served only to direct the bear to them, in this manner he pursued two of them seperately so close that they were obliged to throw aside their guns and pouches and throw themselves into the rivr altho' the bank was nearly twenty feet perpendicular; so enraged was this anamal that he plunged into the river only a few feet behind the second man . . . when one of those who still remained on shore shot him through the head and finally killed him . . . they found eight balls had passed through him in different directions.

Absorbing the mounting tension of these journal entries almost two centuries later, a modern reader almost has to be restrained to keep from shouting aloud at Meriwether Lewis, "For God's sake, order them to stop shooting up grizzly bears going about their own goddamned business!"

Of course no one except the Indians thought to stop shooting up grizzlies for a very long time to come. A twenty-first century American has to pose the question—why, once they'd collected specimens for science, did Lewis and Clark and other nineteenth-century Americans feel such a compulsion to react to animals in the West by *shooting* them? What had history lodged in the American psyche that made the left-and-right, wholesale slaughter of animals—more than 500 million of them is Barry Lopez's estimate, although no one can ever know—such a part of the history of the West, and especially of the grand grasslands of the Great Plains? Why, for example, would the US Army officer and popular writer Colonel Richard Dodge, along with his four companions, feel it a worthy expenditure of their time to slaughter, in three weeks of lounging about on New Mexico's Cimarron River, 127 buffalos, 13 deer and pronghorns,

154 turkeys, 420 waterfowl, 187 quail, 129 plovers and snipe, assorted herons, cranes, hawks, owls, badgers, raccoons, and even 143 *songbirds?* According to Dodge's obsessively kept scorecard, that was a total of 1,262 animals, many of which had functioned only as convenient live targets for bloodlust.

It's a hard thing to know the history of the Great Plains and *not* pose that question. The Lewis and Clark response seemed ubiquitous everywhere one looks. Once I hiked to an Indian rock art panel on the Texas plains where Comanches or Kiowas had portrayed a wagon train with virtually every stick figure traveler brandishing a gun, the sandstone wall carved with jagged, lightning-like lines going in every direction and in such profusion it was clear the artist was attempting to convey a party firing in every direction as the wagons rolled along. Accidental wounds from gunfire, along with drownings during stream crossings, in fact were the principal causes of mortality on the western emigrant trails. But the bigger question: why did we so consistently look at the West through the sights of a rifle?

These initial Lewis and Clark encounters with Great Plains grizzly bears may give us some clues as to why that was. Some of the reasons seem so deeply internalized that virtually the only way we are able to recognize that they aren't universal is to contrast American attitudes towards animals with those of other cultures. At least since the time of the Greeks, and the notion was broadly disseminated through all classes of Western culture by Judeo-Christian traditions, Western Europeans had absorbed the idea that humans were the true measure of the divine on earth, the only one of God's creations made in His image, the only ones possessing that abstract, immortal animation known as a *soul.* According to Genesis 1:28, God had created animals solely for the benefit of humans, for humans to do with as they would. Over that basic idea, the Scientific Revolution of the Age of Reason had layered Descartes's assumptions that, lacking souls or sentience, animals were little more than automatons, living machines with no capacity for self-awareness, not even the capacity to experience injury.

These were fictions that anyone who shot a grizzly and heard it roar its rage and pain—think of the Montana grizzly the Lewis and Clark party shot on May 5 that made no attempt to attack its persecutors but swam to a sandbar "and made the most tremendous roaring from the moment he was shot"— ought to have questioned. But few did. By the Jeffersonian Age, for many Americans individual animals were less teachers of universal truths about being human than they were target practice. Or specimens collected for dispassionate scientific study. Or fiends that represented a danger to civilization and its apparently shaky veneer. Or, worthy opponents against which to pit one's woodcraft, daring, and skills in contests of status.

And as tests of one's technology. Lewis and Clark are exemplars of yet another Western notion that is evident from reading their journals about grizzly encounters, and that is a faith in technology, and the peculiar temptation to test technology's outer limits on what they regarded as challenging and dangerous phenomena. Their grizzly accounts feature a repeated disbelief that the continent held an animal so powerful and tenacious of the will to live that a mere animal could come close to overwhelming American scientific technology. It's the theme Herman Melville explored in *Moby Dick*, wherein nature in the form of a great and dangerous beast drives an American puritan to madness when he can't subdue it.

Lewis and Clark's accounts were not the only ones that filtered in from the West about the grizzly bear, of course. One of the ones that the compilations of bear stories routinely miss was one from the Southern High Plains, a story that passed by word-of-mouth back to places like my home state of Louisiana, perhaps even inculcating the legendary bear killer Ben Lilly with the idea that grizzly bears were the very minions of the devil, and that all of them deserved speedy death at his hands. I am talking now about the story of the first recorded death at a grizzly's hands on the Southern Great Plains.

It was 1821 when this encounter with a grizzly took place on what was christened "White Bear Crick," now known as the Purgatory River out on the plains southeast of Pike's Peak, Colorado. A group of Missouri and Louisiana traders had worked their way up the Arkansas River to trade with the Comanches, and when the cold snaps of November hit they moved towards the mountains to seek winter quarters. For many of the semi-illiterate Southern traders involved, this was their first inkling that the West held anything like a grizzly bear. I still find this account, flavorfully preserved and creatively spelled in the journal of a trader named Jacob Fowler, one of the most chilling grizzly encounters I've ever read, in part because of the bear's single-minded pursuit, which no amount of distraction seemed able to deter.

Somehow it is made even more immediate and easily imagined by the frontier vernacular in which it is told. This is how Jacob Fowler related this remarkable story in the daily journal he kept.

13th novr 1821 tusday: Went to the Highest of the mounds near our Camp and took the bareing of the Soposed mountain Which Stud at north 80 West all So of the River

Which is West We then proceded on 2 1/2 miles to a Small Crick Crosed it and ascended a gradual Rise for about three miles to the Highest ground in the nibourhood—Wheare We Head a full vew of the mountains this must be the place Whare Pike first discovered the mountains Heare I took the bareing of two that Ware the highest. . . . Crossed [Purgatory Creek] and Camped in a grove of Bushes and timber about two miles up it from the River We maid Eleven miles West this day—We Stoped Hare about one oclock and Sent back for one Hors that Was not able to keep up—We Heare found some grapes among the brush—While Some Ware Hunting and others Cooking Some Picking grapes a gun Was fyered off and the Cry of a White Bare Was Raised We Ware all armed in an Instent and Each man Run his own Cors to look for the desperet anemel—the Brush in Which we Camped Contained from 10 to 20 acors Into Which the Bare Head Run for Shelter find[ing] Him Self Surrounded on all Sides—threw this Conl glann [Colonel Glenn] With four others atemted to Run But the Bare being In their Way and lay Close in the brush undiscovered till the[y] Ware With in a few feet of it—When it Sprung up and Caught Lewis doson [Dawson] and Pulled Him down In an Instent Conl glanns gun mised fyer or He Wold Have Releved the man But a large Slut [dog] Which belongs to the Party atacted the Bare With such fury that it left the man and persued Her a few steps in Which time the man got up and Run a few steps but Was overtaken by the bare When the Conl maid a second atempt to shoot but His [gun] mised fyer again and the Slut as before Releved the man Who Run as before—but Was Son again in the grasp of the Bare Who Semed Intent on His distruction . . . the Conl now be Came alarmed lest the Bare Wold pusue Him and Run up [a] Stooping tree—and after Him the Wounded man and [he] Was followed by the Bare and thus the[y] Ware all three up one tree . . . [but] the Bare Caught [Dawson] by one leg and drew Him back wards down the tree . . . I Was my Self down the Crick below the brush and Heard the dredfull Screems of [the] man in the Clutches of the Bare—the yelping of the Slut and the Hollowing of the men to Run in Run in the man Will be killed . . . but before I got to the place of action the Bare Was killed and [I] met the Wounded man with Robert Fowler and one or two more asisting Him to Camp Where His Wounds Ware Examined—it appeers His Head was In the Bares mouth at least twice—and that When the monster give the Crush that Was to mash the mans Head it being two large for the Span of His mouth the Head Sliped out only the teeth Cutting the Skin to the bone Where Ever the[y] tuched it—so that the Skin of the Head Was Cut from about the Ears to the top in Several derections—all of Which Wounds Ware Sewed up as Well as Cold be don by men In our Situation Haveing no Surgen nor Surgical Instruments—the man Still Retained His under Standing but Said I am killed that I Heard my Skull Brake—but We Ware Willing to beleve He Was mistaken—as He Spoke Chearfully on the Subgect till In the after noon of the second day When He began to be Restless and Some What delereous—and on examening a Hole in the upper part of His Wright temple Which We beleved only Skin deep We found the Brains Workeing out—We then Soposed that He did Hear His Scull Brake He lived till a little before day on the third day after being Wounded—all Which time We lay at Camp and Buried Him as Well as our meens Wold admit Emedetely after the fattal axcident and Haveing done all We Cold for the Wounded man We turned our atention [to] the Bare and found Him a large fatt anemel We Skined Him but found the Smell of a polcat so Strong that We Cold not Eat the meat—on examening His mouth We found that three of His teeth Ware broken off near the guns [gums] Which We Sopose Was the Caus of His not killing the man at the first Bite—and the one [tooth] not Broke to be the Caus of the Hole in the Right [temple] Which killed the man at last—

Stories such as this one, circulating through the frontier towns and among the ranks of traders and trappers that became the foundation of many of the West's later settlers, were instrumental in casting all grizzlies as fearsome brutes to be hunted down and shot to death at every opportunity. Building on Meriwether Lewis's term, the grizzly was a "wrathful monster," as the writer Frances Fuller Victor wrote of a Yellowstone grizzly in her 1870 book, *The River of the West.*

In 1991 the writers Tim Clark and Denise Casey compiled a volume they titled *Tales of the Grizzly: Thirty-Nine Stories of Grizzly Bear Encounters in the Wilderness,* which chronicle grizzly/human encounters in the Northern Rocky Mountains from 1804 through 1929. Their collection allowed them to chart what they decided were five distinct periods in the evolution of the American relationship with grizzly bears: (1) A Native American period, when bears were mythic figures, teachers of medicines, helpers, a species whose physiological similarity to humans offered the possibility for transmigration in both directions—a relationship with nature, Clark and Casey assert, that would have been "almost incomprehensible to most modern Americans." (2) An Exploration/Fur Trade period, exemplified by the grizzly encounters of Lewis and Clark and Jacob Fowler, which exposed the fallacy of assumptions about human dominance and faith in technology, and created the initial impressions of grizzlies as the horrible bear, the wilderness fiend that offered Americans a reminder of the dangers of uncontrolled, chaotic nature.

Periods (3) and (4) in this chronology are the periods of conquest and settlement, when homesteaders resolved that it was a Christian duty to eradicate grizzlies and other formidable wildlife in order to liberate the wilderness for God and the Grand Old Party. During this phase, tens of thousands of grizzly bears were shot on sight, and not just to wipe them off the plains for the arrival of the livestock industry. Settlers killed 423 grizzlies in the North Cascade Mountains alone just between 1846 and 1851. In the early twentieth century the Great American War on grizzly bears featured an alliance between livestock interests and the US Biological Survey, whose hunters made official the war on wolves, coyotes, lions, and bears, in the process creating an early federal subsidy for the ranching industry in the West.

That same Progressive era witnessed the fifth period, the official rise of sport hunting and its replacement of market hunting, which now had a black eye. For the animals in the sights, of course, it wasn't so easy to tell the difference. But many sport hunters took to heart President Theodore Roosevelt's advice that "The most thrilling moments of an American's hunter's life are those in which, with every sense on the alert and with nerves strung to the highest point, he is following alone . . . the fresh and bloody footprints of an angered grisly." For hunters, eliminating "bad animals" like predators made sense not just in terms of growing the numbers of huntable elk and deer; going after grizzlies also had become the ultimate nostalgic capture of the vanishing frontier, the hunter's version of a Frederic Remington or Charlie Russell painting. As Roosevelt put it, tellingly, "no other triumph of American hunting can compare with the victory to be thus gained."

Historian Matt Cantwell, in his intellectual history of hunting titled *A View to Death in the Morning*, unearthed an unusual Henry David Thoreau quote that speaks to a point I made earlier in this chapter: "He is blessed who is assured that the animal is dying out in him day by day." America must have been feeling very blessed indeed by the early twentieth century as the rapturous pursuit of bears dwindled their numbers and presumably banished any subconscious fears about human nature.

I find merit in the straightforward chronology of collections like *Tales of the Grizzly*. But my own instinct is to extend the interpretation in at least two ways that seem important, by pursuing the evolution of ideas about bears in both directions from the early twentieth century.

First, as grizzly numbers dropped drastically in the late nineteenth and early twentieth centuries, an interesting phenomenon emerged in the way Americans began to perceive grizzlies, wolves, and occasionally even coyotes. More and more, as their numbers dwindled or as the persecution amplified, ranchers, sportsmen, and Bureau of Biological Survey hunters began to individualize particular animals of all these species and give them their own

By the 1890s hunters, ranchers, and the collapse of the bison herds combined to drive grizzlies off the plains and into the mountains, where they have survived only in the Northern Rockies. Dan Flores photo.

personalities and even names. Once so numerous out on the plains, grizzlies, elk, and other classic Great Plains species had now fled to the mountains. So these last bears are always secreted away up in the peaks. Among grizzlies there was the Wyoming bear known as Big Foot Wallace. There was a notorious California grizzly of the Sierra Nevada called Club-Foot, a Colorado grizzly named Old Mose, a grizzly in Idaho known as Old Ephraim, and a Greybull River bear Wyoming ranchers named Wab, whose life story, in much fictionalized form, the nature writer Ernest Thompson Seton told in his 1900 book, *The Biography of a Grizzly.*

This individualization of grizzlies was an interesting development. It rested on a sentiment, clearly widespread in America at the turn of the century, which had its sources in Darwinian thought as popularized by the natural history writers of the day. Writers of the age, like Seton, Jack London, John Burroughs, Enos Mills, and John Muir, were struggling to erase the Tennyson imagery of a Darwinian world as "nature, red in tooth and claw." The literary devices they used—the personification of animals, an emphasis on animal individuality, cooperation, intelligence and reasoning, and the device of telling their stories from the point of view of the animals (as in London's *Call of the Wild* or James Oliver Curwood's *The Grizzly King*) were designed in part to effect a more favorable regard for animals. Humanitarian animal reformers at the turn of the century even discussed the hitherto unimagined possibility that animals had souls; one eccentric East Coast faction went so far as to found a church to save the souls of the beasts around them. As H. W. Boynton, a critic following these trends, summarized, the message for a world distressed by the implications of Darwinism seemed to be: "If we are only a little higher than the dog, we may as well make the dog out to be as fine a fellow as possible."

Despite the sympathetic and somewhat maudlin view of grizzlies presented in Seton's *Biography of a Grizzly* (with the grizzlies of the plains badlands now long gone and his mountains filling with ranchers and tourists, aging bear Metitsi Wahb commits suicide) and in Curwood's *The Grizzly King* (wherein the wounded but peace-loving grizzly lets his hunter/antagonist walk away unharmed in the end), it took the advent of the Age of Ecology seventy-five years later to begin to rescue predators from a general hatred in America. The real Wab, after all, had met a rather different end than Seton gave him. He was shot by a rancher, the fourth grizzly the hunter had killed that day.

In the minds of many scientists and wildlife managers, the individualizing of animals was long tarnished by the "nature-faker" controversies of the Seton period. With grizzlies long since wiped out on the plains, ranchers, sport, and paid federal hunters steadily extirpated grizzlies across the Mountain West—hunters killed the last grizzly in Texas, in the Davis Mountains, in 1890, the last one in California in 1922, Utah's last big bear in 1923, Oregon's and New Mexico's last grizzlies in 1931, and Arizona's last one in 1935. Professional wildlife management moved under the influence of the Murie brothers, Aldo Leopold, and Eugene Odum in the direction of ever more species-focused directions. Following their leads, the individualistic ideas inherent in the Western worldview gave way in biology to more holism, a stance more biocentric and ecosystem-oriented than before. The new biological holism, however, until recently stopped short of recognizing individuality in animals, let alone rights for individual creatures. Its realm has been the health of species as a whole, and more recently the health of ecosystems. The idea of the Greater Yellowstone Ecosystem emerged as a concept first applied by the famous Craighead brothers to manage Yellowstone grizzlies as a species and as components of a larger habitat.

Prior to twenty-first-century studies that have begun to recognize pronounced individuality in animals like wolves, or urban coyotes, the last noted American environmental thinker who was willing to try for a blend that respected both species and individual animals was John Muir. Between Muir and today's biologists like Stanley Gehrt (who has become fascinated with the idea of individuality in coyotes), animal individuality was long a special target of ire by ecologists and biologists. Although individuality is genetically logical, readily observable in animals in virtually any context, and in fact enjoys practical application in the treatment of "problem" bears and wolves, lingering reluctance about embracing the individual rather than the species seems to spring from the unsavory historical association it has with early twentieth-century nature-faking. Second, and if anything even more frightening to some, animal individuality plays into the arguments of the animal rights groups. Contemporary animal advocates assert an apparently radical doctrine: that individual animals have rights, and that the circle of ethical treatment—which in the Western tradition has expanded through history to confer rights to individuals of groups once denied legal standing, such as women, Native Americans, African Americans, now gay and transgender people—must and ought to be extended to animals on an individual basis.

Earlier in this chapter I mentioned a path not taken, and in closing I'd like to return to that theme. If we are serious about preserving not just the 1,000 grizzlies now left to us, but biodiversity of all kinds in future America, there may be some merit in reconsidering the concept of animal individuality and even analyzing how individual animal rights might be conferred. I cannot say that traditional history stands behind this assertion, because the writers of traditional American history have always assumed that wild animals, especially, are little more than "resources" and often simply wildlands obstacles that inevitably had to give way to progress. A history that judges as individuals those "monster bears" that Meriwether Lewis and Jacob Fowler described—bears whose home territories explorers and traders had entered and that certainly deserved better than being shot on sight as a test of technology and manhood—might go farther towards awakening our environmental conscience than thinking of them as species, resources, obstacles, or even components of an ecosystem.

Of course I fully recognize the logical and practical problems involved in going from *writing history* this way to conferring actual legal standing and *managing* this way. But reading about Native American mythologies, imagery, and rituals associated with bears, you have to be struck by the possibilities that such thinking offers. Maybe the reason there were still 100,000 grizzlies even after 15,000 years of the Indian presence of America was because, as Meriwether Lewis asserted, Indian technology was not up to the task of getting rid of them, although you have to note in this regard that Columbian mammoths were pretty formidable, too, yet the Clovis people apparently still managed to push them into extinction.

All the same, without trying to appropriate anyone's culture or romanticize anyone's past, it is difficult not to conclude that a way of thinking that recognized bears as essentially humans in another form, thus conferred individuality to bears, and thus a corpus of rights to bears—among them the simple right to exist—must have played some role in the historical fact that more than 5 million people and 100,000 bears were able to live together in America for so long. I'm intrigued that Indian grizzly stories do not whitewash bears. The bear personalities in stories from the Blackfeet to the Nez Perce to the Kiowas are complex ones. Almost always the bears possess traits valuable to humans; one Indian culture after another thought of grizzlies as teachers of medicines and herb knowledge, as in a Blackfeet story called the "Friendly Medicine Grizzly." At other times, as in a Gros Ventres story of how the Big Dipper appeared in the sky, grizzlies are "monsters" that lay rapacious waste to human communities and literally chase people into the heavens.

Consistently, though, as in the lusty Athabaskan story "The Girl Who Married the Bear," or the male anxiety tale from the Nez Perce called "The Bear Woman with a Snapping Vagina," the bears are individuals. They are both good *and* evil, are valued and respected in either event on an individual basis, and their inherent *right to exist* is never an issue. In the Indian stories about bears, bears and humans mirror one another. Indeed, one of the most constant themes is that humans and bears play interchangeable roles.

The historical arc of the great bear's story over the five centuries since Europeans arrived is far less nuanced and has a crystal clear direction. Something about the way Americans have thought about bears has been catastrophic to the grizzly, which has undergone a hundredfold reduction in numbers and has entirely disappeared from the core of its ancient range on the Great Plains. Yet in truth there is little that is completely inevitable about history. So we ought not be content that a perspective on bears like that of the natives of the continent is either "incomprehensible" or "too alien." A biologist might say that the bears in the Indian stories are anthropomorphs. Modern nature writers like Bill McKibben will no doubt insist that we have so separated ourselves from the natural world and "humanized" the wild that nature itself is dead and there is no longer a path home. Some historians may continue to write about animals without questioning the assumptions of human dominance. And grizzly bears may never rear up out of a willow thicket on the Great Plains again. All that may happen, and perhaps will. But none of it is inevitable.

A few years ago—it was early August of 2009—a group of us spent five days backpacking into the Bob Marshall Wilderness in Montana. The Bob is a place where the blocky limestone ridges of Montana's Rocky Mountain Front drop away to the plains, to yellow grasslands that roll away, as they always have done, nearly 500 miles east. There had been days of rain before we got into the mountains, and within a couple of miles of the trailhead we began to notice not only wolf tracks on the trail but as well the prints of a gigantic grizzly bear, splayed out in the mud like impact craters on a distant planet. What particularly caught our attention as we hiked in was that the bear tracks were headed out, towards the plains, a country that still lures grizzly bears today.

A week after we got out of the mountains, back in Missoula the local paper carried a headline that shocked all of us. Later on the very day we had hiked out to our cars in the morning, a Forest Service ranger had found an immense male grizzly shot dead and left to rot less than a mile out into the plains. And it was not just any bear. Biologists and rangers had known this particular bear for more than a decade. They had named him "Maximus" because of his extraordinary size; he'd stood 7½ feet tall and weighed 800 pounds. Biologists were certain he was the biggest grizzly in Montana. But what most characterized this bear was his admirable behavior. He was "a good bear," a grizzly that had never gotten in any trouble at all, had left stock alone, retreated into the woods when hikers passed, and ignored their camps. All he was doing was going on a walkabout into the prairies, which made him visible. And got him shot.

A respectful wild grizzly who knew how to live among us deserves a better fate than this. And so do we.

6

In the fall of 1886, William T. Hornaday, taxidermist at the National Museum in Washington, stepped off a train in Miles City, Montana, to undertake a poignant and historic task. The American bison, an animal whose charisma and staggering abundance had for three centuries stood as shorthand for North America to the world, somehow was on the brink of extinction. Except in remote parts of Texas, Montana, and Alberta, where rumors held there might be two or three tiny herds of wildly spooky survivors, a creature whose range had once extended from northwestern Canada to Florida, whose herds sometimes took the better part of a week for mounted horsemen to pass, was tottering on the precipice of total disappearance. Plains hunters like the Blackfeet Indians, who had annually taken 20,000–40,000 of them, had returned from their hunts in 1883 with six. That is why Hornaday was in Montana. Bison were about to fade into memory, and the National Museum at least wanted a representative collection that might become a museum exhibit, since that was all future citizens might ever see of ancient America's most iconic creature.

The Hornaday party's goal was to obtain 20–30 specimens, which the scientist understood might represent as many as half of the wild bison left in the United States. He had narrowed his search to west-central Montana, between the Yellowstone and the Missouri, using the LU-Bar Ranch as headquarters, to hunt a rumored herd of thirty-five in the area. The US army provided support, and two soldiers and two cowboys from the ranch accompanied Hornaday and his assistant, Harvey Brown. On Calf

Creek, a southern tributary of the Musselshell, in October this party began to find buffalo. The stories about the survivor animals were true, though; these buffalo were extraordinarily wild and perceiving themselves pursued, fled nearly fifteen miles across the badlands of eastern Montana. Nonetheless, as dusk was falling on October 16, two of Hornaday's hunters managed to down a huge bull. Because of the lateness of the hour, the party left their prize where it fell with a plan to return the following day.

Here is how Harvey Brown described the scene when they arrived the next morning: "Sunday, Oct. 17th. To our great dismay the noble red men had visited the bull which Boyd & McNannin had killed the day before." Brown's astonishment no doubt captured the expedition's general confusion about what had happened. "All that remained [of the bull] was the head painted red on one side yellow on the other with a red & yellow rag tied to one horn, [and] eleven notches cut in the other [horn]. . . . All around were moccisan tracks."

Hornaday's party went on to take twenty-two buffalo out of this last remnant of animals, a tiny puddle that was almost all that was left of a once vast, now evaporated, ocean of animals. As the director of the New York Zoological Park and a founding member of the American Bison Society, Hornaday would spend much of his next four decades trying to save bison from complete extinction, and he believed in the fall of 1886 that not more than thirty animals remained alive in Montana, the American territory where the last great bison hunts had taken place. He would eventually conclude that at the time of his hunt, only 1,073 bison still drew breath in America.

No one ever identified just who those native hunters were who had located Hornaday's downed bull, or exactly what ceremony they had performed around it during the night of October 16–17, 1886. But from the evidence they left, they, too, seemed to have understood that something truly profound was happening. A bison bull whose head was marked and decorated and painted red and yellow in the night signaled the end of a world, a historical change so traumatic that as the Crow leader Plenty Coups would put it, "After that, nothing happened."

Like some tremendous, crashing sound that ended abruptly just at the moment we turned to listen—that is how the buffalo story strikes many of us in the twenty-first century. For the past hundred years, Americans interested in history and the wilderness continent have realized that the collapse of the bison as a species was a signal event, a watershed in Great Plains history and the history of the United States. It seemed a grand finale to three centuries of conquest across North America, like the Pleistocene extinctions an irreversible step in replacing an old world with a wholly new one. Yet from a Big History perspective, it is also an event quite similar to ones described in the stories of traditional Great Plains people, about times when—usually because of human hubris—buffalo went away. In those stories buffalo always returned, although the measures required to effect that result took unusual efforts of will, and usually the genius of a culture hero. This time the Grand Forces of the modern world have kept buffalo at bay for a very long time. But they remain a meaningful animal not only because the future is always uncertain, but because they, like us, are Americans.

Why does the buffalo matter? It strikes some as a slightly comic and ungainly holdover from a faded world, yet the truth is that this single animal's end-game exemplifies the whole declensionist story of the relationship between Americans and nature over the past five centuries. The buffalo was the essence of ecological adaptation to North America, perfectly suited to the grasslands of the interior of the continent from Alberta and Saskatchewan southward to Texas and Mexico. It was the wildebeest-plus of the American Serengeti, since the Pleistocene extinctions had left it with few grazing competitors, allowing it to attain a biomass wildebeests were never able to achieve. It was a survivor of the great extinctions and of more than 100 centuries of dying at human hands, and yet in the space of less than a century we very nearly erased it from existence. No other environmental story in American history, and there is plenty of competition, produced quite so dramatic an ending.

What, exactly, happened to bison so quickly and finally, an animal that weathered drastic climate change and witnessed scores of other species die out around it 8,000 to 14,000 years ago, but somehow couldn't survive us? Even while their populations were crashing, and certainly since then, there have been many interesting and competing theories.

To most Americans, the buffalo story is the shorthand example of American environmental history in general. It is evidence, if nothing else, of inevitability, of what has happened as civilization has marched around the globe. The imagery of it is perfectly captured in John Gast's famous nineteenth-century painting, *The Goddess of Liberty*, wherein a blonde giant in angelic white garb strides across the Great Plains stringing telegraph wires behind her as wolves, buffalo, and Indians slink away to the margins of the canvas. What killed the buffalo, this imagery implies, was progress, technology, the march of civilization that could brook neither traditional people nor the great ani-

For nearly a million years horses and bison were the keystone grazers of the American Serengeti, where their interactions with the grasslands and its predators fashioned an ecology similar in many ways to zebras and wildebeests in East Africa. Dan Flores photo.

mals of the wilderness. The "inevitable" story as history has told it is one most of us can recite. In the twenty years following the Civil War, maybe as many as 100 million buffalo ended up as bones on the plains in a maelstrom involving railroads, chemical tanning processes, steadily more deadly firearms, and a racist social policy—a secret conspiracy involving the federal government, the military, and a few thousand private hide hunters all cooperating to bring the Plains Indians to subservience by "slaughtering their commissary" to make way for the modern world.

Who knows what the Indians who danced around and painted Hornaday's bull thought about why bison had disappeared? When the US Peace Commission had entertained Indian theories about the matter in 1868—when bison were appreciably diminishing but before railroads and the hide hunt had penetrated very far north—the Northern Plains peoples well understood that bison were going away and they offered various explanations, most of which laid the blame on either the whites or the Métis. One Western Lakota told the commissioners that bison were becoming so few because they couldn't abide the smell of white people. Once the great herds were finally gone, Indians like the Kiowas of the Southern Plains believed the bison had returned once again to the earth, their original point of origin. Still later, the Lakota elders whom photographer Edward Curtis interviewed on Pine Ridge in 1905 told him the whole matter was *wakan*: what had happened to bison was a mystery that probably had to do with divine punishment for some unfathomable transgression.

The Indian understanding of the bison issue took place in the context of traditional histories that in fact included past examples when bison had disappeared, at least regionally for some groups. The modern buffalo, as opposed to the Pleistocene forms, had actually co-evolved as a new species in the presence of native people, who in turn had fashioned around the swelling herds the longest-lived, sustained economy in continental history so far. When Euroamericans first saw the Great Plains and wrote their descriptions of it, they saw it as a *pays sauvage*, or *despoblados grandes*, or a grand *wilderness* freshly made by divine hands. In fact what they were seeing was a landscape intensively managed for many thousands of years by dozens of successive cultures. On the Northern Plains, that sequence included peoples known as the Mummy Cave, Oxbow, McKean, Pelican Lake, Besant, Avonlea, and Old Women's cultures, all of which deliberately set fire to the Great Plains to maintain the country as a great bison/pronghorn/elk/wolf savanna. The Great Plains was not wilderness. It was Indian America.

That bison were still here when the Europeans arrived is fairly reliable evidence that the 8,500-year-old ecology that emerged in the West after the Pleistocene extinctions had come to some kind of dynamic equilibrium. Bison populations, grassland carrying capacity, and predation—including Indian populations and level of hunting stress—over more than eighty centuries of time had settled out into a sustainable balance. It was dynamic, with good times and bad. There were periods when intensive droughts pushed bison and Indians both eastward and westward to wetter places. At least once, during the Altithermal 5,000 years ago, warm and dry conditions so decimated the Southern Plains that climate shifted the bison mass, and the people who hunted them, north of present Colorado for many hundreds of years. Judging from comparative archaeology, there were in fact plenty of periods when bison were regionally quite scarce. But the herds' ecological fit to the Great Plains grassland was such that even with the ebb and flow of climate, even given comparatively wasteful methods of Indian harvest like the buffalo jump, the system endlessly rebounded.

That kind of continuum provoked a natural and entirely appropriate awe from the native peoples. At least in the minds of buffalo-hunting Indians interviewed in the early twentieth century, they conceived the bison savannas as operating on a mysterious plane, the workings of which they intuited in part through what we would call native science, but primarily through religious explanation. Most buffalo hunting peoples believed the bison to have been present early in creation. Like the other great forces of the universe—the sun and moon, the sky overhead—in this kind of cosmic explanation, bison could never disappear entirely and en masse. Much as we are all utterly convinced at this moment that there is no force capable of erasing the night sky of its stars, bison were beyond time and history.

In the Plains Indian creation accounts that undergirded this kind of understanding, the most important animals are there at the beginning of time, with the creators, before humans join the world. So it is not just themselves as flesh that animals like bison offer as gifts for humans. Among the Cheyennes, it was Thunder and Buffalo that gave fire to their culture hero, Sweet Medicine. And among the Mandan-Hidatsas a buffalo bull gave their culture hero, Lone Man, tobacco. In Indian Agent James Walker's famous version of Lakota cosmogony, after creating *Maka* (Earth) and *Skan* (Blue Sky), *Wakan Tanka* then fashioned the *Oyate Pte*, the Buffalo People.

Somewhat in the same manner that the Greeks regarded their gods as partly mortal, most plains tribes thought of buffalo in their worldly form in the same terms as humans—they had families and societies, opinions and memories. They were a people. And, like people they possessed *souls* that survived after death. Thus to kill a buffalo did not destroy it. In some traditions, buffalo had the ability to renew themselves after death. The Cree version of the idea was called *akwanaham otoskana,* "animal covers its bones." According to ethnographer James Mooney, Siouan informants told him that if you left the head, tail, and four feet of a buffalo at the place of its death, the animal would regenerate. He faithfully took down the account: "We came to a herd of buffalo. We killed one and took everything except the four feet, head, and tail and when we came a little ways from it there was the buffaloes come to life again and went off."

Although bison regenerated, the hunting tribes understood that animal masters controlled the buffalo, which made access to them tricky and fraught with taboos and sanctions designed to convey proper respect for creatures willing to sacrifice themselves for the human good. Among the Cheyennes, access to buffalo came at the sufferance of legendary figures Coyote Man and his daughter, Yellow-Haired Woman. The principal regulation among the Cheyennes was "Do not express pity for any suffering creature." That was an insult that would cause the animal masters to take their charges away. Like most buffalo hunters the Cheyennes had a story about a time when the buffalo "all disappeared." Erect Horns, the culture hero of the Suhtai division of the Cheyennes, persuaded them to return by engaging in a particular ritual. Later in the beginning time of Cheyenne history, when the people had forsaken another culture hero, Sweet Medicine, "the buffalo and all the animals disappeared" again. But when Sweet Medicine returned he showed the Cheyennes how to do a ceremony that would call on the animals of the plains to reappear once more.

Like the Cheyennes, the Blackfeet and the Gros Ventres have legendary stories about what happened when the buffalo disappeared, a calamity finally righted by their culture heroes—Napi among the Blackfeet and Nee Aut (Nix'a nt) in the case of the Gros Ventres—who turned themselves into dogs, found the cave where the gods were holding the animals, and drove them out. The Blackfeet called the entity that kept buffalo away "Buffalo-Stealer." When he was unhappy he kept buffalo secreted away in a cave up Cut-Bank Canyon. The Mandans, too, had a traditional story about a time when all the buffalo disappeared. In this case it was because Hoita, the Speckled Eagle, had quarreled with Lone Man (the first Mandan) and as punishment decided to withhold all the animals inside Dog Den Butte. After involved negotiations Lone Man finally convinced Hoita—who was the Mandan master of the animals—to release them to the people.

How did the culture heroes perform these miracles? They did so primarily through reestablishing the kinship between human beings and the animals, and often they created ceremonies to recharge those kinship ties through marriage and symbolic erotic encounters between people and animals. Thousands of years and hundreds of generations living alongside plains animals had fashioned among Indian people a fascinating body of cultural stories that credited the buffalo's willingness to surrender itself to hunters to the mythic kinship ties (inter-marriage, adoptions, and sexual relationships) between the two species. Among the Arikaras, for example, after their cultural hero, Man-Who-Kills-Game-Easily, awoke from a vision, he had sex with a buffalo cow and then taught the people a stick-and-hoop game that symbolized power over the animals through sex. The Arikara Buffalo-Calling Society used this symbolism to call buffalo by invoking the erotic tie between human and animal.

Through yearly rituals and ceremonies designed to call buffalo or replenish plains animals generally, stories such as these lived on through the nineteenth century as explanations of how plains ecology worked. Thanks to the 1830s Missouri River artists George Catlin and Karl Bodmer, we are at least nominally conversant with the outer skin of these ceremonies. The artists portrayed animal-costumed dancers re-creating the ancient stories, along with special lodges and altars that represented the mountains or caves where the gods hid buffalo and other animals when they were displeased. Parts of the ceremonies featured ritualized, symbolic sexuality designed to stimulate bison fertility. But those acts also served as community reminders of the ancient ties.

Among the Cheyennes, two of the arrows in Sweet Medicine's Sacred Arrow Bundle gave Cheyennes the power to kill as many buffalo as they wanted. They associated the opening of the Sacred Arrow Bundle with the Massaum ceremony, a great animal dance at Bear Butte that re-created Coyote Man's and Yellow-Haired Woman's release of the animals in mythic time. Cheyennes performed the Massaum well past 1850. Other of their bands set up a Lone Tipi at their summer Sun Dances, representing the mountain from which Erect Horns had released the buffalo and reanimated the earth and vegetation and the animal life of the plains.

In part because of Catlin and Bodmer, but also because of American fascination with the sexual and fertility aspects of these ceremonies, the most famous of all the animal-calling rituals on the plains were the Snow Owl and Okipa ceremonies of the Mandans and the related Red Stick ceremony of the Hidatsas. Both Snow Owl and Red Stick featured experienced buffalo hunters costumed as buffalo bulls. In Snow Owl, young men beseeched the "bulls" to have sex with their wives so they could acquire the sort of mastery over the animals possessed by the older men. The Hidatsa Red Stick was similar but began with a dance by young women who performed symbolic sex with twelve buffalo bulls represented by a line of twelve red sticks planted in the ground. In the nineteenth century, descriptions of these ceremonies are the

Latin passages that appear in published accounts by witnesses like the Lewis and Clark party.

The elaborate Mandan Okipa ceremony, whose poorly grasped presentation in George Catlin's *Letters and Notes on the North American Indians* made it famous, in part was a reenactment of the mythic story of the release of the animals from Dog Den Butte by Speckled Eagle. In the Okipa this symbol of renewal occurred on the third day of the ceremony. The Okipa represented virtually the entirety of Northern Plains ecology replenished and renewed through symbolic sex between Mandan women, who figuratively became "Buffalo Cows," and Mandan men transmogrified into "Buffalo Bulls." While the Ghost Dance of the 1890s never symbolized these kinship and sexual ties to the animals of the plains, it was in fact another effort at ecological renewal that called on the buffalo, particularly, to reemerge from the earth and overspread the world again. Buffalo-Coming-Out, a Southern Cheyenne priest in western Oklahoma, repeatedly performed ceremonies entreating the bison to reemerge from "Hiding Mountain" (Mount Scott) in the Wichita Mountains, which both Kiowas and Cheyennes believed held the herds. But eventually even Buffalo-Coming-Out gave up the attempt.

It was against this ancient and poetic world, informed by kinship and reciprocity, that Europeans introduced their own views of animals to the continent. Instructed by Christianity and Western science, both of which regarded animals as soulless creatures existing for service to humanity, Europeans who became Americans were most influenced towards animals, frankly, by capitalism. The emerging global market was an economic system resting on genius, for it released the selfish gene in human nature to act on the world in self-interest, pronouncing the result "economic freedom," good for the individual and hence the society and state. But it was a system that could and did convert the living, nonhuman world into a congress of resources, inert matter waiting to be organized into wealth. And because of the intoxicating range of goods it marshalled, even among native people with a different way of seeing the world (but of course with their own human nature intact), it proved an irresistible force.

American military men, journalists, and historians did not print or seriously endorse the Indian explanations for what had happened to the buffalo or how they might return. Across much of the twentieth century the history of what happened to the bison settled into a kind of set piece whose simplistic but still shocking story almost everyone came to accept. Much as the "Lost Cause" explanation for the US Civil War over time came to eclipse slavery as the central cause for that conflagration, probably for the same historical reasons the emerging twentieth-century story about the bison's demise redirected blame in a way more pleasing to those down the timeline. That is to say, the US federal government increasingly emerged as the culprit behind it all. To be sure, by the second half of the twentieth century most historians—with the exception of the Canadian historian Frank Gilbert Roe—had abandoned the bison story to popular writers, who were not inclined to be critical users of their sources. So by the time writers such as Mari Sandoz, Wayne Gard, Tom McHugh, and Dee Brown were publishing in the 1950s, 1960s, and 1970s, their consensus interpretation was that a well-planned and secretive US government policy had marked the buffalo for extinction.

As these writers told the story, it was not that Washington had anything personal against buffalo, but that 1870s administrations had developed a policy to force Plains Indians to accept reservation life by robbing them of their food source. That meant a planned war on the animal. Just as the monumental loss of life in the Civil War seemed more palatable to subsequent generations if the South had fought to preserve states' rights rather than the ownership of slaves, twentieth-century Americans seemed to prefer a bison story that placed the blame for the disaster not on individual self-interest, or capitalism, but on "the inevitable march of civilization" and increasingly on "a federal conspiracy" involving Washington and the US Western Army. After all, hadn't some of the hide hunters themselves left memoirs claiming the government had regarded them as heroes? Apparently none of these very readable popular writers, or their legions of readers, thought to question whether those who pulled the triggers might have been motivated to whitewash their roles in the slaughter.

The truth is, the story of the demise of the bison had not begun with this sort of explanation at all. In 1889, William T. Hornaday himself got into print the first book in the post-bison era to grapple with what had befallen the great herds. His *Extermination of the American Bison: With a Sketch of Its Discovery and Life History*, published by the US Government Printing Office, offered up a cause-effect relationship that, uncomfortably enough for American economic policies almost entirely wedded to a model of unregulated capitalism, placed the blame for the bison's collapse squarely on the market. To Hornaday's thinking, an unregulated market hunt, pursued not only by white hide hunters but by many other diverse groups—with the slaughter pressed on not by governments but by market forces, especially the great fur companies—had been entirely sufficient across a century's time to destroy the bison. In his version of what had happened, greedy, decidedly unsavory hide hunters had delivered the coup de grace to a bison population collapse that had shocked the world. But according to Hornaday, the horse-riding, bison robe–trading native peoples of the plains had also been participants in the project of killing bison for profit. Regardless of who was doing the killing, it was the profit motive, for wealth and status, that had wiped the animals out.

The role of an unrestrained market in decimating bison was Hornaday's great insight about wildlife generally. Indeed, in 1913 he would go on to argue it as a fundamental principle in American wildlife decline in his book *Our Vanishing Wild Life: Its Extermination and Preservation*. Until the US Congress passed the Lacey Act in 1900 regulating the interstate shipment of market-killed wildlife (it came three decades too late for the bison), the US federal government had never imposed restrictions of any kind on capitalism's insatiable appetites for killing wild animals on the western frontier. Left to the natural forces of supply and demand, the result was that the international market had systematically pushed beavers, Pacific fur seals, various species of whales and salmon, and eventually bison and pronghorns and other large Great Plains fauna to the point of their eradication. But in the first decades of the twentieth century, when Hornaday's newly formed American Bison Society began its three-decade private effort at what we should now recognize as an act of endangered species recovery, it was his book's indictment of the *perpetrators* of the market hunt that struck a nerve. Particularly hide hunters and their descendants, and ultimately even some historians, would resent and deny that white frontiersmen, let alone Indians, had been seduced into killing bison purely out of market-driven self-interest.

The first to respond to Hornaday's charge were the surviving hide hunters who had pulled the triggers from the 1860s through the 1880s. As early twentieth-century nature writers and the Progressive conservationists who established the beginnings of basic wildlife protection mourned in public about the near extinction of the bison, former hide hunters reacted. Some, like Charles Buffalo Jones of Kansas, expressed sorrow at what they had done and sought atonement by rescuing the last animals. According to historian Merrill Burlingame, by the 1920s general disapproval of the bison slaughter moved the descendants of many of the hide hunters to destroy all records of their ancestors' complicity in the great bison hunt.

Others, though, were more combative. Texans John Cook and J. Wright Mooar publicly and angrily defended their roles in the buffalo slaughter. According to famous Texas hide hunter Mooar, who frequently led parades in his home state celebrating the passing of the frontier and scoffed at conservationists who mourned the loss of the bison, "any one of the many families killed and homes destroyed by the Indians would have been worth more to Texas and civilization than all of the millions of buffalo that ever roamed from the Pecos River . . . to the Platte."

Mooar's pride in the role he had played for civilization captured a sentiment already becoming widespread at the time. Indians and bison, many Americans decided, were victims of the march of civilization, and civilization was "inevitable." Even so committed a preservationist as Sierra Club founder John Muir seemed to share Mooar's essential ideas about the predestination of it all: "I suppose we need not go mourning the buffaloes," Muir wrote. "In the nature of things they had to give place to better cattle."

It was former hide hunter John Cook's 1907 memoir, *The Border and the Buffalo*, however, that introduced a striking new explanation for what had happened to the buffalo. Far from being villains in a wildlife morality tale, hide hunters like himself had been national heroes—not petty frontier capitalists out for profit but, indeed, men deserving of national thanks and medals of honor. In fact, in Cook's telling the hide hunters had been the executioners on the ground of an actual US government policy to eradicate the bison in order to clear the Great Plains of the Indians. Cook asserted that US military posts on the plains not only encouraged hide hunters to kill as many bison as possible but actually handed out free ammunition to the hunters. Then he went on with what became the "smoking gun" for this argument, what has become the most widely quoted single "speech" in the entire history of the bison story, appearing again and again in books on the plains wars and on bison, and today on scores of websites ranging from that of the Bison Field Campaign to websites for t-shirt sellers. Most Americans probably encountered it via the 1970s international bestseller by Dee Brown, *Bury My Heart at Wounded Knee*. It has appeared in books as recent as a 2012 biography of William T. Hornaday himself.

The problem with this most famous quote in the entire history of the American bison is simple: almost all its details are fabrications.

To convey the hint of invention that was there all along in Cook's hide hunter memoir, the unrepentant killer of thousands of buffalo introduced his smoking gun with the telling misdirect, "So the story goes." Scoundrels uncounted have gotten off scot-free via literary devices like this, and so, too, does the perpetrator of this "story," as Cook never identifies the actual source of the dubious tale he was about to make famous.

What Cook told his twentieth-century readers was that in 1875, with the Texas legislature considering a bill to outlaw the buffalo hide hunt in the Texas Panhandle, General Philip Sheridan himself had hastily journeyed to Austin to bring Texas in line with the official policy and keep it from making "a sentimental mistake by legislating in the interest of the buffalo." Even with the initial hint that what he was relating was hearsay, Cook was not squeamish about putting words in Sheridan's mouth. Here is the speech ("so the story goes") Cook attributed to him:

> These [hide hunters] have done in the last two years and will do more in the next year to settle the vexed Indian question, than the entire regular army has done in the last thirty years. They are destroying the Indian's commissary, and it is a well-known fact that an army losing its base of supplies is placed at a great disadvantage. Send them powder and lead, if you will; but for the sake of a lasting peace, let them kill, skin, and sell until the buffaloes are exterminated. Then your prairies can be covered with speckled cattle, and the festive cowboy, who follows the hunter as a second forerunner of an advanced civilization.

Instead of censuring buffalo hunters, Cook has Sheridan say, America "ought to give them a hearty, unanimous vote of thanks" and ceremoniously present each of them a medal "with a dead buffalo on one side and a discouraged Indian on the other."

It is a great speech, almost a rival to George C. Scott's memorable delivery in front of the American flag in the opening scene of the movie *Patton*, and it appears as key evidence in every twentieth-century book crediting "a government/military conspiracy" for destroying bison in the nineteenth century. Unfortunately, there is every reason to believe it was pure fabrication. No corroborating account in any form exists that Philip Sheridan ever so testified before the Texas legislature. In fact, there is no evidence that the nineteenth-century Texas legislature ever considered a bill to outlaw or regulate the hide hunt (the *Texas* legislature in the forefront of an unprecedented environmental law?); at the national level Texas politicians were sarcastically dismissive of federal bison bills. But it was such a good story that after getting endlessly repeated by writers who failed to think critically about the source or to pursue corroborating evidence, Cook's version—that he and other hide hunters had patriotically slaughtered bison on behalf of the military, federal government, and civilization—in the popular historical memory entirely eclipsed Hornaday's condemnation of the unregulated market. In the era of the Cold War and Vietnam, New York presses published several popular books on bison; everyone seemed to prefer an explanation like this to one that questioned the excesses of capitalism.

So if we pose the question: why did the buffalo, a genus that had survived the arrival of humans, the Pleistocene extinctions, and 100 centuries of contraction and expansion, come within the barest whisper of disappearing a century ago, a different and more complex answer, one based on multiple causes, now seems to hold sway. Of the array of causes, it is fairly evident from the sources that Hornaday was right all along. The market was the undermining force that almost had bison joining the passenger pigeon. But in the past quarter-century we've come to understand that there were other causes of varying intensity, and we now know roughly how and when several of these causes converged to create a perfect storm that broke apart an ecology that had functioned on the Great Plains since the end of the Pleistocene.

Among the things we have recognized now that we hadn't in the 1970s was the influence of climate on bison. In the mid-1970s archaeologist Tom Dillehay began to investigate the presence and absence of bison bones in plains archaeology sites preserving long-term deposits. His conclusion was that the relative abundance and scarcity of bone deposits over time indicated highly variable populations of bison, and that variability was keyed to a fluctuating Great Plains climate. The Altithermal, or Great Drought, an extremely warm/dry time dating from 8,500 years ago down to 4,730 years ago, produced drought conditions so severe on the Great Plains that both bison and people all but abandoned the Southern Plains. Yet another dry episode, the six-century-long Scandic Drought, shrank plains bison herds between about AD 300 and 900, and another—the Pacific Drought, which lasted almost 300 years, from 1250 to 1525—not only impacted bison and other animals but brought down major American civilizations, particularly the Chacoan Empire in the Southwest.

But the work of Dillehay and others also pointed to times of wet, cool weather that grew bumper crops of grasses and swelled the bison herds so that they sometimes spilled out of the Great Plains both eastward and westward. In the few hundred years before the time of Christ the Great Plains was wet and lush. Grasslands, bison, and bison hunters spread southward, as evidenced by the most southerly bison jump ever discovered, the Bonfire Shelter jump site on the Mexican border, where hunters drove so many bison off a cliff of the Pecos River about 500 BC that the animals' rotting remains spontaneously combusted (the "bonfire"), blackening the cliff face. More than a thousand years later, a wet cycle called the Neo-Atlantic Episode (850 to 1250) again grew huge bison herds as well as allowing corn growers on the plains to push agricultural villages far up the grassland rivers well beyond the 100th meridian.

Dry conditions had prevailed on the Great Plains over the three centuries immediately prior to the time Europeans were first becoming a presence in the Americas. But at the very moment when Coronado's party was pushing out onto disconcertingly vast prairies in search of Quivira in the 1530s, another major climatic change set in across the entire Northern Hemisphere. We call this one the Little Ice Age. For plains buffalo, and for buffalo hunters, the Little Ice Age turned out to be a tremendous catalyst for herd expansion and for a revolutionary new hunting culture based around the acquisition of horses. Like previous wet/cool climate regimes, the Little Ice Age climate favored what botanists call C4 grasses—the buffalograss and grama grasses that buffalo particularly favored—as opposed to spring season bunchgrasses (fescues and needle-and-thread) and woody vegetation. The result was a bison efflorescence.

Because Europeans were on hand to document the effects, we know more about how the Little Ice Age influenced bison than we do about the previous climate fluctuations. It clearly created such a biomass of buffalo on the plains that at the time Europeans were establishing their colonies the herds were spilling out of the Great Plains both eastward across the Mississippi and westward down the Columbia and Snake river systems. There was such an overflow of animals, evidently, that when virgin-soil epidemics of Old World diseases decimated populations of Indian hunters in the South and East, the buffalo mass squeezed like toothpaste into every nook-and-cranny prairie from Pennsylvania to Georgia, and across Oregon, Idaho, and northern Utah.

Between 1500 and 1700 the much cooler, moister weather of the Little Ice Age was devastating agriculture in Europe and advancing glaciers in the Alps and the Rockies. For buffalo hunters on the Great Plains of America, though, the Elysian Fields were at hand. Absent as a component of Great Plains ecology for some 8,000 years, horses set free by the 1680 Pueblo Revolt in New Mexico and the abandonment of Spanish missions in Texas exploded across the plains and the West. Within fifty years both horses and the culture of riding and caring for horses had reached the northern extent of horse possibilities among the Crees, Assiniboines, and Blackfoot in Alberta and Saskatchewan. Former hunter-gatherers, like the Comanches of the western deserts and the Siouan speakers of the Great Lakes woodlands, moved east and west to horses and bison. On the eastern border of the prairies, the corn-growing villages launched some of their divisions onto the plains to become full-time bison hunters with names like Cheyennes and Crows. Good weather, horses, and enormous herds of bison all converged, for perhaps ten human generations, to produce a suite of cultures now famous all over the world.

The moment was grand, but it was brief. It did produce mind-bending numbers of bison for a time, although no modern method we can devise for determining their carrying capacity on the Great Plains indicates there ever could have been 60 or 100 million of them. Under optimum conditions somewhere in the range of 25 million seems the best estimate. But the Little Ice Age's optimum, grass-happy conditions began to dissipate during the first half of the 1800s. Western tree-ring studies show wet conditions continuing from 1800 to about 1821. After that nineteenth-century plains weather gradually began to cycle towards dryer, warmer conditions that were increasingly less favorable for grass and hence for buffalo. By 1840 spotty droughts had begun to crop up all over the plains, settling finally into a major dry period from 1858 to 1866 that climate historians consider the end of the Little Ice Age. That end came in a form that made it much worse on grazing animals than any regional drought, for it seems to have occurred simultaneously across almost all of the Great Plains. Two Texas scholars, in an exhaustive study of drought on the Southern Plains, have concluded that between 1698 and 1980, the absolute driest decade on record was not the 1930s Dust Bowl, or "The Time It Never Rained" in the 1950s, but the years from 1856 to 1864.

Climate change, then, we are now certain, was one of the causes of bison collapse in the nineteenth century. The practical effect of the end of the Little Ice Age on buffalo was even more profound than it would seem. By 1850 the bison's former drought refuges east and west of the Great Plains had now filled in with people. Now a part of the United States, New Mexico had a population of 50,000 and Mormon Utah was rapidly climbing towards that figure. American settlers were already in western Oregon, and mining strikes were about to draw large human populations to Colorado and Montana. German and Czech emigrants had settled on the edge of the Southern Plains in Texas, and America's Indian Removal policies had filled Oklahoma and Kansas with more than 87,000 eastern and midwestern Indians, many of whom hoped to hunt bison themselves. There was no direction for bison to flee the growing dry and overcropped plains grasses. As a result, anthropologist Reid Bryson believes the end of the Little Ice Age reduced the Great Plains' carrying capacity for buffalo by as much as 40–60 percent. At the war's conclusion in 1865 there almost certainly weren't 40 or 50 million bison, but more likely 10 or 12 million, which helps put the comparatively slight figures we have from the subsequent hide hunt into a semblance of reality.

The larger point here is that the backdrop of drought enabled a perfect storm of causation to form around bison in the middle of the nineteenth century, well before the hide hunt ever began. The 1840s and 1850s was the heyday of white homesteader caravans along the Overland Trails to Oregon and California, manned by travelers armed to the teeth who shot at everything that moved on their way west. Too, in historian Elliott West's words, the caravans with their oxen, mules, horses, and cattle were nothing short of "great grass-gobbling machines" in a landscape where grass was becoming critical. In fact, another clear causation in the decline of the bison herds was the growing population of horses in the West, not only sometimes very large Indian pony herds, but especially the rapidly proliferating wild horse bands. Unlike pronghorns, horses have a significant dietary overlap with bison, and they competed for water sources, as well. In the eighteenth and nineteenth centuries, for the first time since the late Pleistocene, horses were once again grazing competition for bison on the wild plains, drawing down the carrying capacity for bison every year that the horse herds grew.

The overland caravans, with their oxen and cattle—along with wild cattle ranging across much of Texas—were very likely also the sources for another effect, with consequences whose extent are so far unanswerable but may have been quite significant. Old World livestock introduced exotic new animal diseases, like the rinderpest that decimated wild herds during droughts in Africa in the nineteenth century. The exotic diseases anthrax and bovine tuberculosis were both present in the remnant bison that survived into the 1880s. Texas Ranger Charles Goodnight's 1867 account of a twenty-five-mile-long stretch of the Concho River Valley in Texas filled with buffalo dead from some unknown cause is a tantalizing hint of disease.

In addition to a backdrop of climate change, disruption from overland travelers, new competition from expanding horse populations, and likely even the effects of exotic diseases, first and last as a cause in the collapse of a bison phenomenon 100 centuries old, there was the market. And the market was not just an influence on the 5,000 or so hide hunters who rode onto the plains to shoot down bison to sell their tongues and hides in the 1860s, 1870s, and 1880s. Responding to the trade the Spaniards, Americans, and British offered—firearms and other metal goods, eventually even luxury items that functioned in Indian societies the same way they do in ours, to enhance status and set some people apart from others—nineteenth-century Indian peoples all over North America became ensnared by the global economy. Who can't relate?

Getting captured by the lure of "things" became a phenomenon across the entire globe, one of the most visible effects of market globalization across the past five centuries. On the Great Plains, one of the prize items the market sought were buffalo robes that Indian women painstakingly processed, often over a week's labor. The robe trade in exchange for industrial goods became a major hunting motive for the horse-mounted buffalo people at least as early as the 1820s. In that decade the fur companies, America's first great corporations, traded for and shipped to New Orleans nearly 100,000 Indian-processed buffalo robes annually. As a result of steamboat success in transporting bulky products, by the late 1830s the American Fur Company alone was sending 70,000 robes a year down the Missouri. By the 1840s the yearly figures for the wharves in St. Louis were in the range of 85,000–100,000 robes. And the Hudson's Bay trade eventually nearly rivaled the trade farther south, reaching a zenith of 73,278 robes in the early 1840s.

And yes, there were always Indian leaders who saw the danger in this kind of incorporation into the market. A Hunkpapa headman named Little Bear preached the virtues of ending trade with the whites as early as the 1830s; he was still doing so in the 1850s and his warnings were still falling on deaf ears, since he seems to have been the only Teton leader who felt so. Up and down the Great Plains the result of the market and the robe trade were the same, a literal re-creation of Plains Indian identity around the market, with mounting inter-tribal competition for every remaining pocket of buffalo preserved in war zones between tribes—pockets that got gobbled up, one by one, as expansionist groups like the Lakotas and the Comanches and their allies displaced tribes with prime remaining buffalo pastures. "We stole the hunting grounds of the Crows," one Cheyenne later boasted, "because they were the best." As the Nez Perce hunter Yellow Wolf confessed, "I killed yearlings mostly. It was robes we were after more than meat."

You can see the results of all these causes converging at mid-century in a transparent way in the sources Indian peoples themselves kept. The Kiowa Calendars, for example, a history of that tribe their historians painted on buffalo robes, began referring to severe shortages of buffalo on the Southern Plains during the 1840s. Among the Western Siouan groups, their version of tribal histories are called Winter Counts, and these show that in 1842, 1843, and 1844, the most significant events for those years were the elaborate buffalo-calling ceremonies their shamans were performing, and with mounting earnestness. Ever pragmatic, the Comanches were unconvinced the bison herds would dwindle away, but they had another source of animal protein in Texas and Mexican cattle stolen in their raids. If the bison herds failed to appear, they were willing to forego the hunt and let the buffalo "breed a year or two without molestation." Few others among any of these peoples were prescient enough to grasp all these complexities. So, as in Indian conversations with the Peace Commissioners in the 1860s, while Indian leaders weren't necessarily unanimous in their explanation for why the herds were visibly thinning, generally they tended to ignore their own culpability and blamed the whites on the trails, or the Métis hunters coming down from Canada.

With only 10–12 million buffalo left when the Civil War released thousands of men to seek their fortunes by going west with their guns, American hide and tongue hunters armed with the best killing technology available at the time began to lay waste what was left, the beginnings of an industrial-scale hunt that ended in buffalo hide belts driving corporate factories in the East and Europe. Some of the hide hunters may have believed bison were inexhaustible, but it's a safe bet that few if any indulged the idea that ceremony could cause the animals to reincarnate or to boil up from a cave or mountain in a fresh, inexhaustible supply. They knew they were wiping out the noblest of American species, the very emblem of the continent, but the Billy Dixons, Frank Mayers, and George Causeys of the world justified their selfishness in the classic American manner: what was good for them was also for the common good. And bison after all (as one of them put it), "were walkin', bellerin' gold pieces."

The historian Richard White has a single word for the callous disregard for life, the rotting stench that signaled the arrival of civilization to the plains, the brief and inconsequential economic returns of eradicating the buffalo: pathetic.

So was there, as so many Americans believe, a "secret conspiracy" on the part of the government and the military to destroy the American bison? When they wrote their memoirs, the hide hunters insisted they were the private executioners of a deliberate policy to kill buffalo and control the Indians. However self-serving that claim might strike us now, however unsupported their claims of "government/military support" have turned out to be, invoking a conspiracy has been a stroke of genius more than once in carrying off a historical argument.

What looks closer to the truth is that post–Civil War government in the United States quite publicly struggled with questions about wildlife and the market. Members of both political parties in Gilded Age America were disciples of classical economics, of letting the "higher, natural" laws of the market work, and with Southern Reconstruction ending and Black Southerners losing their voting rights, the party of Lincoln became especially interested in the support of the new American corporations. And the corporations regarded laissez-faire with all the sanctity of religion. Besides, at the federal level America had never passed a bill to protect any animal from market hunting, and would not do so until 1900. The bison issue without question also had a fellow-traveler in the complicated matter of Indian policy, which was in a state of transition from treaty making to the reservation and acculturation period in the 1870s. Americans across the nation were widely debating "the plight" of western Indians then.

The cruelties and excesses of animal slaughter on the Great Plains after the war did capture the attention of Congress, initially with a resolution introduced in 1872 by Senator Cornelius Cole of California to protect "the buffalo, elk, antelope, and other useful animals" from "indiscriminate slaughter and extermination." It went nowhere. In 1874 a Republican representative from Illinois named Greenburg Fort introduced a bill to make it unlawful for any non-Indian to kill "any female buffalo, of any age" in the western territories. By making the act of killing *female* bison illegal, the bill apparently had preservation of the species in mind as opposed to outlawing the hunt entirely. After considerable debate, both houses of Congress passed Fort's bill in 1874, but before female buffaloes could be protected, President Ulysses Grant killed the new law by neglecting to sign it. Word on the floor of Congress was that Grant was a supporter but had been distracted and missed the brief window. So Fort reintroduced the same bill again in 1876, and again it survived the House, but it never got out of committee in the Senate. In the wake of the Little Bighorn and Custer's death that summer, no bill to curtail the buffalo slaughter ever came up for a vote again. Market hunting of American wildlife would remain unregulated by federal law for another quarter-century.

Because the "Indian question" of the day was related to wildlife protection, and the country had politicized Indian policy, there were opinions of every stripe about whether saving bison would prolong Indian assimilation. For conservatives like Texas representatives John Hancock and J. W. Throckmorton, saving buffalo was little other than misplaced "sentimentality." The most famous figure in the history of this story to weigh in was Grant's interior secretary, Columbus Delano, who wrote (rather than testified) that if it sped Indian acculturation, he "would not seriously regret the total disappearance of the buffalo from our western prairies." GOP representative David Lowe of Kansas, on the other hand, thought depriving Indians of their food source ran contrary to civilized Christianity. And no less than General Philip Sheridan, in a widely circulated 1879 telegram to Washington questioning the continued buffalo slaughter by hide hunters on the Northern Plains, believed if such rampant destruction weren't halted the result would be Indian starvation and "great dissatisfaction to all friendly Indians who depend largely upon the Buffalo for subsistence." The general who today appears on t-shirts with an invented quote about giving buffalo hunters medals of commendation, actually wrote: "I consider it important that this wholesale slaughter of the Buffalo should be stopped." So much for hide hunter patriotism and John Cook's "so the story goes."

This debate in Congress over buffalo took place in public, not in secret. And judging from the outcome of the votes on the bison bills, if there was an unwritten policy to kill buffalo, Congress wasn't in on it. There undoubtedly were military men (the writer Colonel Richard Irving Dodge seems to have been one) who agreed with Secretary Delano, but clearly Sheridan and other officers did not. What seems actually to have been the case was that instead of a policy of destruction towards bison, the Grant administration and those to follow decided to have no policy at all. In the absence of a policy, as the conservatives realized, the market was going to do what the market does. So after 1876 the buffalo remained as they had been—another wildlife commons, open to unregulated exploitation—and if Indian and white pursuit of them led to their annihilation and to Indian acculturation, few would mourn the "inevitable" outcome.

But buffalo hunters as national heroes, deserving of medals and widespread public applause for their patriotic acts? That was John Cook's and J. Wright Mooar's fantasy. Funny, though, that in Canada, where neither white hide hunters nor a "secret government conspiracy" played any role in the buffalo story at all, the result turned out exactly the same: on behalf of the fur trade, the market hunt ended up killing all the buffaloes on the Canadian plains, and even sooner than the final hunt, in 1882–1883, down in Montana. Nobody got any ticker-tape parades in Calgary.

The former hide hunter Charles "Buffalo" Jones, the Texas ranching couple Charles and Mary Goodnight, conservationist/writer William Hornaday, the Canadians James McKay and Charles Alloway—these were the handful of bison advocates who saved the animal from extinction. But from the beginning they had help from native people. One was a Pend Oreille Indian named Samuel Walking Coyote, who along with his Salish wife, Mary Sabrine, brought six bison calves from eastern Montana across the Rockies to the Flathead Reservation in western Montana. Those three bulls and three cows became the nucleus of a famous herd called the Pablo-Allard herd. The mixed-blood Lakota Fred Duprees was another, who caught five calves on the Yellowstone and sold his animals in Canada. In fact, Michel Pablo was also part Indian, and James McKay was a Métis.

From the 1880s into the early twentieth century, when the American Bison Society emerged with the express purpose of rescuing bison from extinction, these were the individuals who saved buffalo in the northern West. The rescuers of the slightly smaller Southern Plains bison were the Goodnights, who preserved a small herd on their ranch in Palo Duro Canyon, Texas, and Buffalo Jones. Convinced the hide hunters had not killed every last bison on the Southern Plains, between 1886 and 1889 Jones made forays from southwestern Kansas to West Texas in search of remnant pockets of animals. The old hide hunter knew his country; his biggest catch was fifty-six calves in the Texas Panhandle. As he later wrote, "I am positive it was the wickedness committed in killing so many that impelled me to take measures for perpetuating the race which I had helped almost destroy."

The saviors' motives were not entirely spotless. Walking Coyote was probably the exception, but the rest all hoped to establish a profit-making venture

Reduced from 20–30 million by the unregulated market for Great Plains wildlife during the nineteenth century, enough bison have survived in the twenty-first century to serve as a core of animals to re-wild a Yellowstone-sized prairie preserve. Dan Flores photo.

with buffalo, domesticating them, interbreeding them with cattle, and selling purebred animals to various Wild West shows, zoos, and circuses. Eventually their animals—some biologists argue a total of only eighty-eight, the most serious genetic bottleneck buffalo have faced—became the nucleus of bison placed with parks and on bison ranges such as the national bison range the Roosevelt administration created on the Southern Plains in 1905, now the Wichita Mountains National Wildlife Refuge.

The driving force behind the exchange of animals and the creation of rescue herds was William T. Hornaday's brainchild. Founded in 1905, not disbanded until 1936, when it believed its work was done, the American Bison Society deserves accolades but with an asterisk the size of a basketball. Unlike the Sierra Club, its membership was overwhelmingly male and almost entirely eastern (of its 723 members in 1908, all of 6 were from the Great Plains). But it was the society's vision for a buffalo future that has colored the bison story ever since. The buffalo's male saviors from the East entirely endorsed the conversion of the Great Buffalo Savanna to a privatized empire of ranches and farms and cattle as bovine replacement. They saw their mission as saving buffalo from extinction, but not as an endangered species that should be recovered in the wild in its original habitat. What the society envisioned instead was a system of parks and refuges where modern Americans could stand and gawk at buffalos in a form of Old West nostalgia tourism. A century later it sounds suspiciously like the plot of a Kurt Vonnegut science fiction novel.

To its credit, the American Bison Society did save buffalo, and in an age when America allowed passenger pigeons and Carolina parakeets to vanish and the Bureau of Biological Survey to do all in its power to banish the wolf from the world. But this was a peculiar rescue. It made the American bison, as recently as 1870 the continent's most numerous wild animal, into a trendy sort of ranched beef animal, or a symbol merely, a circus beast from history, saved as a faunal badge of conquest in the way a butcherbird pins its victims on a barbed-wire fence to display its prowess. Saved, but unlike pronghorns, grizzlies, even wolves now, not really free, and certainly not wild.

In our time, with bison populations in parks and refuges and as ranched beef animals (whose products we can buy in chain grocery stores) now well beyond a quarter-million, with forty-odd Indian tribes involved with the modern Intertribal Bison Cooperative in restoring buffalo on Indian reservations, buffalo are back in our lives in a way they haven't been in a century. Given the steady and unabated human outmigration from the plains states, along with a future climate that may exceed Altithermal proportions, a different kind of buffalo future is possible. If, in another century, Americans looked back on the twenty-first century and saw some sort of immense wild buffalo/wolf preserve in place on the plains, would they regard it as another of our celebrated acts of world-class conservation, on the scale of setting Yellowstone aside as the world's first national park in the nineteenth century, or creating the Wilderness Preservation System in the twentieth? That would be a grand coda to the buffalo story of the nineteenth and twentieth centuries.

Because Indians remain major players in the buffalo story, along with science and economics and politics there is still ceremony. Over dinner several years ago with Fred DuBray, one of the original founders of the Intertribal Bison Cooperative, Fred told me a story from the beginning days of the ITBC. When he and other Great Plains residents had the idea of bringing buffalo back to Indian reservations in the West, an elderly Lakota woman had taken them aside and said, in effect, "Best you ask the buffalo if they *want* to come back."

I was intrigued. I was a captive audience. "And?" I asked. Fred took a couple of bites, swilled his drink, dabbed at his mouth with a napkin. He had a great sense of timing.

"Well, we did a ceremony and asked them," he said.

"And what did they *say*?"

"They said they wanted to come back," Fred replied. "But they said they didn't want to come back and be cows. They said they wanted to be buffalo. They wanted to be wild again."

7

Against all the odds of history, ecology, and time, the American West in the second half of the twentieth century was a wolf-less world. As late as the 1960s occasional transient wolves continued to drift up from Mexico's mountains into an America that had only coyotes, gray wolves that probed at their ancient homelands in places like Arizona and New Mexico. And wolves out of Canada, in the 1980s, trotted secretively down into Glacier National Park in the US Northern Rockies. Yet the Great Plains, the part of America where wolves had existed for thousands of years in demonstrably the greatest abundance of any region on the continent, by the start of the new century had been No Wolf's Land for seventy-five years.

Nonetheless, in a canyon on the plains of West Texas in the mid-1990s I stood riveted by a wolf that was staring directly at me through the yuccas from a distance of no more than fifty feet. She was ebony-black, this wolf, and at such close range I could see that she was a muscular and reflexive miracle in the prime of life. She looked huge, although I knew that the thick wool beneath her four-inch growth of guard hairs was one of the things that gave her size, that she probably weighed less than 80 pounds. Her legs were long, brindle-colored, tapering down to delicate ankles where bone and sinew executed a 90-degree flare into padded feet half-again bigger than my palm. Gliding away through the mesquite and cactus, she moved on those feet like black water pouring, her fox bush of a tail carried low, her hindquarters slightly lower than her withers as she trotted, rendering her movements vaguely hyena-like. But it was when she stopped to stare back at me over that sharp, refined muzzle that I most felt her primal, wolf power. Her eyes were yellow-amber, and they did not break contact furtively as can those of a dog, but emitted presence—a probing intelligence—unwaveringly into mine. There was explication in that look. It made you understand, somehow, why this animal above all the other native creatures of America has always engendered both fierce hatred and consuming love.

The look in those yellow wolf eyes, I thought then and still do, speaks to the heart of the wolf dilemma on this continent. Wolf eyes remind us of the untamable land that frightened us Americans into an orgy of destruction of the wild. But they also reflect back to us the spirit of a continent that we're someday going to have to embrace if we're ever going to be people of this place, true "Americans."

The wolf I was watching had a name. I had named her Ysa, short for *Ysambanbi*, a word from the Comanche language that means "Handsome Wolf." It was in fact the name of a prominent Comanche *nomnekaht*, or war leader, who 200 years earlier travelers often found camped in the High Plains canyon where I was watching my black wolf. The name was apt, for at three years old she was truly a beautiful animal. Ysa and her mate, Wily—a strapping, cream-colored cross out of Arctic tundra wolf and McKenzie River husky parentage—were my "wolves," or wolf-hybrids. They both had some small percentage of domestic canine ancestry, although short of sequencing their genomes I don't think anyone could say how much "dog" and how much "wolf" was there. As with most of these often-maligned animals ("Worse Than Pitbulls" was the title of a program airing on national television at the time), it doesn't take much wolf ancestry to color behavior sharply, and Ysa and Wily acted like dogs about the same way wild buffalo act like feedlot cows. Not a great deal, in other words.

Wolf/dog hybrids were something of a phenomenon in the United States back then, and about as welcome to many Americans at the turn of the twenty-first century as home-grown terrorists. As Susan Stewart of Knight-Ridder News Service put it in a review of a documentary on the return of the wolf, "What is wolf behavior? Basically, wolves kill little animals. . . . Wolf fascination," she went on, "may succeed with those viewers who have not lately been reading *Little Red Riding Hood*." As for her, "Mary, her little lamb and the Christmas season are too potent as symbols to leave any room for wolf sympathy." In modern America, any animal that's seen as a threat to little girls,

A gray wolf, a grizzly, coyotes, and ravens share a carcass, a classic American Serengeti scene now possible again. Jim Peaco photo, 2013. Wikimedia Commons.

cuddly lambs, and Santa Claus has a definite spin problem. But wolves' stock was on the rise among many, and in the absence of wild wolves in the countryside, wolf-hybrids had become popular.

I can't say why most people who do something as impractical as acquiring wolf-hybrids do so, and I confess I was as leery as the next person of the truck driver from the Texas Panhandle who called one day wanting to know where he could get a wolf-hybrid to train as a guard/attack animal, and who hung up on me when I told him that animals that were high-percentage wolf were far too shy around people to work as guard dogs. What I can say, though, is that my own experience with wolf-hybrids was grounded in a kind of quest for native authenticity in a landscape—the Southern High Plains—that had every last buffalo stripped from it by 1878, every last wolf by 1924, and almost every last blade of grass in my own time. I think I was driven a little crazy by this, and in the longing to repossess the essence of what had gotten banished from the Great Plains, I ended up committing sins I never intended to commit.

In retrospect, the cuddly-lamb types—and of course the cattlemen and the sheepmen—were no doubt right about this part: owning wolf-hybrids may be a symptom of a disturbed personality, or at the very least a personality that has drifted hard in the direction of excessive romance. What sort of illumination this casts on the wolf in Great Plains and American West history could be peripheral. Somehow, having done it myself, I think it isn't.

We know for certain from evolution and from human history that with the exception of our primate cousins, wild canids have been intimately associated with us longer than any other large animals on the planet. One of the best biological clues for the temporal depth and intimacy of human relationships with other animals is shared diseases. We humans share fifty diseases with cattle (including one of the deadliest killers of humanity, smallpox, evolved from cowpox), forty-six with sheep, forty-two with swine. But we share the most diseases of all, sixty-five, with canines. Freudian-era psychologist Caveath Read, in his 1920 volume *The Origin of Man*, one of the first books to advance a Darwinian explanation for human behavior, argued that early humans may actually have modeled their social and cooperative life after that of the canid packs they saw around them. The evolving human mind, he wrote, was "a sort of chimpanzee mind adapted to the wolfish conditions of the hunting pack," and Read proposed that when the fossils of humanity's earliest ancestors were found, they should be named *Lycopithecus*—"wolf-ape."

Like humans, wolves evolved to be so ecologically flexible that by their first couple of million years they had become cosmopolitan, spreading across the globe. Emerging from North American roots to spread across virtually the entire planet, wolves (again like us) ramified into many different regional types, genetically related pools of animals specific to particular geographic settings. When North American biologists got around to studying wolves here, these types acquired something like the status of regional Indian tribes. Less than three-quarters of a century ago, American taxonomists had designated a whopping twenty-three subspecies of *Canis lupus*, the gray wolf, and another three of *Canis rufus*, the red wolf, that were found across North America.

In the minds of twentieth-century wolf biologists like Stanley Young and Edward A. Goldman of the federal Bureau of Biological Survey, or biologist Raymond Hall of the University of Kansas, their taxonomic exercises represented what they believed to be the ancient wolf reality of the continent—a great many wolf "tribes" worthy of recognition. By 2012, however, when the US Fish and Wildlife Service published a monograph titled *An Account of the Taxonomy of North American Wolves*, biologists had come to an entire rethinking of American wolves. That monograph concluded that North America's wolves sprang from two origins. All members of the Canidae come from an American evolutionary line dating back 5 million years. But while coyotes and some related wolves remained in North America, the ancestors of America's gray wolves migrated to Asia and Europe and only returned home to America via the Bering land bridge roughly 20,000 years ago. They also returned at three different times in three separate, unique waves of animals. Utilizing both classic morphology but also a host of new genetic studies, this taxonomic rethink shrank the number of gray wolf subspecies from the twenty-three Young and Goldman had designated in the 1940s down to only four.

Thus modern wolf science has concluded that most of the former wolf subspecies were actually just local variants of four Asian gray wolf and two American wolf species. The gray wolves include the white wolves of the Arctic, *Canis lupus arctos* of the extreme north of the continent, along with a western Rocky Mountain wolf, *C. l. occidentalis*, found from the Montana Rockies northward along the mountains of the West to Alaska. The new taxonomy still regards the small gray wolves of Mexico and the American Southwest, *C. l. baileyi*, or the Mexican wolf, as a distinctive gray wolf. But the wolf with the greatest American range of all, extending across a huge swath of the United States, from the Pacific across the whole of the Great Plains, and on to the western Great Lakes and northward through much of the eastern half of Canada, was *Canis lupus nubilus*. This was the famed "buffalo wolf" of so much Great Plains history.

But there is also the American wolf line, distinct from the above gray wolves. By 2012 wolf taxonomy recognized the original range of the red wolf, *Canis rufus*, as stretching from Central Texas across the South and up the Eastern Seaboard to Canada. And it reclassified the wolf of the eastern Great Lakes—formerly believed to be a subspecies of the gray wolf—as its own species, *Canis lycaon*. Most importantly for the purely American wolves, the new wolf taxonomy claims that the wolves of eastern America were ancient continental wolves that had come from the same evolutionary line that produced coyotes: "Coyotes, *C. rufus*, and *C. lycaon* are modern representatives of a major and diverse clade that evolved within North America."

As for the brawny plains lobos, or buffalo wolves, that produced so many flights of description in nineteenth-century Great Plains travel, as I write this in my house outside Santa Fe, New Mexico, I am surrounded by buffalo wolf country, old buffalo wolf den sites, buffalo wolf folklore. Over in West Texas

I know that buffalo wolf stories still get told—stories of all the wolves in an upper Red River valley poisoned out in one season by a Comanche market hunter; of cowboys pulling wolves apart with ropes, from horseback; of professional wolfers like Allen Stagg and Jack Abernethy poisoning 200–300 wolves a year on the Texas Panhandle's XIT Ranch in the 1890s; of an en masse late nineteenth-century wolf self-exodus westward from the plains into Colorado and New Mexico, like persecuted Jews searching for a refuge from a wolf inquisition; of the last wolf in the Texas Panhandle, gutshot with a .22 and run down and dispatched with a Model-T.

But neither here in New Mexico, nor in West Texas, Kansas, Nebraska, or the Dakotas are there buffalo wolves on the plains any longer. One of the animals that defined the very nature of this country for 20,000 years, whose adaptive strategies set a pattern for mammalian life here, got wiped clean from the whole vastness of Great Plains topography. Climate change was not the reason for this mass extirpation. We were.

I mark it a measure of the America I was born to that I made it to my forties and had to drive myself 4,000 miles from my natal Louisiana home before I saw my first wolf in the wild.

It was the summer of 1990 and a traveling companion and I were in British Columbia, driving the Alcan Highway in a kind of tribute to the last great American wilderness when out of the mundane world of blaring twentieth-century music and whining rubber on asphalt, an ancient dream-like form loped up out of my subconscious (it almost seemed) and in flesh-and-blood trotted across the road in front of us. Enclosed in our technological shell, hurtling across the continent at 60 mph, we were still looking at the vastness around us as scenery. But twentieth-century British Columbia was not like the twentieth-century Great Plains. It was biologically alive and was one of the continental places that has simply been too vast, cold, and remote for prior humans to have killed almost every last charismatic animal.

I was driving and rounding a curve with the low Northland sun in my eyes when I saw the motion of her, a rocking-chair rhythm coming up the highway embankment fifty yards ahead. By the time she was halfway across the road and had turned her head to fix me with her eyes, I knew exactly what she was. Perhaps dredging up from some eons-old genetic memory, I recognized the lope and I knew the look, and I knew she wasn't a coyote, or a dog. I have to write that the memory of that beautiful young female wolf, alive and unafraid in her home country, loping across a late-afternoon British Columbia road, still makes the hair stand up on my neck.

When we drove back from Alaska several weeks later, Wily, a year-old male wolf cross that had been abandoned in an Anchorage kennel, rode in the back of the Jeep, a late twentieth-century White Fang bound for warmer climes.

If you're into self-revelation, it's hard to get more exposed anywhere on the planet than on the Llano Estacado of West Texas, and crouching on hands and knees, I was exposed. Except for shorts and a pair of moccasins, I was naked in the sun and Texas dust, nothing but a flimsy spray of yuccas to protect me. Eyeing me with alarm, dung beetles waddled away in the short grass, performing their handstand technique to roll away their delicacies, a strategy enabling them to keep a complicated array of beady eyes on me all the while. They obviously didn't think much of my chances in this encounter.

Fifty yards away I could see two pairs of sharp canine ears emerging out of another big clump of soapweed. Something about their intensity signaled to me that another rush was coming, but before I could figure out how I knew that, there was a perceptible gathering, almost a compression. Then a moment of held breath, and suddenly two large, four-legged forms were exploding out of the yuccas, noses and ears aimed at me like gunsights. The lanky bodies approached so rapidly and directly and with such lack of wasted motion that I should have been able to register knife-edge detail, but it was a bit like trying to pick out the stitches on a Nolan Ryan fastball. Instead there was a slur of Cubist images—open red mouths, a tongue streaming saliva into the air, yellow eyes unblinking and fixed—carried by a thumping rhythm that put me in mind of something very elemental.

The fifty yards took less than three seconds. Twenty feet from where I crouched, dripping sweat into the dirt, the careening forms parted. One—the bigger, cream-colored one—low-hurdled me without missing a stride. It made no attempt either to bite or slash. The black one was smaller and quicker, and waited until I was distracted by the hurdler before whirling behind me, exposed fangs gleaming curved and white in the sun, and snapping the end of my ponytail. *Gotcha!*

Wily trotted up to give me a quick kiss and then jaw-wrestled with Ysa while I regained my composure after their charge. It was the fall of 1991, almost eighteen months after I'd brought Wily home from Alaska. Through one of those complicated sequences of events that karma or the gods (or living in the country) seems to set one up for, I'd been bequeathed a second wolf. Ysa, now an eight-month-old, jet-black female pup who was supposed to be 90 percent "Eastern timber wolf" (a red wolf, among which a black color phase is common?), had by then joined Wily in their acre-sized pen.

Getting rushed by a couple of wolf-hybrids is obviously not quite the same thing as witnessing life from the perspective of a wolf's prey, but that's been a harder thing for humans to experience than you might think. Except where rabid animals are concerned, wolves just don't attack or prey on people. Some biologists argue that wolf parents, which have to teach their pups almost everything about how to survive in the world, only give them certain prey templates. Human beings aren't one of them. Historians are able to document only three wild wolf attacks on humans across the entire twentieth century. The most famous wolf attacks on people in all of history occurred in 1767 in Languedoc, France, when wolves are supposed to have killed and feasted on more than 100 people, mostly children. The story is hard to document, and some versions claim the guilty animals were actually wolf-hybrids, whose dog nature made them more aggressive and less afraid of people.

My favorite part of this story has always been the practical and entirely modern solution proposed by the Languedoc politicians. Supposedly they recommended that the French government round up all the wolves in the province and then relocate them (properly rehabilitated, wouldn't you think?) across the Channel, among the peasants of England.

All the wolves now remaining in North America were on hand for at least 20,000 years of one of the grandest canine barbecues in world history. Before the last millennia of the Pleistocene ended, the direct ancestors of our modern wolves had joined short-faced bears, various saber-toothed and scimitar cats, false cheetahs, steppe lions, and running hyenas in pulling down camels, sloths, giant long-horned bison, and perhaps mammoth calves in the Pleistocene Great Plains world of ancient America. That world, a place of science fiction giants that hardly seem real to us now, nonetheless bequeathed to wolf descendants their proper place in the scheme of North American ecology. As Great Plains trader and author Josiah Gregg put it in the 1840s, "Although the buffalo is the largest, he has by no means the control among the prairie animals; the sceptre of authority has been lodged with the large gray wolf."

You vegans who contribute to the Fund for Animals and Defenders of Wildlife, wolf partisans who send your money to Wolf Haven to "adopt" your very own wolf, all you consumers of cutesy wolf mugs and medallions and wolf-adorned electric toothbrushes and t-shirts should make sure you look the wolf in the eye and envision a wolf's life for what evolution truly intended it to be. Because what wolves do is hunt down, kill, and eat other animals. Not nearly so omnivorous as coyotes or bears, wolves like mammal flesh, and they prefer it freshly killed. As "in" as the charismatic wolf has become for many environmentalists since the 1980s, we ought to acknowledge that since the Pleistocene extinctions took away hyenas and short-faced bears and all the big American cats, the wolf has been the most efficient killer of large mammals, especially big ungulates, of any American predator. Seven-hundred-pound grizzly bears like to eat army cutworm moths and grass and marmots, things that die, to be sure, but not quite so dramatically as an elk or a bison dies. While wolves will pursue mice and rabbits and other small stuff, they prefer caribou, deer, elk, buffalo, moose. Wolf kills are marvels of athleticism, speed, endurance, and teamwork on the part of the wolves. For their prey a fatal encounter is marked by terrified flight, resistance, and the horrible capitulation of a crippled and overwhelmed animal.

Unless and until we re-create some facsimile of it on the modern Great Plains, we are never going to know exactly how this ancient predator/prey ecology worked in the part of America where it was a routine, daily spectacle for so many thousands of years. Indian oral traditions can give us some inkling about the details, but not much. Accounts by naturalist-oriented nineteenth-century travelers such as Lewis and Clark, Josiah Gregg, or John James Audubon often tell us more but it is difficult to know how well these pre-Darwinian observers understood what they saw. Modern wolf/prey interaction studies in other landscapes are probably the closest we can get, but these are incomplete and we are still learning from them. How can we grasp the full dimensions of the buffalo wolf's impacts on the bison herds, in any case, without either free-roaming plains herds or viable populations of buffalo wolves interacting with them?

About the time wolves were becoming darlings of the environmental movement, in biology circles it had become fashionable to argue against predation as a balance-of-nature factor in controlling prey populations. But this was short-lived ecological revisionism. Beginning in the 1920s, when ecologists began to probe the possible beneficial effects predators might have on nature, the classic view was that the predator/prey relationship worked mechanically, that predators were the key to holding prey populations under some carrying capacity limits fixed by prey resources, and that the relationship worked as a rhythmic oscillation around a steady line. As rabbit or deer populations increased, in other words, the number of bobcats or wolves also increased until a point was reached where predation was capable of curbing prey population growth. Declining numbers of prey in turn suppressed predator population growth, until the scenario commenced once again.

This concept, which has a name—the Lotka-Volterra Equations—furnished evidence from predation that ecosystems worked in simple, linear, mechanical fashion. For much of the twentieth century predator biology used the Kaibab mule deer disaster, when deer went through an efflorescence after federal hunters eliminated big predators from Arizona's Kaibab Plateau and the mule deer population destroyed its browse, then crashed spectacularly, to demonstrate the critical role of predation in keeping prey within natural carrying capacities.

In the 1940s, though, an ecologist named Charles Elton discovered that the records of the Hudson's Bay Company, whose trappers had been harvesting furbearing animals from the Boreal forest of Canada for almost two centuries, indicated something otherwise. While the HBC trapping records did show regular cycles in the populations of snowshoe hares and lynx, the cycles didn't match the assumed equation. Hares seemed to have four-year cycles, while lynx populations revolved around a ten-year cycle. Predator revisionism was born. A subsequent and more critical look at these HBC records by later researchers, however, indicated that the hares and lynx had been trapped in different areas, so any attempt to combine the data painted a false picture. Nonetheless, Elton had set predator rethinking in motion.

At mid-century Durwood Allen's work on moose and wolf interactions in Isle Royale National Park in Michigan showed what seemed to be wild swings in the populations of both species. Working with animals we now believe are one of the few remnant populations of buffalo wolves left in America, Allen also demonstrated the precarious nature of predation: wolves commonly "tested" more than a dozen moose before they were successful in bringing one down. By then predation revisionism was in full swing, and in 1973 a New Zealand ecologist, Graeme Caughley, published a soon-famous paper asserting that predators played little or no role in controlling populations of many prey animals, that for some ungulates an autogenic (internal) mechanism slowed or stopped population growth when it approached critical carrying capacity in a local habitat. Furthermore, Caughley argued, for a variety of reasons the famous Kaibab episode probably hadn't meant what ecologists thought, and likely was a hoax, anyway!

Here in the twenty-first century predator revisionism seems to be in retreat. Studies from the western Canadian provinces, from Alaska, from Minnesota, and now from the Northern Rockies of Montana, Idaho, and Wyoming, where wolves are part of the ecology, all seem to demonstrate a significant role for wolves in establishing the dynamic equilibrium of nature. In southeastern Alaska, wolf predation is said to have exerted strong evolutionary pressure on the behavior and habitat selection of mountain goats. In Alaska and the Yukon, in one controversial study, biologists labeled wolves and bears the chief influence on moose and Nechina caribou demographics, crediting wolves with taking some 30 percent of the moose population annually. In Minnesota, in a particularly compelling study done by well-known biologist and wolf advocate David Mech, the biologist assessed wolves as a key cause (among several interacting ones) responsible for a deer herd collapse in the Superior National Forest in the 1970s. Elk and deer hunters, used to decades of sport without competition from predators, have taken note.

One step in understanding the role wolves played on the Great Plains 150–200 years ago is with a central insight or two from Chaos Theory. Natural systems like the bison/wolf ecology of the ancient Great Plains should be characterized by wide swings of population variation within a normal equilibrium. Disturbances in such a system are inevitable, and if they are of sufficient magnitude they can cause the whole system to rachet suddenly to a new equilibrium.

The Pleistocene Extinctions were one such disturbance, a massive shift that struck the West roughly 10,000 years ago. Unlike many plains animals, wolves and bison both survived the sudden loss of some thirty-two genera of animals, although modern bison represented a dwarfing within their genus. As dwarf bison proliferated to fill all the grazing niches left vacant, lacking competitors they multiplied into the millions, a remarkable flood of one species that cycled, depending on the weather, between 20 and 30 million animals on the plains. Buffalo wolves, left with only coyotes or occasional packs of red wolves as competitors, were perfectly positioned to enjoy another 10,000 years of fat living on the grand prairies of the West. In the bison/wolf era, wolf numbers on the Great Plains likely oscillated between 1 million and 1.5 million of the big gray predators. Starting 100 centuries ago this was the new equilibrium, and it lasted almost to our modern present, specifically until the 1880s.

When early American diarists like Meriwether Lewis, John James Audubon, and John Charles Fremont first observed wolves on the Great Plains, they called them the "shepherds" of the buffalo herds. Trader Josiah Gregg said of plains lobos that although there were "immense numbers of them upon the Prairies," only when bison were present, or when trading caravans, hunting parties, or Indian bands traveled across the plains, did an observer see wolves in great numbers. In the latter case the attraction was the potential to scavenge the offal from human hunts. Many accounts from the 1820s on describe wolves approaching from all directions in response to hearing rifle fire echo across the open plains. Dr. Michael Steck, traveling the Santa Fe Trail across the Southern Plains in 1852, gives us a sense of what it was like to be on the wild American Serengeti then. Anytime there were buffalo present, he wrote, wolves were so common that "we see immense numbers of them. A common thing to see [is] 50 at a sight. In the daytime never out of sight of them, see Hundreds in a day."

Connections between particular bison herds and particular wolf packs—the "shepherd" phenomenon—seem accurate in describing contained places like the modern Wood Buffalo National Park in Canada. But the analogy may not have worked quite that way on the open plains. Specific wolf packs probably did not migrate with the bison herds as they shifted north and south, summer and winter, since under normal conditions, wolves are territorial. A wolf pack, which commonly consists of the alpha breeding pair and from one to two litters of its pups, establishes a home range that, to be sure, may encompass forty or fifty square miles. But it has boundaries, near the center of which is usually the den site. In what biologists call Optimal Foraging Strategy, areas adjacent to wolf dens got hunted harder. Wolves don't hunt periphery areas where pack boundaries overlap as thoroughly, creating a phenomenon that both biologists and anthropologists have noticed in North American ecology. Such wildlife buffer zones occurred where Indian tribal boundaries met, as well, and produced the same outcome: they allowed the buildup of relatively unmolested prey animals where territories met.

Individuality is marked in wolves, and it must have meant that the packs developed many different strategies for hunting bison on the plains. Josiah Gregg, an amateur naturalist who was one of our best sources on plains wildlife, claimed that "certain it is" that plains gray wolves "overcome many of the largest buffaloes, employing perhaps different means of subduing them." Gregg believed the commonest method was "that, while running, they gnaw and lacerate the legs and ham-strings till they disable him, and then he is killed by the gang." Artist George Catlin preserved for us a wondrous pair of watercolors portraying a wolf pack attacking a grown, but ailing, bison bull. Catlin's art—showing even a dying bison bull hooking and kicking his attackers and tossing lobos like bowling pins—underlines the risk to wolf life and limb. Some wolf packs may have learned how to stampede bison off cliffs, then feasted on the animals mangled and killed in the fall. There are anthropologists who believe that Indian hunters learned the technique of the bison jump from this wolf strategy.

But William Clark, on April 22, 1805, when the Lewis and Clark expedition was ascending the Missouri River through what is now North Dakota, described by far the most common buffalo wolf hunting technique. As Lewis recorded it, "Capt. Clark informed me that he saw a large drove of buffaloe pursued by wolves today, that they at length caught a calf which was unable to keep up with the herd. the cows only defend their young so long as they are able to keep up." What William Clark had noticed was an old Plains Indian observation. For every ten of those cuddly little yellow-red calves following their mothers in the late spring, the Pawnees said, wolves usually ran down and devoured about four.

"See those circles in the grass?" travelers on the overland trails would say, pointing to revegetating buffalo wallows. "They're wore down by mother buffalos trying to protect their calves from the wolves."

Long centuries of peaceful relations with the native peoples had taught plains wolves not to fear human beings. It's not that wolves acted aggressively—Europeans consistently expressed scorn at what "cowards" wolves in the West were. It was instead their tameness that attracted the notice of European and American travelers. Virtually every diarist of the early nineteenth-century West said something about how trusting wolves seemed to be, trotting in front of their horses like dogs, or sitting curiously on a sandbar as their flatboats passed within feet. William Clark finally yielded to some unfathomable urge and actually killed a wolf walking by close enough that he could stab it with a bayonet, evidently just because it was tame and he could.

But soon enough, with everyone traveling the West armed to the teeth and taking shots at almost every wolf they saw, wolves learned to keep their distance, at least out of rifle range. But that sort of casual persecution was only a taste of the changes about to come in rapid succession across the nineteenth century. For 10,000 years after the Pleistocene Extinctions wolves had lived and died and taken (roughly speaking) an allotted third of the natural increase of the teeming wildlife of the West, while native people watched and admired and emulated them, and sometimes called on their power. Then in the 1820s Plains Indians got caught up in the market hunting of buffalo, and in the 1830s wagon trains of emigrants began to course the plains, followed by mining parties in the 1850s. Wolves to this point were doing very well on the offal resulting from a mounting human harvest of animals. Even the return and spread of wild horses across the prairies was also a boon, maybe more to mountain lions than to wolves, although wolves certainly relearned an old canid knowledge from the Pleistocene: how to prey on colts.

The end game for Great Plains wolves began in the midst of these good times. Made from the seed of an East India fruit, strychnine was in commercial production in Pennsylvania as early as 1834. It was cheap, completely unregulated, and a key tool of biological warfare against the natural world in America for much of the nineteenth and twentieth centuries. In an age that was inured to carnage, it was also a horrific killer. Within 10–20 minutes a tablet of strychnine gulped down as part of a predator's meal would wreak such havoc on its central nervous system that it launched the victim into wrenching waves of convulsive cramping. A strychnine-poisoned wolf died from asphyxiation, but not before the poison wracked it with such violence that death left it in a signature pose, a corpse with a rigidly arched spinal column.

By the 1850s, trading posts in Westport, Missouri, where overland travelers struck out across the Great Plains, regularly stocked strychnine for western travelers. This is how predator pelts began to join the international fur trade in that decade. With strychnine pellets in their saddlebags, travelers and traders could lace every dead bison or horse they saw with the poison, hang around a day or two to see what happened, and reap the benefits. Confronting strychnine, Great Plains predators—and all sorts of collateral targets like ravens and magpies and eagles—were suddenly vulnerable to humans as never before.

The commercial buffalo harvest of the 1860s–1880s created unprecedented boom-time conditions for wild canines, but it also inaugurated this first chemical warfare against them. The wolf bonanza of all time clearly was the American slaughter of the remaining few million buffaloes, for fun and sport but mostly for the money derived from their hides and tongues, from 1872 to 1884. For a few years wolves and coyotes lived large off the blood sport. But even creatures as numerous as bison eventually began to dwindle away before the onslaught; ultimately the market hunters had to expand their target species to elk, pronghorns, bighorn sheep, and deer. Ultimately there were between 5,000 and 20,000 hunters on the Great Plains in those years. No one then, or anyone now, has ever been able to measure a war on the wild on the scale they conducted it, but millions of living creatures lost their lives as a result.

When the old bison/wolf/Indian equilibrium flew apart, with the Indians herded onto reservations and bison literally erased from the Great Plains, wolf populations were briefly at their highest point in a hundred centuries. The wildlife slaughter had been a wolf Elysian Fields. Another dynamic ratchet had clicked into place, a new equilibrium that was slow to form but involved the replacement animals, domesticated stock like cattle and sheep, raised by ranchers who would brook no losses to predators. To the wolves, sheep and cattle must have seemed animals that *needed* killing—all of them helpless, infirm, and lame-witted. To the ranchers, to the livestock associations, to professional wolfers, to the governments that backed their actions, wolves were a visible and hateful symbol of the wilderness that civilization was on a mission to suppress. By 1880 the great western wolf war had become a war to convert the ancient wilderness to a money-making pasture for cows and sheep.

Our ancestors on the Great Plains shot, roped, gassed, stomped, and strangled wolves. They trapped them with the steel leghold trap invented by Sewell Newhouse to replace the wild with "the wheatfield, the library, and the piano," Newhouse said. Wolf hunters hung wolves from trees as if they were human outlaws. Some states tried biological warfare; in Montana, a 1905 state law required veterinarians to infect captured wolves with sarcoptic mange and release them to spread the disease. But mostly we poisoned them. In the adage of the New West: the wolf didn't destroy the cow; the cow destroyed the wolf. It was as if civilization was taking revenge on the animal that more than any other has reminded the civilized how brief is our separation from the animal.

Between 1901—that's when professional wolfer Ben Corbin published his book, *The Wolf Hunter's Guide*, explaining the wolf war in terms of Christianity, democracy, and the depravity of wolves—and 1924, when the Predatory and Rodent Control (PARC) division of the federal Bureau of Biological Survey was distributing 3.5 million strychnine baits across the West annually, we successfully cleared the West of all but a few pockets of wolves. The period from 1850 to 1925 featured the greatest mass slaughter of wolves in world history. Territorial and state legislatures were usually in the pockets of live-stock associations in the West, and they made bounties on predators almost government's primary reason for being during the period. Kansas bountied wolves in 1864, Colorado Territory in 1869, Montana Territory in 1883, and Wyoming plus the territory of Arizona/New Mexico in 1893.

In the bounty phase of the predator war, another of my home-base states, Montana, provides a truly classic example of the mindset of a century ago. Be-tween 1883 and 1928, Montana paid bounties on 111,545 wolves and 886,367 coyotes, a ranching subsidy during the territorial stage that devoured a stun-ning two-thirds of Montana's annual budget! The state paid bounties on 23,575 wolves in 1899, but wolf populations had collapsed so dramatically by 1920 that in that year Montana paid out bounties on only 17 of them. By con-trast, bountied coyotes remained consistent—about 30,000 a year—across the whole span of Montana's bounty period. At the point in 1914 when Con-gress reoriented the federal agency called the Biological Survey to its twenti-eth-century mission of destroying American predators, western states were paying out a million dollars a year to annihilate the animal that had been the top predator on the Great Plains for 10,000 years.

Now, with new federal help in the form of Biological Survey hunters, who largely opted for mass-poisoning with strychnine as the quickest method to annihilate wolves, the few remaining Great Plains lobos stood little chance. As their numbers dwindled, ranchers and bureau hunters began to bestow names on the last, elusive individual animals. Two-Toes was one of the last on the plains, a Wyoming wolf that hunted east of the Laramie Range and finally got trapped there by bureau hunter Albert McIntyre in 1916. The no-torious Custer wolf died in South Dakota in 1920, accused and convicted of sins against cattle only a T-Rex could have perpetrated. Out on the Colorado plains, hounds ran down one of the last wolves in 1919, and bureau hunters trapped three more there the next year.

The last pack out on the grasslands where Colorado, New Mexico, Kansas, and Oklahoma join possessed two celebrity alphas, a male called Whitey and a female known as Three-Toes. The equally legendary bureau hunter Stanley Young got Whitey through blind-set traps and sheer luck in 1921. With the pack's pups also killed, that left Three-Toes as the last wolf on the Colorado plains. When she could find no male wolves, she bred with a ranch dog and whelped a litter of hybrids, believed the last litter birthed by a wild wolf on the Great Plains. Three-Toes finally fell to bureau hunter Roy Spangler the same year that Snowdrift, a white wolf in the upper Missouri country, became the last plains wolf killed in Montana. The year was 1923. The next year pic-nickers shot a wolf with a .22 in the Texas Panhandle and ran it down in their Model T, clearly an omen of the changing times. There are no more stories of wolves on the Great Plains after that.

There was the possibility then, of course, as there is now, that wolves flee-ing into the Rockies and into the country's new national parks might bear litters that would recolonize the plains. Except that starting in 1898, park personnel actually began poisoning wolves inside national park boundaries. Yellowstone even invited Vernon Bailey of the Biological Survey to show their rangers proper mass extermination techniques, and between 1914 and 1916 the world's first national park destroyed 83 coyotes and 12 wolves inside park boundaries. Yellowstone's tally through the demise of the last remaining wolves in the park, in 1926, was 136, 80 of them puppies. Meanwhile, Glacier National Park, bordering Montana's Northern Plains, had a superintendent named James Galen who was so thrilled with the state's experiment with bio-logical warfare against predators that he wrote the state veterinarian in hopes of releasing mange-infected animals into Glacier. His Washington superiors thought poison would be more effective, and Glacier proceeded to tally 14 poisoned wolves in the park by 1920.

While the last population of buffalo wolves secreted themselves away in dense forests in the upper Midwest and on the islands in Lake Superior, in the American West it was only in the mountainous, forested Far North—in Alaska, Alberta, and British Columbia—that there were still healthy popu-lations of wolves. Even there, Canadians poisoned 17,000 wolves to protect their caribou herds in the 1950s, and by 1960 a rabies eradication program had reduced Alberta's wolf population from 5,000 to about 500. But at least *some* wolves were still in the Far North. Except in these few places, by the mid-twentieth century we had entirely erased wolves, along with wolf preda-tion and wolfsong, from the interior American West. Coyotes, flexible, adapt-able, capable of living in civilization's shadow, reaped the benefit, assuming most of the wolf's former range across the continent.

The age of the wheatfields, the libraries, the pianos—and growing re-morse for what we had done—was upon us.

Nature abhors a vacuum. Years ago a wildlife biologist friend explained to me the logic of coyote control in Texas. He and his graduate students had arranged to poison, trap, and helicoptor-gun every last coyote off a large West Texas ranch, in part to see if the startling computer models of coyote recovery under such pressure held up in the real world. At tremendous expense and effort they pulled it off, but in less than a year, through in-migration and expanded litter sizes of other coyotes in the region, the coyote population on the ranch was up to 80 percent what it had been when they had commenced their scorched-earth policy. The computer modeling proved out. "What'd the rancher say about that outcome?" I asked. "Hell," my friend laughed, "he read our report, spat in the dirt, and opted for continued wholesale coyote control anyway." The wolf vacuum in the American West may have lasted a little longer than the coyote vacuum on that Texas ranch, but not by much. Their return has needed our help, though.

Something fundamental in American thinking about nature began to change in the second half of the twentieth century. Maybe it wasn't a full-on paradigm shift, since there has been a fierce and nasty backlash against environmentalism starting with the Reagan administration and the rise of the Republican Right. But as a result of the Age of Ecology in the 1960s and 70s, which fed on an embrace of biologist/author Aldo Leopold's "biocentric" respect for other creatures, and certainly on a healthy dose of the youthful idealism that has always driven American history, the wolf became a beneficiary. Credit Richard Nixon, too. Awkwardly trying to surf the environmental wave, one of the game-changers he bequeathed us was the Endangered Species Act of 1973. And one of the things that act brought us was federally mandated *recovery* of charismatic endangered animals like red and gray wolves.

Unlike those West Texas coyotes, the wolves have needed our help. But where the barriers weren't impossible ones, they aided their own cause. In the 1980s Alberta's wolf population had rebounded to some 4,200, and it was only a matter of time before all those elk and moose and deer in places like Glacier National Park attracted wolf attention. While biologists for the US Fish and Wildlife Service were working on wolf recovery plans—they completed an initial plan for reintroducing the Mexican wolf into the Southwest in 1982, and released the Northern Rocky Mountain Wolf Recovery Plan five years later—wolves were eyeing the vacuum in the American West and making their own plans.

Whether creatures as intelligent as wolves can reason is as much a philosophical as a scientific question. The creamy-white female wolf that made continental history in the late 1980s might well have been engaged in deduction. Whatever her reasons, where others had hesitated, she denned—the first time close enough to the US border that in November 1985 her litter, known as the Magic Pack, entered Glacier National Park and became overnight celebrities. The white wolf whelped her second litter on Montana's Flathead River in 1986. It was probably the first litter of wolves born in the American West in fifty years. Biologists gave her a blue-collar name, Phyllis, and fittingly her descendants that began colonizing Montana were strapping big examples of *Canis lupus irremotus*, the Rocky Mountain wolf. A male radio-collared on the Sun River in 1993, where the Rockies meet the Northern Plains, weighed 120 pounds. Phyllis might have been famous in the United States, but in Canada she was just a wolf. In 1992 a Canadian hunter shot her. She was running with dogs, he said, and everybody hates dogs that rebuke our domestication and learn to go feral from a *wolf*.

By the early 1990s wolves were on their way back into the American West, at least partially of their own volition. But not entirely. After years of epic battles, wolf recovery had come up with new strategies like "experimental, non-essential populations" (translation: endangered species of animals actually *could* be shot if they depredated on livestock) and offers by the environmental group Defenders of Wildlife to *pay* ranchers for any stock wolves might kill. So under the recovery provisions of the Endangered Species Act of 1973, the Fish and Wildlife Service in 1995 released Canadian gray wolves into remote Rocky Mountain locations in Idaho and Montana. And most famously of all, into Yellowstone National Park. A few years later the Mexican Wolf Recovery Team made a similar release of Mexican wolves into the Blue Range of southeastern Arizona. North American gray wolves were now on a mission from the gods, repopulating the earth after the devastation of a great war.

A female wolf becomes sexually mature in the winter before her second birthday, and for my wolf hybrid Ysa that time arrived in the winter of 1991–1992. Ysa's pups were born during a cold, rainy night, and maybe it was the rain— maybe it was her inexperience—that decided her not to have them in one of the mine-shaft-sized dens she'd excavated. Instead she bore them on the flat, open ground, and since she couldn't keep them in a warm pile without a depression, she lost five. That left two males and two females, which she moved into one of the dens once the rain stopped. For months she and Wily had

My female wolf-hybrid Ysa and her pups with Wily. Dan Flores photo.

been howling—probably the first wolf howls in that part of West Texas since the 1920s—and hearing only coyotes and their own echoes in the Southern Plains wolf vacuum. Maybe that's why she had that whopping litter.

From the time I first pulled the pups out of the den when they were three weeks old—little walruses with ears already erect and muzzles already elongating, already growling at one another—I handled them almost daily. But I wanted to watch my wolf-hybrids raise and teach their pups. What I failed to anticipate was that they would teach them to be something very close to wild animals.

Neotony, or the biological tendency of offspring to spend a significant percentage of their lives in the company of their parents, is one of the things we humans share with canids, and I got to see some remarkable teaching close up that spring. I saw the vocalizations and expressions the pups resorted to in order to prompt their parents to regurgitate meals for them. I witnessed Wily's instruction in how to avoid rattlesnakes, and I was rapt at Ysa's cat-like demonstrations of how to pounce hapless plains woodrats that idiotically kept blundering into their pen. I had dreams about the pups' wild circuits around their enclosure with their parents, tails tucked under and rollicking along in a lope that looked like gray waves surging above a green surf. One dusk a pair of coyotes took possession of the low hills across the road and started to yip and yodel. The wolves froze, peered for a moment at the coyotes . . . and then threw back their heads and joined in, the pups' adolescent howls breaking into yips and barks that were indistinguishable from the high-pitched yodeling of the coyotes.

They were all individuals. One, a little female that was a clone of her dad, was curious and happy and friendly. Two—a male and female—were near-twins, yellow-eyed with striking wolf markings and gray pelage, achingly beautiful in their nervous alertness. Another male I called Big Boy was James Dean sullen. And wild. A few months later his new owner left him with a vet I also used, who later told me what transpired. Administering Big Boy's shots, both vet and assistant left the room for a minute. When they returned Big Boy had vanished. After looking everywhere in the clinic for him for more than an hour, the vet had to call the owner with the news that they had somehow lost his wolf. Four days later, searching for a rare medicine, an assistant climbed up on a chair and opened the door of a cabinet that was at ceiling level. Inside, tucked behind bottles and boxes and utterly silent, was the six-month-old wolf, hidden away in a cabinet whose door he had pulled shut.

A couple of years after they had their only litter, Wily and Ysa accompanied me on a move that spanned much of the American West. After almost fifteen years as a plainsman, I switched allegiances, from the sere, dusty, horizontal yellow to the vertical blue and green of the Rocky Mountains. Just as the Northern Rocky Mountain Wolf Recovery Team was finally releasing the first wolves in seventy-five years to inhabit the sprawling public lands mountains of Idaho and Montana, I moved from Texas to Montana and bought land and built a house in the Bitterroot Valley, dead in the midst of new/old wolf country.

It was a remarkable stroke of luck, a chance to witness the historical flipside of those final motions of wolf annihilation in the 1920s. I was on hand for the birth of the first wild wolf pups to be whelped in the Bitterroot Valley of Montana in three-quarters of a century. I got to sit out on my deck at night and hear wolves howling in the nearby Sapphire Mountains. I drove past wolves hit by cars on the highway into town. The local papers daily ran wolf stories. By the late 1990s the Three-Mile wolf pack, a large pack of wolves that fairly quickly had established themselves in the Bitterroot, were hunting elk in the ridges just above my house. Wolf-deprived for all my life, I had landed in the middle of wolfsong redux in the West.

One spring, driving home late from Missoula near midnight, within a mile of my house five big canine forms loped across the dirt road at the edge of my headlamps. I knew at once they were part of the Three-Mile pack, and as quickly as I could enlist reflexes I flipped on the brights in my Jeep and swerved to a stop so my lights bathed the grassy slopes where they now trotted, their eyes lit green like fireflies receding across a pond. I leaped into the cold night, straining to see, then jumped back in the Jeep, jockeying to position it for better light, all for a very specific reason.

At a party in Missoula a couple of years before, a wolf biologist had told me that the Three-Mile pack included several black wolves, news that had silently made the hair stand on the back of my neck. Wily, the wolf hybrid I had hauled to Texas from Alaska in 1990, was gone by then; he had been my constant companion for nine years before his allotted time ran out. But Ysa, my yellow-eyed, coal-black female wolf, had been with me in Montana for only a few months when one October afternoon, after a couple of high-speed circuits around the pasture, she had turned and trotted up the driveway. And disappeared. Although Wily and I had roamed the hills for months looking, calling, and howling for her, we never saw her again. In a state as bristling with firearms as Montana, I had strong intuitions about her fate. But there had always been some small hope: there were wild wolves in the mountains by then, and she would have come into oestrus that winter.

Watching those five pairs of illuminated green eyes recede from view that night, I strained till my eyes crossed trying to see a black form among them. Of course I thought to call her name, and on occasion since, prodded by the unresolved mystery of what happened to her, have wished mightily that I had. But in fact I did not shout her name into the Montana night. I watched the green fireflies disappear, then drove on home.

A decade after that midnight wolf sighting near home, my fiancée Sara and I are standing shoulder-to-shoulder with thirty or so other people alongside the slender pavement that winds gracefully through Yellowstone's Lamar Valley. It is September 2013, and like everyone else here, many of whom now make pilgrimages from around the country and the world to do this, we are peering through a spotting scope trained on a scene unfolding in the sagebrush half a mile away. A herd of pronghorns is fording the shallow Lamar River on dainty legs directly in front of the crowd, but that is not what has everyone riveted. The Gray Wolf Restoration Team released seven wolf packs from Canada into Yellowstone in 1995 and 1996, and this morning a pack called the Junction Butte pack—descendants of the wolves that fought for control of the prized Lamar Valley in the 1990s—has pulled down a bison across the river. In September 2013 the Junction Butte pack consists of eleven wolves, led by a gray alpha female the wolf watchers call "Ragged Tail" and a tall, thin male known as "Puff," a moniker from his puppy years when sarcoptic mange left him with mere patches of fur. The wolf cognoscenti here regard Puff as the best hunter in the park, and he has proved it this morning.

The problem for the wolves is that 1,500 pounds of bison on the ground has not just lured in magpies, ravens, eagles, and coyotes. It has also attracted grizzlies, specifically a large boar and a sow trailing three young cubs. The roadside watchers are thus privileged to see a genuine ancient spectacle. It is a fury of sound and motion marked by distant snarls and piercing barks as the wolves circle and feint while the grizzlies charge and swipe with huge paws, birds swirl and dive above the melee, and coyotes and bear cubs watch from a safe distance, the cubs looking more than a little stunned by the wild action around them. In the early twenty-first century, this is the one remaining place in the Lower Forty-Eight where human observers can still witness this classic confrontation of the American Serengeti, featuring all the remaining charismatic species (save wild horses) that once defined the Great Plains in the eyes of the world.

I adore getting to see something like this in Yellowstone, or knowing that the park's Northern Range elk herd—twenty years ago a wildly overpopulated, aspen-destroying machine of 17,000 animals—is now down to 6,500. My regret is for the iconic homeland of all these animals, the Great Plains, so given over to private lands, crops, and livestock that wolf recovery in our time has had to unfold exclusively in the public lands of the Mountain West. From those first releases in Wyoming, Idaho, and Montana in the mid-1990s, wolf populations in the Northern Rockies shot up to 1,700 animals in barely more than a decade. Northern Rockies wolves had soon colonized Washington and Oregon, and transient wolves began appearing in California, Utah, and even as far south as the North Rim of the Grand Canyon in Arizona. With this success the Fish and Wildlife Service in 2011 pronounced Rocky Mountain wolves "recovered" under the Endangered Species Act and turned management over to the states involved. Idaho and Montana promptly established wolf hunting

The new 2015 endangered Mexican gray wolf recovery rule will allow wolves to repopulate parts of the Southern Plains for the first time since federal hunters exterminated gray wolves from the plains in the 1920s. From the US Fish and Wildlife Mexican Gray Wolf Recovery Plan, 2015.

seasons (Montana wolf hunters killed 230 in the 2013–2014 season). Wyoming's Old West attempt to return wolves to shoot-on-sight vermin status, however, resulted in the federal government reestablishing control over wolves there, as well as in the western Great Lakes states, in 2014.

The Northern Plains, home to so much wolf history, has lain outside the official recovery areas, but of course it has not taken wolves on either side of the plains long to work their way back to their ancient haunts. In 2011 a black male wolf that biologists had radio-collared near the Grand Tetons showed up 300 miles out on the plains, in eastern Montana and Wyoming. The following year a wolf killed near Custer, South Dakota, turned out to be a buffalo wolf from the Great Lakes population on the other side of the plains. Conceding that a wolf had tried to colonize South Dakota, the state's wildlife director was quick to assure the public that "there's no place for wolves in South Dakota." South Dakota, he averred, was just too "inhabited" for wolves.

Unpredictably, it appears that the best possibility for a return of gray wolves to the Great Plains after the aberration of the past century will come out of the beleaguered, far less successful Mexican wolf recovery program in the Southwest. Using wolves from a captive breeding program centered around a single pregnant female wolf captured in Mexico in 1980, this wolf recovery project has limped along since 1998 with releases into a tiny, 7,000-square-mile mountain range in eastern Arizona that has struggled to sustain the fed's modest goal of 100 wild wolves there. But a lawsuit by environmentalists produced a miracle in 2015. Now there is a new Mexican Wolf Recovery Rule that will not only triple the number of wolves in the Southwest, to a goal of as many as 325, but redraws the boundaries of the recovery area to drape across 154,000 square miles of Arizona and New Mexico.

South of the Interstate 40 corridor, extending from the California border on the west to the Texas border on the east, is now to be wolf country. At long last, almost exactly a century after private wolfers and federal hunters wiped out the last wolf packs on the Southern Plains, south of a line from Amarillo to Albuquerque there will be slender, graceful Mexican gray wolves, coming again to re-wild at least this part of the American Serengeti.

LOVING THE PLAINS,
HATING THE PLAINS,
RE-WILDING THE PLAINS

8

And what a splendid contemplation too, when one (who has traveled
these realms, and can duly appreciate them) imagines them as they
might in future be seen (by some great protecting policy of government)
preserved in their pristine beauty and wildness, in a magnificent park.

—George Catlin, on the Missouri River, 1832

The vanishing prairie is as worth preserving for the wilderness idea as the
alpine forests.

—Wallace Stegner, "The Wilderness Letter"

I know almost nothing useful about W. H. Auden, the twentieth-century British writer-critic, except that once he wrote
these lines, which I committed to memory: "I cannot see a
plain without a shudder—'Oh God, please, please, don't ever
make me live there!'" There's an exclamation point at the end of
that sentence. Auden's sentiment, I think—and most modern
Americans I feel sure would agree with it—captures the early
twenty-first-century view of the matter nicely. The Great Plains
is not, by any standard measure of aesthetics, an admired part
of America these days, a loved landscape of our contemporary
times the way we love the mountains or the oceans or even the
deserts. As even Deborah Epstein Popper, a proponent of a future Buffalo Commons on the plains remarked during a tour of
the Southern Plains of Oklahoma and Texas in the early 1990s:
"This is terrible country! . . . There is *nothing here*. It is un-country.
It shouldn't be allowed to exist!"

Anyone who has driven an automobile across the country Popper is describing recognizes her feeling. Through the car windows a vast emptiness of space assaults the senses. The horizon encircles the world like the rim of an immense plate, and no matter how fast you drive it recedes in front of you, eventually placing you in a kind of Twilight Zone of suspended forward motion. The wind buffets and rocks your car. There are stretches where, if you roll down the windows, the country smells like a dustier Iowa, with more than a hint of ammonia, feedlots, and hog farms. Other than the frequent sight, oddly in these sere expanses, of thousands of waterfowl threading the blue bowl overhead, you see virtually no wildlife—maybe a few pronghorns if you look really hard, more likely a coyote rocking across the road. You probably don't see a single prairie dog. Much of the day the harsh light is almost too bright to look at, or at least it is when the light isn't diffused into a brown pall by agriculture going airborne. Tiny burgs memorable for the amount of windblown waste snagged on chainmesh fences loom and recede along laser-straight highways. Billboards unintentionally advertising the plains social order—Jesus, cowboy boots, farm machinery, banking loans, pesticides, the Denver Broncos—actually become welcome breaks in the monotony. A pervading notion characterizes such drives: "I wish to God I'd have flown."

So we react to the modern world of the Great Plains. But it was not always so. There was a time not so long ago when the reactions were very different. To stoke our sense of wonder at the variability of human response to place, let me quote a few of them. They are about the same place I just described, and that is a remarkable thing.

The first is from Sir William Dunbar, a Scottish scientist from Natchez, Mississippi, whom President Thomas Jefferson engaged to help him lead what would have been the first American exploration into the heart of the Southern Plains. Situated as he was on the forested edges of fascination with the country farther west, Dunbar re-created for Jefferson the sense of excitement western travelers had about the Great Plains two centuries ago.

"By the expression plains, or prairies," he told the president, "it is not to be understood a dead flat without any eminences." He went on: "The western prairies are very different; the expression signifies only a country without timber. These prairies are neither flat nor hilly, but undulating in gently swelling lawns, and expanding into spacious valleys." Dunbar had not been into the interior himself but he had spoken with those who had. "Those who have viewed only a skirt of these prairies speak of them with a degree of enthusiasm, as if it were only there that nature was to be found truly perfect." Dunbar finally ended his passage this way: "They declare that the fertility and beauty of the vegetation, the extreme richness of the valleys, the coolness and excellent quality of the water found everywhere, the salubrity of the atmosphere, and above all, the grandeur of the enchanting landscape which this country presents inspires the soul with sensations not to be felt in any other region of the globe."

There were "wonderful stories of wonderful productions," Dunbar told Jefferson. Travelers spoke of mountains of pure or partial salt, and silver ore lying about in chunks on the prairie. But especially compelling were the stories of the wildlife riches of the great prairies. There were bears, "tygers," wolves, and buffalo and other herds of grazers beyond imagination, even great herds of horses that had gone wild. There were stories of giant water serpents, although Dunbar did not credit those. But all the rest he believed to be real. It filled him with wonder, which he passed on to the American president.

Dunbar himself never got to see the region of those wonderful productions, but on one of the maps Jefferson was perusing—an untitled map assembled by American General James Wilkinson in 1804—the country Dunbar described was already labeled the "Great Plains." But many Americans in the Jeffersonian Age did get to see and experience the wonder of these Great Plains. Among several such passages from Lewis and Clark's ascent of the Missouri River into the western savannas, Meriwether Lewis wrote, on September 17, 1804, as the party was just entering the plains in today's South Dakota, that "the shortness and virdue of the grass gave the plains the appearance throughout it's whole extent of beatifull bowling-green in fine order." None of the party could quite believe the wildlife spectacle before them: "a great number of wolves of the small kind, halks [hawks] and some pole-cats were to be seen. . . . this senery already rich pleasing and beatiful was still farther heightened by immence herds of Buffaloe, deer Elk and Antelopes which we saw in every direction feeding on the hills and plains."

Lewis's exploring contemporary, Zebulon Montgomery Pike, in 1806 found the High Plains of the Arkansas River country rather more barren than Lewis's bucolic scene. He thought the Southern Plains a match for the "sandy desarts of Africa." That same area of the plains inspired the Stephen Long exploring party of 1819–1820 to pronounce the central and southern stretches of the plains "unfit for agriculture" and a "barrier" to the continuing expansion of Americans westward. They did note, though, that "travelling over a dusty plain of sand and gravel, barren as the deserts of Arabia" was actually never tedious because of the thrilling wildlife spectacle, whose closest analogue once again was Africa. On the Arkansas, Captain John Bell wrote, they were endlessly in sight of "thousands of buffalo on both sides of the river." Naturalist Thomas Say, the official discoverer of the coyote, added less romantically that the vast herds of animals they saw were never without a roiling, noisy, raucus accompaniment of "famine-pinched wolves and flights of obscene and ravenous birds."

Americans and those who weren't citizens of the continent were startled and curiously amazed by descriptions like this. The writer Washington Irving was enthralled enough to go himself and then write *Travels in the Prairie*. New York novelist James Fenimore Cooper wrote a Leatherstocking novel about the plains. The painter of Indians, George Catlin, was besotted and did his best, which often wasn't so great, to capture prairie landscapes, as with his *Big Bend on the Upper Missouri*. Germans who trained with the legendary naturalist Alexander von Humboldt explored around the world, but one of the places they sought out was the American plains. Prince Maximilian of Wied-Neuwied was one, who brought with him the amazing animal painter Karl Bodmer. It was Bodmer, with epic paintings like *Landscape with Herd of Buffalo on the Upper Missouri*, who went west with talents that could take the measure of the Great Plains. His collection of watercolors done on the Missouri in the early 1830s are some of our very best American Serengeti time-travel enablers. And there was John James Audubon. Of course. Audubon and his sons did almost the full suite of plains fauna, an ecological portrait gallery, from their 1843 trip up the Missouri. And in 1849 Francis Parkman told readers what it was like to "Jump Off" from the East into the great prairies in one of the celebrated books of the century, *The Oregon Trail*.

Even after the Civil War, when travelers, naturalists, and artists going west were responding to the Hudson River School's focus on American mountains, the plains remained unforgettable for many, at least until the slaughterhouse of the market hunt commenced. The Russian nobleman, Grand Duke Alexis, went on his Great Plains safari in 1872, continuing a tradition of European elite hunter/adventurers on the Great Plains that went back to Sir William Drummond Stewart and Sir George Gore. American military officer Richard Irving Dodge wrote several books about the plains for an avid readership. So did George Armstrong Custer's wife, Elizabeth. Teddy Roosevelt fled the East and family deaths to live on two ranches in the Dakotas, writing books like *Ranch Life and Hunting Trails*. Across the Atlantic, the plains—as ever—continued to intrigue the same set of eclectic adventurers who searched out the sources of the Nile or became white hunters in East Africa. The naturalist Ewen Cameron and his well-born photographer bride, Evelyn, went to the Montana badlands on their honeymoon in 1889 and never left.

Even in the twentieth century, after the previous three-decade slaughterhouse had rendered the plains eerily silent but before modern agriculture ripped the grass off much of the country, the region could still entrance. For the bohemian Mabel Dodge, journeying by train to New Mexico, the plains seemed a desert, but a beautiful one "that rolled away for miles and miles, empty, smooth, and uninterrupted. . . . I thought I had never seen a landscape reduced to such simple elements." Young Georgia O'Keeffe, seemingly sentenced to a career as an art teacher in Outback Texas during World War I, out on the undulating sweeps near Canyon marveled at how you could just drive or walk "off into space." To which she added: "It is absurd the way I love this country." Writing her friend Daniel Catton Rich as late as 1949, O'Keeffe told him: "Crossing the Panhandle of Texas is always a very special event for me . . . driving in the early morning toward the dawn and rising sun—The plains are not like anything else and I always wonder why I go other places."

Other twentieth-century women artists, like Mari Sandoz and Willa Cather, reacted similarly to the country that had produced them. As Cather told a back-home newspaper in 1921: "I go everywhere. I admire all kinds of country . . . But when I strike the open plains, something happens. I'm home. I breathe differently. That love of great spaces, of rolling open country like the sea—it's the grand passion of my life. I tried for years to get over it. I've stopped trying. It's incurable."

Even without the great herds and their predators, with the landscape itself still largely intact the Great Plains struck many as terrestrial poetry. But people who got to see the "entire heaven and entire earth," uncountable wildlife speckling the undulating sweeps, never forgot it. Not surprising, then, that America's poet laureate of the nineteenth century, that ultimate American lover of being in the world, got captivated. Walt Whitman saw the plains for the first time after the Civil War, when the animals and native inhabitants still held sway and the frontier was then hosting one of the greatest dramas in the world. His reaction was simple and direct: "I am not so sure but that the prairies and plains, while less stunning at first sight, last longer, fill the esthetic sense fuller, precede all the rest, and make North America's characteristic landscape."

There's an obvious question to pose here. What has happened to make the modern reaction to the Great Plains so different now? How, in other words, do you get from Walt Whitman and Willa Cather to "un-country"?

The answer self-evidently has to do with the extraordinary transformation the Great Plains underwent at our hands in the late nineteenth and early twentieth centuries. In effect we dismantled and demolished a 10,000-year-old ecology, very likely one of the most exciting natural spectacles in the world, in the space of a half-century. There were people who made careers out of that loss, among them the artists Charlie Russell and Frederic Remington and the writer Zane Grey, and what they mourned was what they saw as life in "the wilderness," a thrilled-to-the-marrow life among native people and thronging wildlife and nature. As Grey believed, the West had offered the world one last chance to live in a state of nature as natural men and women. And then modern America had withdrawn the offer.

For women especially tuned in to the plains, like Cameron and O'Keeffe and Cather, it was not wildlife beyond imagining but a sense of freedom derived from a vast, uncluttered space of grasslands that appealed so strongly. "Space" and "like the ocean" served as code-words for the freedom available to independent women on the open grasslands of the plains in the early twentieth century. The novelist Mari Sandoz mourned the loss of the world of the Indians and in her books wrote longingly of the wild creatures that had blanketed her home state of Nebraska, but in the twentieth century she also thrilled to the effect of space O'Keeffe and Cather mentioned.

But historical forces that mounted in intensity as railroads and ranching and farming arrived destroyed much even of that Great Plains. The war on plains wildlife was the unkindest throat-slitting in the creation of "un-country," but there was more. Act two was the agricultural assault. Because level, grassy plains did not appear to present the kind of obstacles to agriculture other landscapes did, with the animals removed, from the 1850s to the 1930s, homesteading policies privatized the overwhelming bulk of the American Great Plains. In western Kansas/eastern Colorado, the Big Breakout—that term referred to plowing the grasses under—took place under the nineteenth-century homestead laws and in the decades on either side of the twentieth century. In Oklahoma the land rushes resulting from Indian allotment was the trigger. Settlers broke out western Nebraska, the Dakotas, eastern Montana, and eastern New Mexico after Congress passed the Enlarged Homestead Act in 1909. In Texas, with its anomalous lands history and long devotion to privatization, the sale and breakup of the XIT Ranch in 1915, along with disposed railroad tracts, brought farmers by the trainload to the Llano Estacado and Rolling Plains there.

The losses to the foundations of plains ecology, the loss of the grasses themselves, are staggering to contemplate. Conservation biologists now hold up the tallgrass prairie, whose extent on the southern Blackland Prairie agriculture took down to less than 1 percent of its original coverage, as one of the unforgivable sins against nature in continental history. Losses in the areal extent of the grasslands in the mid-grass and shortgrass plains are also mind-boggling. By 2001 Saskatchewan had only 19 percent of its native prairie left. North Dakota possessed only 28 percent of its remaining prairie at the beginning of the century, and that was before the Bakken oil boom. Texas has an average of 20 percent of its prairie today, although the part of the High Plains I know best, the central Llano Estacado, is in far worse shape. Lubbock County, where I lived, by the 1980s had lost 97 percent of its native grasslands. Literally all that remained was in Yellow House Canyon, a grassy gorge too rugged to plow up and plant to cotton. It was the very spot I sought out to homestead.

The contrast between the Great Plains and Rocky Mountains in Lewis and Clark's day was clear in the party's longing to escape the wildlife-poor mountains and return to the plains. In our time, two centuries of history have accomplished an entire reversal: the federally managed Rockies are now home to most of the West's wildlife, which fled there from the plains, while the privately owned Great Plains has become a monument to the American sacrifice of nature.

But this is a three-act story. Once we thrilled to the Great Plains. Then we wreaked havoc on its ecology and many came to despise the result. For the past three-quarters of a century, a third phase—undoubtedly not the last—has been building momentum. As a result of some bad historical misses, to an extent stage three is still a vision. But there have been some successes, too.

Re-wilding the Great Plains with its traditional charismatic big animals means finding landscapes where the antelope can play. In our time, environmentalism and conservation biology recognize natural grasslands and prairie ecosystems as some of the most under-preserved natural regions around the world. Despite an international push to set aside grand grassland parks to preserve the charismatic wild animals of the African plains—Serengeti National Park in Tanzania, Masai Mara National Reserve in Kenya, Kruger National Park in South Africa—conservation in the United States ironically overlooked or bypassed our own Great Plains in the federal preservation agenda. It's beyond ironic that the first visionary call for an American national park, George Catlin's in 1832, was for a park on the Great Plains, because the National Park Service has long been an embarrassment in its apathy towards plains parks. That began to change in the 1930s, but not before there were too many huge misses.

The major American conservation initiatives that gave us our national forest and national park public lands a century ago focused on western landscapes that were too high, too rocky, or too rough to farm. That meant mountain ranges and western canyons, places like the Rockies, Sierras, Cascades, and the Colorado Plateau became the bastions of the public lands. Except for a scattering of island mountain ranges on the Northern Plains, the powers that fashioned the western public lands almost entirely ignored the Great Plains, a country deemed grassy enough to ranch, with few impediments to farming, therefore ripe for homesteading. During the initial phase of national park history the scenic ideals of the Romantic Age also meant sublime scenery, by the standards of the age (and Old World tastes) almost always landscapes of great vertical relief.

Thus Yellowstone and Glacier and Rocky Mountain national parks, along with the great canyons like Yosemite, Zion, and the Grand Canyon, became the *ne plus ultra* examples of American parks, not merely monumental, but monumentally *vertical*. No landscapes on the plains seemed very interesting to a park service with this kind of value system. Although early on the NPS did accept three Great Plains parks—Sullys Hill in Nebraska, Platt in Oklahoma, and Wind Cave in South Dakota—the three totaled fewer than 30,000 acres altogether compared to 2.2 million acres for Yellowstone alone. Eventually the NPS downlisted all but South Dakota's Wind Cave, which did acquire a herd of pure and free-roaming bison, although the park never grew beyond 33,000 acres. Other than Wind Cave, almost the only Great Plains nature preservation of the early twentieth century came when Teddy Roosevelt's administration proclaimed a small mountain range in southwestern Oklahoma the Wichita Mountains Wildlife Refuge in 1905.

As the park service moved slowly away from what parks PR man Robert Sterling Yard called the "Scenic Supremacy of the United States" towards some incorporation of ecosystem values in its criteria for parks, a new problem for the plains surfaced. Until passage of the Land and Water Conservation Fund Act in 1964, the park service had no acquisition budget, and that became an almost insurmountable obstacle in parts of the plains, where private ownership of the grasslands had reached the point where almost every potential site for a plains park that might house remnant plains animals confronted the obstacle of buying up private lands. In the 1920s the pioneer of community ecology, Victor Shelford, and a group called the Committee of Ecology of the Grasslands began to press for large Great Plains preserves based on ecological factors rather than scenic spectacles that would humble European visitors. They studied eleven sites, found four more than acceptable, and eventually submitted one (spanning three-quarters of a million acres in Nebraska and South Dakota) to the park service and Congress. But nothing came of it.

The philosophical direction the park service took in its early years was the result of the personal vision of its first director, a New Englander named Stephen Mather. Mather developed a set of evaluative criteria for new additions to the parks and national monuments system that his successor and protégé, Horace Albright, followed well into the 1930s. The prime directive in Mather's criteria was a large, preferably contiguous area with natural features so extraordinary as to be of national interest. Mather wanted scenic parks, and he wanted them to be of a particularly unusual and impressive quality. So while scientists like Victor Shelford were thinking in terms of preserving representative ecosystems, the park service had the Mather scenery inertia to overcome. Consequently, as park service personnel began to look beyond the mountains and to heed the scientists' interest in the Great Plains, they concentrated their efforts not on the rolling, grassy uplands most typical of the region, but on the more dramatic badlands and canyon lands country, the plains' erosional equivalents of the Colorado Plateau. Plains history and the success of Yellowstone had them thinking about animals, too, but scenery was always first.

The problem was that no landscapes on the Great Plains measured up when compared to the scale of a Zion or a Grand Canyon. In the 1920s and 1930s the NPS disappointed the ecologists by turning down one proposal after another. But one area of the plains, the South Dakota Badlands, set the plains on the road eventually to a second plains national park.

Local advocates had proposed the yellow-and-cream South Dakota Badlands as a park as early as 1909, and since much of its acreage consisted of
"excess" Indian lands and parcels passed over in the homesteading process, it
was a prime candidate for a park service with no money. But as a badlands its
sparse grass cover seemed too thin for wild herds in the Yellowstone model.
And plenty of people in the park service held the proposed "Teton National
Park's" lack of vertical relief against it. At the time the broadly experienced
Roger Toll was the chief investigator for new parks in the NPS. Toll visited the
area in July of 1928 and within days decided that "it is not a supreme scenic
feature of national importance." The Badlands, he explained to his Washington superiors, "are surpassed in grandeur, beauty and interest by the Grand
Canyon National Park and by Bryce National Park."

Sixty percent of the Badlands had remained part of the public domain,
though, and when the state of South Dakota agreed to acquire and transfer to
the NPS 90 percent of the private holdings, Toll proposed a consolation. He
recommended that the NPS use the Antiquities Act (whose targets were landscapes of unusual archaeological or geologic interest) to proclaim 68,000
acres of the area a national monument. Congress quickly approved Badlands
National Monument in 1929. Eventually enlarged to some 250,000 acres, it
became the Great Plains' largest chunk of public lands with President Roosevelt's proclamation opening it in 1939. Bison were gone, pronghorns very
nearly so, and across the gray and saffron mounds and cliffs, hunters had
already wiped out the famous local population of Rocky Mountain bighorns
decades before. All three species could be (and were) recovered, but the Badlands' often sparse grass cover and relatively small size kept it from becoming
a plains version of Yellowstone's wealth in wildlife.

Something similar happened with North Dakota's Little Missouri Badlands, which the NPS initially found "too barren" for a national park. At first
local ranchers opposed the idea of a park vehemently. But rancher opposition
swirled away with the Dust Bowl and the Depression, and the NPS finally acquired the area in 1947—but as a historical/memorial park based on President
Theodore Roosevelt's presence in the area. With its pronghorns and bison
herd and, eventually, wild horses, North Dakota's Theodore Roosevelt National Park came closer to the Great Plains ecosystem park Shelford and the
ecologists were calling for. But the park's two units were small, barely 70,000
acres total, and coyotes excepted, the NPS allowed none of the big predators
like the grizzlies (and eventually wolves) that roamed Yellowstone.

The public lands reserve on the Northern Plains that would eventually have the most promise as a Catlin-like wild possibility began life modestly in 1936 as the Fort Peck Game Range, initially managed by the Bureau of Biological Survey. The bureau had sent its well-respected ecologist, Olaus Murie, to report on the area surrounding the reservoir that the Corps of Engineers was creating on the Missouri River, expecting Murie to suggest a waterfowl refuge. Murie's conclusion was that the broken, badlands-studded valley held much greater promise as a preserve for big wild animals. From small things, large results. By the 1970s the Game Range had become the Charles M. Russell National Wildlife Refuge, and soon enough it was the second-largest one in the Lower Forty-Eight. For re-wilding the Great Plains, its steady accretion in size made it a real possibility, and grassland conservationists began paying very close attention.

And the Southern Plains? During the 1930s, when scientists were trying to pull the NPS in the direction of ecosystem thinking, actually it was on the Southern Plains where—at least for a few years—park personnel finally began to toy with the idea of a large ecosystem Great Plains park, one that would have gone far towards recapturing the plains' wildlife spectacle and ancient poetry with an Africa-style park. With an omnibus parks bill in 1978, the NPS would eventually upgrade both Badlands and Theodore Roosevelt to full national park status, and along with Wind Cave and Saskatchewan's Grassland National Park, established in 1981, these gave the Northern Plains a fair start in the direction of eventual re-wilding. The Southern Plains, on the other hand, would end up entirely lacking a national park of any size. The plains below the Arkansas River does possess a scattering of national wildlife refuges and very small national monuments, notably Alibates Flint Quarry in the Texas Panhandle and Capulin Volcano on the New Mexico plains. But in the twenty-first century, the Texas, Oklahoma, Kansas, Colorado, and New Mexico plains remain "un-country." How that happened is quite a story.

It is also historically odd. With the exception of the Black Hills, Palo Duro Canyon—the great canyon the Red River carved through the Llano Estacado plateau in West Texas—was probably the most famous landscape on the Great Plains. A Comanche hideaway and home to Charles Goodnight's ranch, Palo Duro was both a scenic and vertical jewel inset into vast grasslands. It seemed a perfect locale for the large Great Plains park ecologists were hoping for. The Texas congressional delegation began bringing Palo Duro up as a potential park as early as 1908. But the big canyon had long since gone under private fence, and the truth was that only a handful of people had ever seen it, at least until a young Georgia O'Keeffe exhibited paintings of it in New York in 1917. Once when it was opened to the public, 14,000 people showed up to see it on one day.

A 60-mile long, 800-foot deep roar of color, Palo Duro not only had historic and scenic values, it also exposed 250 million years of North American geology going back to the Permian Age. Goodnight and his wife, Mary, had preserved a small herd of distinctive Southern Plains buffalo on their ranch in the canyon, and above the canyon rim there were intact grasslands where thousands of pronghorns and wild horses had once roamed, and could again. Texas was already planning a small state park there in the early 1930s, and Palo Duro had some local champions, among them writer and historian J. Evetts Haley, who was writing a biography of Goodnight. Even Enos Mills, "the John Muir of the Rockies," journeyed to West Texas to support a national park in Palo Duro. But it seems to have been Horace Albright's chance layover in Amarillo in 1932, leading to a perusal of photographs of Palo Duro, that led the director to decide to add the big plains canyon to an upcoming investigative tour of possible Texas park sites by Roger Toll.

Until his untimely death in a car crash later that decade, Toll was a one-man-make-it-or-break-it whirlwind for the NPS, the man whose opinion basically gave the West most of the national parks it got in the 1930s and 1940s. At the time of his Texas tour in the winter of 1933–1934, Toll was still very much a Mather-style scenery advocate. But at park service offices in Washington the ecologists evidently regarded his upcoming examination of Palo Duro Canyon as the master-stroke of plains preservation they hoped for. While Toll journeyed to Texas, the scientists were assembling maps and materials for the creation of a million-acre "National Park of the Plains" around Palo Duro, a huge swath of territory half the size of Yellowstone that would have included the canyons but also adjacent grasslands all around the canyon rims with the idea of restoring key wildlife like bison and pronghorns.

In company with Haley, Toll spent four days in Palo Duro in January 1934, traversing much of its sixty-mile length from a series of waterfalls at the upper end down to the stunning Narrows gorge of a dramatic side-canyon called Tule, which explorer Randolph Marcy had described in 1852 as the most dramatic scene he'd ever witnessed. Toll was impressed: he regarded Palo Duro as scenically superior to the Badlands he had recommended for monument status six years earlier. But whereas the Grand Canyon was monumental, like the Dakota Badlands, Palo Duro nudged Toll's scenic meter only up to "interesting and picturesque." In sum, as Toll wrote in his report, the NPS's scale of sublimity made Palo Duro "not well qualified for a national park as its scenery is not of outstanding national importance." He told the new NPS director, Arno Cammerer, that unfortunately, "It would rate below the present scenic national parks." Toll was also concerned about real estate values in Texas, where land wasn't quite as inexpensive as it had been in the Dakotas.

Even as Toll was damning Palo Duro with faint praise, ecosystem values continued to gain ground in the NPS. And the West Texas canyon had now caught the eye of the NPS. The service's new Everglades National Park in Florida, established for its ecological values instead of classic scenery reasons, demonstrated that NPS interest in ecosystems was now serious. And new parks like Acadia (Maine), Shenandoah (Virginia), and Great Smoky Mountains (Tennessee/North Carolina) demonstrated that it wasn't impossible to create national parks in regions lacking a public domain.

A Texas Democratic Senator named Morris Sheppard now stepped up to champion a Great Plains preserve in West Texas, more to aid the collapsing farm economy of the 1930s, you suspect, than because he was an advocate of re-wilding the Southern Plains. As High Plains farming fell apart in the Dust Bowl and the federal government took back thousands of acres of former homesteads, Sheppard began to press for a different form of federal economic salvation for the Dust Bowl region by having President Roosevelt make Palo Duro into a national monument by proclamation.

Noted geologist Herman Bumpas, an advisor to the NPS, became an inside supporter of this idea. As Bumpas told park officials in Washington, a Palo Duro Canyon National Monument seemed almost a necessity in another of the service's new themes: public education about the natural world. Located just south of Route 66, the famed principal automobile route across the country in an age when Americans were taking to the road in record numbers, Palo Duro could play the geological role of the "First Chapter of Genesis" for tourists heading west on the Mother Road, Bumpas said, since its bottom-most geological strata ended exactly where those at the rim of the Grand Canyon began.

So in October 1938, the park service initiated a second review of Palo Duro Canyon. This time the idea was far more modest than the earlier vision of a Great Plains park half the size of Yellowstone. The planned Southern Plains national monument of 134,658 acres would be twice the size of the Theodore

Roosevelt unit, although not quite up to Badlands size. By this point in the evolution of the park service, the evaluation strategy was much more systematic than when Roger Toll's visual comparison of a landscape with Glacier or the Grand Canyon could decide its fate. From the Santa Fe regional offices, eight NPS experts in as many fields descended on Palo Duro during March and April 1939.

The end result was an eighty-nine-page document assessing everything from the botany and wildlife of the canyon to its geological and historical significance. The national monument report naturally included a detailed estimate of the acquisition cost, too, a figure that ran to $294,000, plus $264,000 to fold in the 15,000-acre state park. The boundaries were to extend from the waterfalls section 35 miles down the canyon to a place called Paradise Valley, owned by Charles Goodnight's old ranch, the JA. The boundaries excluded Tule Canyon and its spectacular gorge, but future monument expansion no doubt would have taken in that section. As an indication that the park service had not yet fully embraced the idea of ecological restoration on the plains, the 1939 report did not include any significant description of bison or pronghorn restoration, let alone wild horse recovery. By that year the grand idea of a large, restored Southern Plains Yellowstone seems to have evaporated.

Of the scientists, it was the geologists who were most excited. Geologist Charles Gould made an eloquent plea in his section of the report. "From the standpoint of Geology and scenery," he wrote, "Palo Duro is well worthy of being made into a national monument. It is the most spectacular canyon, carved by erosion, anywhere on the Great Plains of North America."

In Washington the Santa Fe field team's recommendation in favor of monument status met with mixed reviews. Those who had actually seen Palo Duro were uniformly in favor of national monument status. But again, in a region of the West that almost entirely lacked public lands, the most important element was cost. What the NPS required in the 1930s was a state government or a group of wealthy patrons to step up and write the check for a new park or monument. When word got out, public support did come in, but it was mostly from places like Denver, Albuquerque, and Oklahoma City. The Texans in whose state the new national monument would reside, however, seemed oddly ambivalent. And ambivalence was the swan song for Palo Duro National Monument. When Senator Sheppard inquired about the status of the monument in 1940, Interior Secretary Harold Ickes told him that Interior stood "willing to recommend the establishment as a national monument of approximately 135,000 acres of land" once donors stepped forward to acquire the property. In Maine, North Carolina, Tennessee, and Virginia, wealthy donors and public campaigns were raising money in that same decade to acquire new park lands. But in Texas? No wealthy oil visionary from the Lone Star state stepped forward the way the Rockefellers were then doing in Jackson Hole, Wyoming, to create Grand Teton National Park.

So ambivalence, or apathy, or perhaps just ideological opposition to public lands killed a large national monument in West Texas that could eventually have served as a core for re-wilding parts of the Southern Great Plains. Losing an expansive Southern Plains national monument—to say nothing of that earlier, Catlin-like vision of a million-acre Great Plains Yellowstone around Palo Duro—were the biggest missed opportunities on the plains in the twentieth century. Texas's park division has managed since to double the size of the state park to about 30,000 acres and has created another 16,000-acre park 35 miles south along the Caprock escarpment that now has a free-roaming bison herd rounded up on the JA Ranch. Those just aren't much consolation for those who know Palo Duro's larger story.

With the release of the new Mexican gray wolf recovery rule in 2015, wolves sooner or later are going to be on the Southern Plains again. *Wild Earth Journal* has even published a re-wilding proposal for a biological corridor encircling the Caprock escarpment of the Llano Estacado where wolves and lions might thrive. But it takes public lands for a vision like that to work. In 2006 and 2007 the Nature Conservancy released highly detailed, fine-grained biodiversity/ conservation studies of both the Southern Plains and Central Plains ecoregions. They were optimistic that on the Central Plains, primarily in New Mexico, Colorado, Kansas, and Nebraska, 50 percent of 56 million acres of areal grasslands remain intact and unplowed. But 92 percent of the entire area is in private hands, only 3 percent in federal ownership, and remaining grasslands are patchy across all of it. On the Southern Plains, primarily Texas, Oklahoma, and New Mexico, conditions are even worse, with less intact grasslands and a mere 3.6 percent of the landscape in public (federal plus state) ownership.

Many small-scale conservation opportunities exist on the Central Plains and Southern Plains, but the burden of plains history rests heavy here, with little hope for re-wilding on a scale that would inspire national and international excitement. In the nineteenth century this country was sometimes called the "Zahara of North America," a wilderness its explorers said "seems particularly adapted as a range for buffaloes, wild goats, and other game." Whether anything like the opportunities of the 1930s ever stands so willing and fetching before us again appears dubious now.

In the 1950s and 1960s residents of the Great Plains and even those outside the region took for granted that we had resolved the disaster of the Dust Bowl with improved farming practices and (naturally) "technological fixes." Of course we had also managed by the 1940s to tap into the Ogallala Aquifer, with such an apparent abundance of clear, pure water surging through the well casings that the country from Texas to Nebraska launched into an era of unprecedented growth, symbolized by factory farming that often went on even during the night. Everyone from those happy generations assumed that like the rest of the West and the country, the arc of history for the region was onward and upward towards unlimited growth and population. Then, in the 1970s, the aquifer began to drop, rapidly and to depths that made pumping the water up no longer so cost-effective. Dust returned, too, and in the 1980s came census reports showing steady out-migration and falling revenues all across the plains. At that point something like a new consciousness emerged about the Great Plains, and serious reappraisal of the burden of modern plains history began.

The Colorado geographer William Riebsame has tried out evolutionary models to assess how American society actually did respond to the Dust Bowl. Riebsame contrasted true adaptations with mere "resiliency," or a tendency to rebound to its previous strategies of inhabiting a place following a major disturbance. In short, Riebsame tends to think that many of the changes Great Plains society made to combat the Dust Bowl, and now the drawdown of the Oglalla Aquifer, have tended to be resilient rather than adaptive. Contour farming, listing, and center-pivot irrigation were all merely technological refinements of what we had been doing when the crises struck. The ideas and machines that seemed to "fix" the Dust Bowl, in his view, in reality were adjustments to the market, not to nature in a semi-arid, windswept setting that's subject to periodic drought and has never done anything quite so well as grow grass and support wild grazers and predators.

What makes the future of the Great Plains scary is, of course, predicted global climate change, and at rates far faster than anything humans have ever experienced. Climate science has repeatedly singled out the Southern and Central Plains, especially, as among America's regions that will be hard-

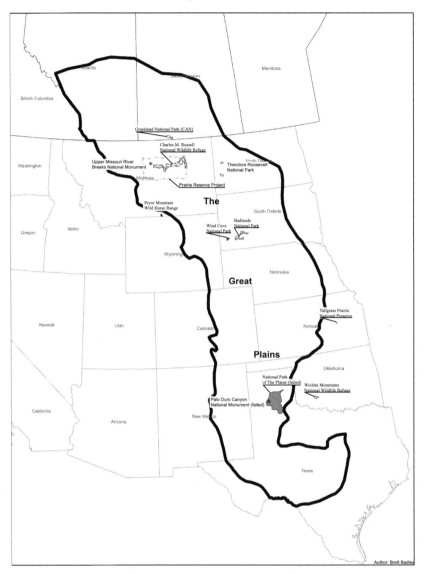

By the twenty-first century the American Serengeti shows only a small scattering of successfully preserved national landscapes, along with some regrettable failures in a region of the West that nearly got bypassed by the national parks movement. Only Montana's American Prairie Reserve holds the potential of a future Yellowstone of the Great Plains.

it by global change. Some scientists have asked us to imagine not just a repeat of the Dust Bowl, which was only a decade-long phenomenon, but mega-droughts that could change the plains so drastically as to feature a significant and rapid advance of Chihuahuan Desert conditions northward. So it seems self-evident to many that the Great Plains is on the cliff edge of a major paradigm shift, and it could be one that might make the world of the past more appealing than it has ever been. The plains artist Charlie Russell spent his whole career, even into the 1920s, trying to re-create what he thought of as a dreamtime world on the plains. He had seen the plains when "the land belonged to God" briefly, in the 1880s, and mourned the loss of it his entire life. Something like what he dreamed, we may get to live.

A new vision for the Great Plains is out there. As Frank and Deborah Popper have come to argue with respect to their Buffalo Commons idea, plains out-migration, the emergence of Indian peoples as major environmental players, endangered species recovery of wolves on the western borders of the plains, and a new excitement about ecological restoration generally are making their Buffalo Commons idea a reality, just on a smaller and more decentralized scale than they had originally envisioned.

This is no doubt a correct assessment as far as it goes. There is a great deal of private, grass-roots, and even state-based re-wilding going on across the plains. There are groups like the Southern Plains Land Trust in southeastern Colorado, which is seeking to acquire High Plains acreage for restoration. The Nature Conservancy now has an office in Amarillo to assist Texas Parks and Wildlife's long-running efforts to enlarge its Llano Estacado parks and maybe create a large, High Plains state park where buffalo, pronghorns, elk, and hopefully wild horses can roam at large again. The Great Plains Restoration Council in Denver is working as an information clearing-house for hopes to create a million-acre Buffalo Commons somewhere on the plains. Nonprofits like the American Buffalo Foundation and the High Plains Ecosystem Restoration Council are attempting to advance that cause, too. There are similar groups in the Black Hills, pushing for a "Greater Black Hills Wildlife Protection Area," and in Nebraska (where the focus is on the Sand Hills), in Kansas and Oklahoma (focused on the Flint Hills and tallgrass prairie), and in North Dakota, where the battle against the consequences of fracking and energy development rage on.

Because on the Northern Plains there is more public land in the form of

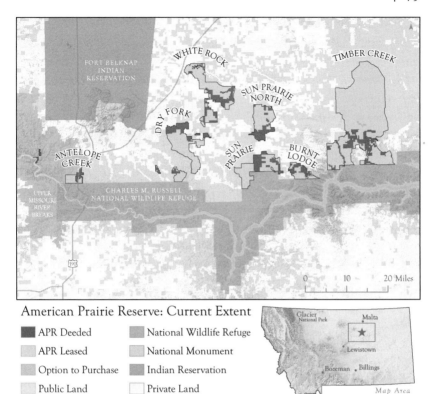

American Prairie Reserve: Current Extent

- APR Deeded
- APR Leased
- Option to Purchase
- Public Land
- National Wildlife Refuge
- National Monument
- Indian Reservation
- Private Land

The most exciting prospect for re-wilding the Great Plains with its nineteenth-century charismatic fauna is the American Prairie Reserve, which seeks to merge already protected federal lands with incisive private acquisitions to create a twenty-first-century wildlands on the Northern Plains even larger than Yellowstone Park.

parks, national grasslands, and Bureau of Land Management parcels, and because Indians there managed to retain tribal reservation holdings in a way that didn't happen on the Southern Plains, the best hope for a grand George Catlin plains wildlands now lies in the north, and specifically in the state of Montana. Even the Sierra Club, for decades interested only in mountains, has become a prairie advocate for this area. It has had its own evolving proposal for High Plains biological corridors linking preserved "core" areas, modeled on the Yellowstone-to-Yukon idea for the Northern Rockies, but has now bought in on the exciting re-wilding project that is unfolding in Montana.

Conservation biologists say that to work in re-wilding terms, a Catlinesque plains park should at least cover 2.5 million acres, about the size of Yellowstone (although some of them insist that 10–20 million acres would be a more effective size). Getting some re-creation of the historic Great Plains on this scale would be an act of conservation statecraft on the level of creating the first national parks in world history, or passing a Wilderness Act that has protected so much American nature. Restoring historic Great Plains nature would be a cultural goal for the United States that its citizens, and no doubt the citizens of the world, would celebrate for centuries.

There is nothing quite so grand as a 10-million acre Great Plains park under way in the real-life world, but there is something close to this vision. It acquired life from President Clinton's 2001 proclamation of an Upper Missouri River Breaks National Monument extending downstream from the White Cliffs section of the Wild and Scenic Missouri River. The new monument drapes along 150 miles of the river—the river of Lewis and Clark, Catlin, Maximilian and Bodmer, Audubon, and Teddy Roosevelt—that was so important to plains history. If we can merge this 377,346-acre National Monument with the Charles M. Russell National Wildlife Refuge farther downriver, now grown to a whopping 915,814 acres, then federal managers would have the makings of a Yellowstone-sized chunk of the plains located in a state that already has wolves and grizzlies in its mountains and buffalo and Spanish mustangs readily available nearby. Of course there are obstacles, plenty of them. The national monument is managed by the BLM and the wildlife refuge by the Fish and Wildlife Service, for one thing. Far more importantly, both are highly checkerboarded with private lands and ranchsteads and livestock grazing throughout.

During the lead-in to President Clinton's announcement of the new national monument, the Nature Conservancy released the first of its Great Plains studies, *Ecoregional Planning in the Northern Great Plains Steppe*, examining the prairie sections of five states, plus two Canadian provinces. That study argued that with 60 percent its grasslands intact, with that percentage going as high as 95 percent in the western parts of the study area, and with significant public lands already in place, in the twenty-first century the Northern Plains—"where landscapes spanning across millions of acres represent perhaps the most intact grasslands in North America"—was unquestionably the best re-wilding candidate on the American Great Plains. Private in-holdings scattered through the public lands, however, were going to be a major issue. An international assessment by ecologists of grasslands around the world a

In the White Cliffs on the Wild and Scenic Missouri River. Dan Flores photo.

few years later also singled out eastern Montana as one of only four global candidates for plains conservation on a large scale. By that time another international environmental group, the World Wide Fund for Nature, had begun an effort to identify critical acquisition properties in the area with a solution in mind for merging the public parcels.

American Prairie Reserve, a nonprofit set up to turn this grand, Yellowstone-like vision into reality, opened offices in Montana in 2001 to see if the Rockefeller family's strategy of buying up private lands to create Grand Tetons Park might work in the twenty-first century. The organization has raised more than $80 million (there are big-time donors from both coasts as well as thousands of small donors) and it has an epic plan: to acquire a critical half-million private acres in order to stitch together the existing public lands along the Missouri into a restored Great Plains preserve that could approach 3.5 million acres in size, almost half again larger than Yellowstone Park, for stocking a bison herd, at a minimum, of 10,000 animals. As with most visionary endeavors, misinformation abounds, including articles in the conservative press carrying inflammatory titles like "Bison-Loving Billionaires Rile

Ranchers with Land Grab." But many major players, including the National Geographic Society, which produced a 2010 film about the idea—*American Serengeti*—are all in.

Because re-creating the American Serengeti does mean acquiring private lands from ranchers who often are rabidly against the idea of reversing the flow of history and despise any thought of reintroducing bison to the plains, what American Prairie Reserve has been cautious about publicly proclaiming is that it would love to see grizzlies and wolves colonize the Reserve from their strongholds in the western mountains. But ultimately what its board and supporters truly want restored is the whole suite of animals on the historic plains, using Yellowstone as a template for the world-class Great Plains park we never got. The Reserve's Hilary Parker told me flat out: "Make no mistake: Our goal is nothing short of re-establishing all of the megafauna of the original plains." Its supporters, the Bozeman-based Ecology Center and the Predator Conservation Alliance, have a High Plains Ecosystem Recovery Plan that envisions re-creating all the ecological processes of the Northern High Plains—classic re-wilding, in other words, with wild bison ranging free in large numbers and grizzlies and wolves and fire all returned to the region. And perhaps, with some nudging and a new appreciation for the long evolution of horses on the continent, even the wild horses that helped give the historic plains some of the magic and poetry of the American Pleistocene.

Admittedly this is a romantic vision. It will without question be difficult to make happen in the twenty-first-century political climate. What it does hold out is a promise of sustainability resting on what this plains world wants to be, on its ancient ecological base. Because, simply enough, what has always worked best on the Great Plains was what was there all along.

A pair of ecologists, Fred Samson and Fritz Knopf, have been arguing for two decades that for preserving biological diversity in North America, the Great Plains has become "perhaps the highest priority" in conservation. The first time I read their argument about prairie conservation I knew a statement like that was going to strike some readers, utterly bored by the plains in their present, skinned form—and almost surely never having read Lewis and Clark, Audubon, Cather, or O'Keeffe—as ridiculous, some kind of bad joke perpetrated by science nerds who don't quite get that it's not funny.

Not long after, though, three friends and I had the chance to load our gear into canoes and head off for a float trip adventure on the Wild and Scenic stretch of the Upper Missouri River. After two days of leisurely paddling down the river we were lucky enough the second afternoon to be the only ones to set up camp in the stunning White Cliffs Narrows of the Missouri. The feeling from the morning that followed has never left me.

Sunrise that next morning came on like something out of a Karl Bodmer painting. I had awakened maybe an hour before dawn, looked around at the setting while barely conscious, then had let the murmuring river carry me away . . . only to be yanked, wide-awake, out of my sleeping bag a few moments later as slanting yellow sunlight caught the cliffs across the river with the blinding, reflective glare of a searchlight. It was like someone had turned on a 300-watt light in a darkened room, and it had me out of my bag and standing at water's edge with my mouth open in what I realized, after a moment, was a form of shocked recognition of *something* that retreated just around the corners of my mind.

I had never been on the Missouri River before. But standing there under that impossibly lit sky, watching ducks arrowing low over the surface of the water and a small herd of mule deer pogoing away through hoodoos and pedestal rocks at my sudden appearance, while a coyote yipped a dawn serenade across the river, after a few moments it came to me. I had read books and pored over nineteenth-century art and dreamed daydreams of the wilderness Great Plains for much of my life, and now here I stood, on the banks of the Missouri, in the very stretch where Meriwether Lewis had wondered whether these scenes of "visionary inchantment would never have and end." Just downstream from where I stood I knew that two centuries earlier, William Clark, wandering amongst a hundred dead bison washed against the shore, had found wolves in such great numbers and so "verry jentle" that on some unfathomable impulse he killed one with a stab of his bayonet. Karl Bodmer had painted the very cliffs I now watched. He, too, had seen this brittle sunrise light begin to soften to peachier, moisture-filled hues.

This place was déjà-vu for me not from some past life, but from the minds of others, who had made me know what a magical world the Great Plains once had been. The poetry of the plains was considerably fainter in my time on earth, but this particular morning on the Missouri I was hearing enough of the passages to realize that despite all, we had not entirely lost the American Serengeti. Not yet.

SELECTED BIBLIOGRAPHY

INTRODUCTION: AMERICAN SERENGETI

Audubon, John James. "Missouri River Journal." In *Audubon and His Journals*, eds. Maria Audubon and Elliott Coues. 2 vols. New York: Dover Press, 2nd ed., 1986: vol. 1.

Bekoff, Marc. *The Emotional Lives of Animals*. Novato, CA: New World Library, 2008.

Boehme, Sarah, ed. *John James Audubon in the West: The Last Expedition, Mammals of North America*. New York: Harry Abrams, 2000.

Botkin, Daniel. *Our Natural History: The Lessons of Lewis and Clark*. New York: G. P. Putnam's Sons, 1995.

DeVoto, Bernard. *Across the Wide Missouri*. New York: Houghton-Mifflin, 1947.

Fleharty, Eugene. *Wild Animals and Settlers on the Great Plains*. Norman: University of Oklahoma Press, 1995.

Horner, Jack. "Keynote." Montana History Conference, Helena, MT, October 2003.

Matthiessen, Peter. *Wildlife in America*. New York: Viking-Penguin, rev. ed., 1987.

Pagnamenta, Peter. *Prairie Fever: British Aristocrats in the American West 1830–1890*. New York: W. W. Norton, 2012.

Thoreau, Henry David. *The Journal of Henry David Thoreau, 1837–1861*, ed. Damion Searles. New York: New York Review Books Classics, 2009.

Vestal, Stanley. *Jim Bridger, Mountain Man: A Biography*. New York: William Morrow, 1955.

Webb, Walter Prescott. *The Great Plains: A Study in Institutions and Environment*. Boston: Ginn, 1931.

Wilson, Edward O. *Biophilia: The Human Bond with Other Species*. Cambridge, MA: Harvard University Press, 1984.

CHAPTER ONE. EMPIRES OF THE SUN: BIG HISTORY AND THE GREAT PLAINS

Carlson, Paul. *Deep Time and the Texas High Plains: History and Geology*. Lubbock: Texas Tech University Press, 2005.

Christian, David. *Maps of Time: An Introduction to Big History*, 2nd ed. Berkeley: University of California Press, 2011.

Flannery, Tim. *The Eternal Frontier: An Ecological History of North America and Its Peoples*. New York: Grove Press, 2002.

Flores, Dan. "Essay: The Great Plains 'Wilderness' as a Human-Shaped Environment." *Great Plains Research* 9 (Fall 1999): 343–355.

———. *The Natural West: Environmental History in the Great Plains and Rocky Mountains*. Norman: University of Oklahoma Press, 2002.

Hamalainen, Pekka. *The Comanche Empire*. New Haven, CT: Yale University Press, 2008.

Hodges, Glenn. "First Americans." *National Geographic* 227 (January 2015): 124–137.

Johnson, Eileen, ed. *Lubbock Lake: Late Quaternary Studies on the Southern High Plains*. College Station: Texas A&M University Press, 1987.

Martin, Paul. "40,000 Years of Extinctions on the Planet of Doom." *Palaeography, Palaeoclimatology, Palaeoecology* 82 (1990): 187–201.

———. "The Last Entire Earth." *Wild Earth* 2 (Winter 1992–1993): 29–32.

———. *Twilight of the Mammoths: Ice Age Extinctions and the Rewilding of America*. Berkeley: University of California Press, 2007.

Martin, Paul, and Richard Klein, eds. *Quaternary Extinctions: A Prehistoric Revolution*. Tucson: University of Arizona Press, 1985.

McPhee, John. *Rising from the Plains*. New York: Farrar, Straus, and Giroux, 1986.

Spielman, Katherine. "Late Prehistoric Exchange between the Southwest and the Southern Plains." *Plains Anthropologist* 28 (November 1983): 257–279.

Stuart, David. *Anasazi America: Seventeen Centuries on the Road from Center Place*. Albuquerque: University of New Mexico Press, 2000.

CHAPTER TWO. PRONGHORNS: SURVIVORS FROM A LOST WORLD

Byers, John. *American Pronghorn: Social Adaptations and the Ghosts of Predators Past*. Chicago: University of Chicago Press, 1997.

Flores, Dan, ed. *Journal of an Indian Trader: Anthony Glass and the Texas Trading Frontier, 1790–1810*. College Station: Texas A&M University Press, 1985.

———. *Southern Counterpart to Lewis and Clark: The Freeman and Custis Accounts of the Red River Expedition of 1806*. Norman: University of Oklahoma Press, 2002.

Fremont, John Charles. *The Expeditions of John Charles Fremont*, eds. Donald Jackson and Mary Lee Spence. 5 vols. Urbana: University of Illinois Press, 1970–1984.

Geist, Valerius. *Antelope Country. Pronghorns: The Last Americans*. Iola, WI: Krause Publications, 2001.

Gregg, Josiah. *Commerce of the Prairies*, ed. Max Moorhead. Norman: University of Oklahoma Press, 1954.

Knight, Dennis. *Mountains and Plains: The Ecology of Wyoming Landscapes*. New Haven, CT: Yale University Press, 1994.

McCabe, Richard, Bart O'Gara, and Henry Reeves. *Prairie Ghost: Pronghorn and Human Interaction in Early America*. Boulder, CO: University Press of Colorado and the Wildlife Management Institute, 2004.

Moulton, Gary, ed. *The Journals of the Lewis and Clark Expedition, Volume 3: August 25, 1804–April 6, 1805*. Lincoln: University of Nebraska Press, 1987.

Nowak, Ronald. *Walker's Mammals of the World*, 6th ed. 2 vols. Baltimore: Johns Hopkins University Press, 1999.

Puryear, Lela. "Reminiscences of George Clarence Wolfforth." *West Texas Historical Yearbook* 24 (October 1948): April 1884 section.

Schmidly, David. *Texas Natural History: A Century of Change*. Lubbock: Texas Tech University Press, 2002.

Sibley, John. *A Report from Natchitoches in 1807*, ed. Annie Heloise Abel. New York: Museum of the American Indian, 1922.

Urbigkit, Cat. *Path of the Pronghorn*. Honesdale, PA: Boyds Mills Press, 2010.

CHAPTER THREE. COYOTE: THE AMERICAN JACKAL

Beeland, T. Delene. *The Secret World of Red Wolves: The Fight to Save North America's Other Wolf*. Chapel Hill: University of North Carolina Press, 2013.

Bright, William. *A Coyote Reader*. Berkeley: University of California Press, 1993.

Budiansky, Stephen. *The Covenant of the Wild: Why Animals Chose Domestication*. New Haven, CT: Yale University Press, 1992.

Dobie, J. Frank. *The Voice of the Coyote*. Lincoln: University of Nebraska Press, 1961.

Dunlap, Thomas. *Saving America's Wildlife: Ecology and the American Mind, 1850–1990*. Princeton, NJ: Princeton University Press, 1988.

"Family CANIDAE—Wolves, Coyote, Dogs, and Foxes." In E. Raymond Hall and Keith Kelson, *The Mammals of North America*. 2 vols. New York: The Ronald Press, 1959: vol. 2.

Flores, Dan. *Coyote America*. New York: Basic Books, 2016.

Gehrt, Stanley, Seth Riley, and Brian Cypher, eds. *Urban Carnivores: Ecology, Conflict, and Conservation*. Baltimore: Johns Hopkins University Press, 2010.

Gillespie, Angus, and Jay Mechling. *American Wildlife in Symbol and Story*. Knoxville: University of Tennessee Press, 1987.

Grinnell, Joseph, and Tracy Storer. "Animal Life as an Asset of National Parks." *Science* 44 (1916): 375–380.

Hyde, Lewis. *Trickster Makes This World: How Disruptive Imagination Creates Culture*. New York: Farrar, Straus, and Giroux, 1998.

Leopold, Aldo. *The River of the Mother of God and Other Essays*, eds. Susan Flader and J. Baird Callicott. Madison: University of Wisconsin Press, 1991.

Mead, James. *Hunting and Trading on the Great Plains, 1859–1875*, ed. Schuyler Jones. Norman: University of Oklahoma Press, 1986.

Mighetto, Lisa. *Wild Animals and American Environmental Ethics*. Tucson: University of Arizona Press, 1991.

Moulton, Gary, ed. *The Journals of the Lewis and Clark Expedition, Volume 3: August 25, 1804–April 6, 1805*. Lincoln: University of Nebraska Press, 1987.

———. *The Journals of the Lewis and Clark Expedition, Volume 4: April 7–July 27, 1805*. Lincoln: University of Nebraska Press, 1987.

Robinson, Michael. *Predatory Bureaucracy: The Extermination of Wolves and the Transformation of the West*. Boulder: University Press of Colorado, 2005.

Shivik, John. *The Predator Paradox: Ending the War with Wolves, Bears, Cougars, and Coyotes*. Boston: Beacon Press, 2014.

Snyder, Gary. *The Old Ways*. San Francisco: City Lights Books, 1977.

Tedford, Richard, Xiaoming Wang, and Beryl Taylor. *Phylogenetic Systematics of the North American Fossil Caninae (Carnivora: Canidae)*. New York: Bulletin of the American Museum of Natural History, 2009.

VonHoldt, Bridgett, et al. "A Genome-Wide Perspective on the Evolutionary History of Enigmatic Wolf-Like Canids." *Genome Research*, Cold Harbor Laboratory Press, 2011.

"Wolves Thinning Yellowstone Coyotes." *Missoulian* (Missoula, Montana), September 28, 1997.

Worster, Donald. *Nature's Economy: A History of Ecological Ideas*, 2nd ed. New York: Cambridge University Press, 1994.

Young, Stanley, and Harley Jackson. *The Clever Coyote*. Lincoln: University of Nebraska Press, 1978.

CHAPTER FOUR. BRINGING HOME ALL THE PRETTY HORSES:
THE HORSE TRADE AND THE AMERICAN GREAT PLAINS

Abbey, Edward. "Wild Horses." In Edward Abbey, *One Life at a Time, Please*. New York: Henry Holt, 1989: 45–48.

Audubon, John James, *Ornithological Biography* . . . 3 vols. Edinburgh: Adam & Charles Black, 1835: vol. 3.

Becknell, William. "Journal." *Missouri Historical Society Collections* 2 (July 1906): 56–67.

Benson, Nettie. "Bishop Marin de Porras and Texas." *Southwestern Historical Quarterly* 51, no. 32 (1947): 16–40.

Berlandier, Jean Louis, *Journey to Mexico during the Years 1826 to 1834*, trans. Sheila Ohlendorf, Josette Bigelow, and Mary Standifer. 2 vols. Austin: Texas State Historical Association, 1980.

Bexar Archives (Spanish Archives of Texas), Barker Texas History Center, University of Texas–Austin.

Bollaert, William. *William Bollaert's Texas*, ed. Eugene Hollon. Norman: University of Oklahoma Press, 1987.

Bolton, Herbert Eugene, Papers, Pt. 1. Bancroft Library, University of California–Berkeley.

Burnet, David, "The Comanches." In *Information Respecting the History, Conditions, and Prospects of the Indian Tribes of the United States*, ed. Henry Rowe Schoolcraft. 4 parts. Philadelphia: American Bureau of Indian Affairs, 1853: part 1.

California Manuscripts, Provisional Records, Letters Registers, 1794–1823. Bancroft Library, University of California–Berkeley.

Castaneda, Carlos. *Our Catholic Heritage in Texas, 1519–1936*. 7 vols. Austin: Von Boeckmann-Jones, 1958–): vol. 5.

Catlin, George. *Letters and Notes on the Manners, Customs, and Conditions of the North American Indians*. 2 vols. New York: Dover Press ed., 1973.

Clark, LaVerne. *They Sang for Horses*. Tucson: University of Arizona Press, 1966.

Cobo, Father Bernabe. "History of the New World." 1891, Typescript translation, Lawrence Kinnaird Papers, Bancroft Library, University of California–Berkeley.

Dawson, W. M. "Growth of Horses under Western Range Conditions." *Journal of Animal Science* 4 (1945).

De Steiguer, Edward. *Wild Horses of the West: History and Politics of America's Mustangs*. Tucson: University of Arizona Press, 2011.

Dobie, J. Frank, Papers, Items 16771–16776 (includes Bartlett, Collinson, Dwyer, Duval accounts). Ransom Humanities Research Center, University of Texas–Austin.

———. "The Comanches and Their Horses." *Southwest Review* 36 (Spring 1951): 99–103.

———. *The Mustangs.* New York: Bramhall House, 1934.

Flores, Dan. *Horizontal Yellow: Nature and History in the Near Southwest.* Albuquerque: University of New Mexico Press, 1999.

Flores, Dan, ed. *Journal of an Indian Trader: Anthony Glass and the Texas Trading Frontier, 1790–1810.* College Station: Texas A&M University Press, 1985.

———. *Southern Counterpart to Lewis and Clark: The Freeman and Custis Expedition of 1806.* Norman: University of Oklahoma Press, 2002.

Hackett, Charles Wilson, ed. and trans. *Pichardo's Treatise on the Limits of Louisiana and Texas.* 4 vols. Austin: University of Texas Press, 1931–1946.

Hulbert, Richard, Jr. "The Ancestry of the Horse." In *Horses through Time*, ed. Sandra Olsen. Boulder, CO: Roberts Rinehart Publishers for the Carnegie Museum of Natural History, 1997: 13–34.

Jackson, Jack. *Los Mesteños: Spanish Ranching in Texas, 1721–1821.* College Station: Texas A&M University Press, 1986.

James, Thomas. *Three Years among the Indians and Mexicans*, ed. Walter Douglas. St. Louis: Missouri Historical Society, 1916.

Jefferson, Thomas. Papers, Manuscripts Division, Library of Congress, Washington, DC.

Jordan, Terry. *North American Livestock Ranching Frontiers.* Lincoln: University of Nebraska Press, 1993.

Kust, Matthew. *Man and Horse in History.* Alexandria, VA: Plutarch Press, 1983.

La Vere, David, and Kaita Campbell, eds. "An Expedition to the Kichai: The Journal of Francois Grappe, September 24, 1783." *Southwestern Historical Quarterly* 98 (July 1994): 59–78.

Lawrence, Elizabeth. *Hoofbeats and Society: Studies of Human–Horse Interactions.* Bloomington: Indiana University Press, 1985.

Linton, Ralph. "The Comanches." In Abram Kardiner et al., *The Psychological Frontiers of Society.* New York: Columbia, 1945: 47–80.

MacFadden, Bruce. *Fossil Horses: Systematics, Paleobiology, and Evolution of the Family Equidae.* New York: Cambridge University Press, 1992.

Nasatir, Abraham, and Noel Loomis, eds. *Pedro Vial and the Roads to Santa Fe.* Norman: University of Oklahoma Press, 1967.

Neighbors, Robert. "The Nauni or Comanches of Texas." In *Information Respecting the History, Conditions, and Prospects of the Indian Tribes of the United States*, ed. Henry Rowe Schoolcraft. 4 parts. Philadelphia: American Bureau of Indian Affairs, 1853: part 2, 125–134.

Pike, Zebulon Montgomery. *The Journals of Zebulon Montgomery Pike*, ed. Donald Jackson. 2 vols. Norman: University of Oklahoma Press, 1966.

Roe, Frank. *The Indian and the Horse.* Norman: University of Oklahoma Press, 1955.

Ruxton, George. *Adventures in Mexico and the Rocky Mountains.* London: John Murray, 1847.

Sherow, Jim. "Workings of the Geodialectic: High Plains Indians and Their Horses in the Arkansas River Valley, 1800–1870." *Environmental Review* (Summer 1992): 61–84.

Sibley, John. *A Report from Natchitoches in 1807,* ed. Annie Heloise Abel. New York: Museum of the American Indian, 1922.

Sieur de Cadillac Pontchartrain, October 26, 1713 (letter). In Jack Jackson et al., *Mapping Texas and the Gulf Coast.* College Station: Texas A&M University Press, 1990: 5.

Simpson, Gaylord. *Horses: The Story of the Horse Family in the Modern World and through Sixty Million Years of History.* NY: Oxford University Press, 1951.

Wilson, Gilbert. "The Horse and Dog in Hidatsa Culture." *Anthropological Papers of the American Museum of Natural History* 15 (1924): 125–311.

Wilson, Maurine, and Jack Jackson. *Philip Nolan and Texas: Expeditions to the Unknown Land, 1791–1801.* Waco: Texian Press, 1987.

Wolfe, Michael. "The Wild Horse and Burro Issue." *Environmental Review* 7 (Summer 1983): 179–192.

Worcester, Donald. "The Spread of Spanish Horses in the Southwest." *New Mexico Historical Review* (July 1944, January 1945): 225–232.

CHAPTER FIVE. THE MOST DANGEROUS BEAST:
THE GRIZZLY, THE GREAT PLAINS, AND THE WEST

Brown, David. *The Grizzly in the Southwest.* Norman: University of Oklahoma Press, 1985.

Brown, Joseph Epes. *Animals of the Soul: Sacred Animals of the Oglala Sioux.* Rockport, MA: Element Press, 1992.

Cartmill, Matt. *A View to Death in the Morning: Hunting and Nature through History.* Cambridge, MA: Harvard University Press, 1993.

Chauvet, Jean-Marie, et al. *Dawn of Art: The Chauvet Cave, the Oldest Known Paintings in the World.* New York: Harry Abrams, 1996.

Clark, Tim, and Denise Casey. *Tales of the Grizzly: Thirty-Nine Stories of Grizzly Bear Encounters in the Wilderness.* Moose, WY: Homestead Publishing, 1991.

Dax, Michael. *Grizzly West, New West: The Failed Attempt to Re-Introduce Grizzly Bears in the Bitterroot Mountains.* Lincoln: University of Nebraska Press, 2015.

Fleharty, Eugene. *Wild Animals and Settlers on the Great Plains.* Norman: University of Oklahoma Press, 1995.

Fowler, Jacob. *The Journal of Jacob Fowler, Narrating an Adventure from Arkansas through the Indian Territory, Oklahoma, Kansas, Colorado, and New Mexico, to the Sources of the Rio Grande del Norte,* ed., Elliott Coues. New York: F. P. Harper, 1898.

Geist, Valerius. "Did Large Predators Keep Humans out of North America?" In *The Walking Larder,* ed. Janet Clutton-Brock. London: Unwin-Hyman, 1989: 128–140.

Grumbine, R. Edward. *Ghost Bears: Exploring the Biodiversity Crisis.* Washington, DC: Island Press, 1992.

Johnson, Minette. "The Spiritual Significance of the Bear to the Indians of the Great Plains." Unpublished paper in author's possession.

Keiter, Robert, et al., eds. *The Greater Yellowstone Ecosystem: Redefining America's Wilderness Heritage*. New Haven, CT: Yale University Press, 1991.

Kruk, Hans. *Hunter and Hunted: Relationships between Carnivores and People*. New York: Cambridge University Press, 2002.

Ladner, Mildred. *William de la Montagne Cary: Artist on the Missouri River*. Norman: University of Oklahoma Press, 1984.

Mattson, David, and Troy Merrill. "Extirpations of Grizzly Bears in the Contiguous United States, 1850–2000." *Conservation Biology* 16 (August 2002): 1123–1135.

Moulton, Gary, ed. *The Journals of the Lewis and Clark Expedition, Volume 4: April 7–July 27, 1805*. Lincoln: University of Nebraska Press, 1987.

Murray, John, ed. *The Great Bear: Contemporary Writings on the Grizzly*. Anchorage: Northwest Books, 1992.

Nash, Roderick. *The Rights of Nature: A History of Environmental Ethics*. Madison: University of Wisconsin Press, 1989.

Quammen, David. *Monster of God: The Man-Predator in the Jungles of History and the Mind*. New York: W. W. Norton, 2003.

Rockwell, David. *Giving Voice to Bear: North American Indian Rituals, Myths, and Images of the Bear*. Niwot, CO: Roberts Rinehart Publishers, 1991.

Roosevelt, Theodore. *Hunting the Grisly*. New York: P. F. Collier and Sons, 1893.

Seton, Ernest Thompson. *Lives of Game Animals*. Boston: Charles T. Branford, 1953.

Shepard, Paul. *The Others: How Animals Made Us Human*. Washington, DC: Island Press/Shearwater, 1996.

———. *The Sacred Paw: The Bear in Nature, Myth, and Literature*. Washington, DC: Island Press, 1992.

Victor, Frances Fuller. *The River of the West: Life and Adventures in the Rocky Mountains and Oregon*. San Francisco: R. J. Trumball, 1870.

CHAPTER SIX. A DREAM OF BISON

Bechtel, Stefan. *Mr. Hornaday's War: How a Peculiar Victorian Zookeeper Waged a Lonely Crusade for Wildlife That Changed the World*. Boston: Beacon Press, 2012.

Berger, Joel, and Carol Cunningham. *Bison: Mating and Conservation in Small Populations*. New York: Columbia University Pres, 1994.

Bray, Kingsley. "Lone Horn's Peace: A New View of Sioux–Crow Relations, 1851–1858." *Nebraska History* 66 (Spring 1985): 29–47.

Brown, Joseph Epes. *Animals of the Soul: Sacred Animals of the Oglala Sioux*. Rockport, MA: Element, 1992.

Bryson, Reid. "Chinook Climates and Plains Peoples." *Great Plains Quarterly* (Winter 1982): 12–13.

Burlingame, Merrill. "The Buffalo in Trade and Commerce," *North Dakota Historical Quarterly* 3 (July 1929): 262–291.

Callenbach, Ernest. *Bring Back the Buffalo! A Sustainable Future for America's Great Plains*. Washington, DC: Island Press, 1995.

Congressional Globe, 42nd Congress, 2nd Session, February 14, 1872.

Congressional Record, 43rd Congress, 2nd Session, February 2, 1874; March 10 1874; 44th Congress, 2nd Session, February 23 and 25, 1876.

Cook, John R. *The Border and the Buffalo: An Untold Story of the Southwest Plains[,] The Bloody Border of Missouri and Kansas. The Story of the Slaughter of the Buffalo, Westward among the Big Game and Wild Tribes, A Story of Mountain and Plain*. Topeka, KS: Crane, 1907.

Coupland, Robert. "The Effects of Fluctuations in Weather upon the Grasslands of the Great Plains." *Botanical Review* 24 (May 1958): 273–317.

Dillehay, Tom. "Late Quaternary Bison Population Changes on the Southern Plains." *Plains Anthropologist* 19 (August 1974): 180–196.

Dobak, William. "The Army and the Buffalo: A Demur—A Response to David D. Smit's 'The Frontier Army and the Destruction of the Buffalo: 1865–1883.'" *Western Historical Quarterly* 26 (Summer 1995): 197–202.

Dodge, Richard. *The Plains of the Great West and Their Inhabitants* (New York: Archer House, 1959).

Flores, Dan. "Bison Ecology and Bison Diplomacy: The Southern Plains from 1800 to 1850." *Journal of American History* 78 (September 1991): 465–485.

———. "The Great Contraction: Bison and Indians in Northern Plains Environmental History." In *Legacy: New Perspectives on the Battle of the Little Bighorn*, ed. Charles Rankin. Helena: Montana Historical Society Press, 1996: 3–22.

Garretson, Martin. *The American Bison: The Story of Its Extermination as a Wild Species and Its Restoration under Federal Protection*. NY: NY Zoological Society, 1938.

Geist, Valerius. *Buffalo Nation: History and Legend of the North American Bison*. Stillwater, MN: Voyageur Press, 1997: chap. 4.

Hamalainen, Pekka. *The Comanche Empire*. New Haven, CT: Yale University Press, 2008.

Harrod, Howard. *The Animals Came Dancing: Native American Sacred Ecology and Animal Kinship*. Tucson: University of Arizona Press, 2000.

Howard, James. "Yanktonai Ethnohistory and the John K. Bear Winter Count." *Plains Anthropologist* 21 (August 1976): 28–52.

Isenberg, Andrew. *The Destruction of the Bison: An Environmental History, 1750–1920*. New York: Cambridge University Press, 2000.

———. "The Returns of the Bison: Nostalgia, Profit, and Preservation." *Environmental History* 2 (April 1997): 179–196.

Lawson, Merle. *The Climate of the Great American Desert: Reconstructing the Climate of Western Interior United States, 1800–1850*. Lincoln: University of Nebraska Press, 1974.

Ostler, Jeffrey. "'They Regard Their Passing as Wakan': Interpreting Western Sioux Explanations of the Buffalo's Decline." *Western Historical Quarterly* (Winter 1999): 475–497.

Peterson, John. "Buffalo Hunting in Montana in 1886: The Diary of W. Harvey Brown." *Montana, the Magazine of Western History* (Autumn 1981): 2–13.

Schulman, Edmund. *Dendroclimatic Changes in Semiarid America*. Tucson: University of Arizona Press, 1956.

Sheridan, Philip, to E. D. Townsend. Telegram, Chicago, October 31, 1879. Letters Received, Adjutant General's Office, National Archives Record Group 94.

Stahle, David, and Malcolm Cleaveland. "Texas Drought History Reconstructed and Analyzed from 1698 to 1980." *Journal of Climate* (January 1988): 59–74.

White, Richard. *Railroaded: The Transcontinentals and the Making of America.* New York: W. W. Norton, 2011.

Zontek, Ken. *Buffalo Nation: American Indian Efforts to Restore the Bison.* Lincoln: University of Nebraska Press, 2007.

CHAPTER SEVEN. WOLFSONG REDUX

Bednarz, James. *The Mexican Gray Wolf: Biology, History, and Prospects for Re-Establishment in New Mexico.* Albuquerque: US Fish and Wildlife, Endangered Species Report 18, 1988.

Botkin, Daniel. *Discordant Harmonies: A New Ecology for the 21st Century.* New York: Oxford University Press, 1990.

Bowden, Charles, "Lonesome Lobo." *Wildlife Conservation* (January-February 1992): 45–53, 73.

Boyd, Diane. "International Movements of Recolonizing Wolf Populations in the Rocky Mountains." Paper presented at the Second North American Symposium on Wolves, Edmonton, Alberta, August 1992.

Braudel, Fernand. *The Structures of Everyday Life*, trans. Stan Reynolds. New York: Harper and Row, 1981.

Brown, David, ed. *The Wolf in the Southwest: The Making of an Endangered Species.* Tucson: University of Arizona Press, 1983.

Brown, Reagan. *Proceedings of the Predator Control Summit.* Austin: Texas Department of Agriculture, 1980.

Brunner, Jim. "The Mexican Gray Wolf Plan." *Rangelands* 16 (August 1994): 140–142.

Caughley, Graeme. "Eruption of Ungulate Populations, with Emphasis on Himalayan Tahr in New Zealand." *Ecology* 51 (Winter 1970): 53–72.

Chambers, Steven, et al. *An Account of the Taxonomy of North American Wolves from Morphological and Genetic Analyses.* Washington, DC: US Department of Interior Fish and Wildlife Service, 2012.

Coleman, Jon. *Vicious: Wolves and Men in America* (New Haven, CT: Yale University Press, 2004).

Collinson, Frank. "Silver Gray, Arctic, Buffalo, or 'Lofer'—He Was a Big Bad Wolf." *Amarillo Sunday News and Globe*, February 5, 1939.

Dawidoff, Nicholas. "One for the Wolves." *Audubon* (July-August 1992): 38–45.

Eberhardt, L. L., and K. W. Pitcher. "A Further Analysis of the Nelchina Caribou and Wolf Data." *Wildlife Society Bulletin* 20 (1992): 385–395.

Fischer, Hank. *Wolf Wars: The Remarkable Inside Story of the Restoration of Wolves to Yellowstone.* Helena, MT: Falcon Press, 1995.

Fish and Wildlife Service, US Department of Interior. *Reintroduction of the Mexican Wolf within Its Historic Range in the Southwestern United States: Final Environmental Impact Statement.* Albuquerque: US Fish and Wildlife Service, 1996.

Fogelman, Valerie. "A Case of Mistaken Identity: The Eastern Timber Wolf in the United States." Mss. in author's possession.

Fritts, Steven, et al. "The Relationship of Wolf Recovery to Habitat Conservation and Biodiversity in the Northwestern United States." *Landscape and Urban Planning* 28 (1994): 23–32.

Gasaway, William, et al. "The Role of Predation in Limiting Moose at Low Densities in Alaska and Yukon and Implications for Conservation." *Wildlife Monographs* 120 (1992): 1–59.

Gregg, Josiah. *Commerce of the Prairies*, ed. Max Moorhead. Norman: University of Oklahoma Press, 1954.

Gunson, John. "Historical and Present Management of Wolves in Alberta." *Wildlife Society Bulletin* 20 (1992): 330–339.

"Family CANIDAE—Wolves, Coyote, Dogs, and Foxes." In E. Raymond Hall and Keith Kelson, *The Mammals of North America*. 2 vols. New York: The Ronald Press, 1959: vol. 2.

Harrell Family Papers. "The Last Wolf Killed in the Panhandle." Oral History Tape, Panhandle-Plains Historical Museum Archives, Canyon, Texas.

Jones, Karen. *Wolf Mountains: A History of Wolves along the Great Divide.* Calgary: University of Calgary Press, 2002.

Keith, Lloyd. *Wildlife's Ten-Year Cycle.* Madison: University of Wisconsin Press, 1963.

Mech, L. David. *The Way of the Wolf.* New York: Voyageur Press, 1992.

Mech, L. David, and Patrick Karns. *Role of the Wolf in a Deer Decline in the Superior National Forest.* St. Paul: USDA Forest Service Research Paper NC-148, 1977.

Mexican Wolf Recovery Program. Final Environmental Impact Statement and Final Decision: January 2015. www.fws.gov/southwest/es/mexicanwolf/nepa_713.cfm.

Millet, Lydia. "High Noon for the Gray Wolf." *New York Times*, January 18, 2015.

Nowak, R. M. "Another Look at Wolf Taxonomy." In *Ecology and Conservation of Wolves in a Changing World*, L. N. Carbyn et al., eds. Edmonton, AB: Circumpolar Press Institute, 1995.

Paradiso, John, and Ronald Nowak. "Wolves: Canis lupus and Allies." In *Wild Mammals of North America: Biology, Management, Economics*, eds. Joseph Chapman and George Feldhamer. Baltimore: Johns Hopkins Press, 1982: 460–474.

Robbins, Jim. "Wolves across the Border." *Natural History* (May 1986): 6–15.

Robinson, Michael. *Predatory Bureaucracy: The Extermination of Wolves and the Transformation of the West.* Boulder: University Press of Colorado, 2005.

Schwarz, Joel. "Crying Wolf." *American Way* 19 (March 4, 1986): 68–72.

Schwennesen, Don. "Matriarch Wolf Killed in Canada." *Missoulian* (Missoula, Montana), February 12, 1993.

Steck, Michael. "Trail Letter by Michael Steck, 1852," in Marc Simmons, ed., *On the Santa Fe Trail.* Lawrence: University Press of Kansas, 1986: 18–27.

Tedford, Richard, Xiaoming Wang, and Beryl Taylor. *Phylogenetic Systematics of the North American Fossil Caninae (Carnivora: Canidae).* New York: Bulletin of the American Museum of Natural History, 2009.

Wise, Michael. "Killing Montana's Wolves: Stockgrowers, Bounty Bills, and the Uncertain Distinction between Predators and Producers." *Montana, the Magazine of Western History* 63 (Winter 2013): 51–67.

Young, Stanley, and E. A. Goldman. *The Wolves of North America.* 2 vols. New York: Dover Press, 1944.

CHAPTER EIGHT. LOVING THE PLAINS, HATING THE PLAINS, RE-WILDING THE PLAINS

Broach, Elise. "Angels, Architecture, and Erosion: The Dakota Badlands as Cultural Symbol." *North Dakota History* 59 (Spring 1992): 2–15.

Callenbach, Ernest. *Bring Back the Buffalo! A Sustainable Future for America's Great Plains.* Washington, DC: Island Press, 1996.

Catlin, George. *Letters and Notes on the North American Indian Tribes . . .* 2 vols. New York: Dover Edition, 1973.

Cowart, Jack, Juan Hamilton, and Sarah Greenough. *Georgia O'Keeffe: Art and Letters.* Washington, DC: National Gallery of Art, 1987.

DeVoto, Bernard, ed. *The Journals of Lewis and Clark* (Boston: Beacon Press, 1953).

Evernden, Neil. "Beauty and Nothingness: Prairie as Failed Resource." *Landscape* 27 (1983): 3–6.

Glanz, Michael, and Jesse Ausubel. "The Ogallala Aquifer and Carbon Dioxide: Comparison and Convergence." *Environmental Conservation* 2 (1984): 123–131.

James, Edwin. "Account of an Expedition from Pittsburgh to the Rocky Mountains Performed in the Years 1819, 1820." In *Early Western Travels,* ed. Reuben Gold Thwaites. Cleveland, OH: Arthur H. Clark, 1906: vol. 17.

Jameson, John. "The Quest for a National Park in Texas." *West Texas Historical Association Year Book* 50 (1974): 47–60.

Kroll, Andrew, and Dwight Berry. "Carnivores in the Caprock: Re-Wilding the High Plains of Texas." *Wild Earth* 9 (Summer 1999): 35–40.

Lubove, Seth. "Bison-Loving Billionaires Rile Ranchers with Land Grab." *Bloomberg Pursuits* (Summer 2013).

Luhan, Mabel Dodge. *Edge of Taos Desert.* New York: Harcourt, Brace, 1937.

Matthews, Anne. *Where the Buffalo Roam: The Storm over the Revolutionary Plan to Restore America's Great Plains.* New York: Grove Press, 1992.

Miller, Kenton. "The Natural Protected Areas of the World." In *National Parks, Conservation, and Development: The Role of Protected Areas in Sustaining Society,* eds. Jeffry McNeely and Kenton Miller. Washington, DC: Smithsonian Institution Press, 1984: 21.

Mills, Enos. "Address to Amarillo Kiwanis Club on Palo Duro as a Park." *Amarillo Daily News,* October 20, 1921.

Mondor, Claude, and Steve Kun. "The Lone Prairie: Protecting Natural Grasslands in Canada." In *National Parks, Conservation, and Development: The Role of Protected Areas in Sustaining Society,* eds. Jeffry McNeely and Kenton Miller. Washington, DC: Smithsonian Institution Press, 1984: 508–517.

Nature Conservancy. *A Biodiversity and Conservation Assessment of the Southern Shortgrass Prairie Ecoregion.* San Antonio: The Nature Conservancy, 2007.

———. *Central Shortgrass Prairie Ecoregional Assessment and Partnership Initiative*. Nature Conservancy: Final Report, 2006.

———. *Ecoregional Planning in the Northern Great Plains Steppe*. Nature Conservancy: 1999.

Parker, Hilary, Communications and Outreach Manager, American Prairie Reserve. Interview with the author, November 13 and 17, 2015.

Peart, Bob. *A Record of the World Temperate Grasslands Conservation Initiative Workshop, Hohhot, China, June 28 and 29, 2008*. Vancouver: Temperate Grasslands Conservation Initiative, 2008.

Pike, Zebulon Montgomery. *The Journals of Zebulon Montgomery Pike*, Donald Jackson, ed. 2 vols. Norman: University of Oklahoma Press, 1966.

Popper, Deborah Epstein, and Frank Popper. "The Fate of the Plains." *High Country News* 20 (1988): 15–19.

Proposed National Parks, File o-32, Boxes 2948, 2954, National Archives Record Group 79, including Regional Form and Map, National Park of the Plains, Proposed National Parks and Monuments (Box 2948), and "Investigative Report on Proposed Palo Duro National Monument, Texas, May 1939," in File o-32J (Box 2948).

Riebsame, William. "Sustainability of the Great Plains in an Uncertain Climate." *Great Plains Research* 1 (1991): 133–151.

Rothman, Hal. *Preserving Different Pasts: The American National Monuments*. Urbana: University of Illinois Press, 1989.

Rowland, Erin Dunbar, ed. *Life, Letters, and Papers of William Dunbar*. Jackson: Press of the Mississippi Historical Society, 1930.

Runte, Alfred. *National Parks: The American Experience*, 2nd ed. Lincoln: University of Nebraska Press, 1987.

Samson, Fred, and Fritz Knopf, eds. *Prairie Conservation: Preserving North America's Most Endangered Ecosystem*. Washington, DC: Island Press, 1996.

Schmidt, Robert. "The Mega-Chihuahuan Desert." In *Third Symposium on Resources of the Chihuahuan Desert Region*, eds. A. Michael Powell, et al. Alpine, TX: Chihuahuan Desert Research Institute, 1989: 105–115.

Shelford, Victor. "Preservation of Natural Biotic Communities." *Ecology* 14 (1933): 240–245.

Shepard, Jerry. "Singing Out of Tune: Historical Perceptions and National Parks on the Great Plains." Ph.D. diss., Texas Tech University, 1995.

Shepard, John, Colleen Boggs, Louis Higgs, and Phil Burgess. *A New Vision of the Heartland: The Great Plains in Transition*. Denver: Center for the New West, 1994.

Sierra Club website, http://www.sierraclub.org/ecoregions/prairie/html.

Stroud, Patricia Tyson. *Thomas Say: New World Naturalist*. Philadelphia: University of Pennsylvania Press, 1992.

Wallach, Bret. "The Return of the Prairie." *Landscape* 28 (1985): 1–5.

Whitman, Walt. *Leaves of Grass*. New York: Bantam, 1871 ed., 1983.

INDEX